Restoration and 18th Century

Theatre Research

Bibliography

1961–1968

Restoration and 18th Century
Theatre Research
Bibliography
1961–1968

⌣⌣⌣

Edited by
Carl J. Stratman, C. S. V.

Compiled by
Edmund A. Napieralski (1961–1968)

&

Jean E. Westbrook (1961–1966)

Whitston Publishing Company
Incorporated
Troy, New York
1969

PREFACE

At the Chicago meeting of the Modern Language Association Convention in 1961, one Conference was devoted to 17th and 18th century drama and theatre. Two results voted by the members of the Conference were: 1) to continue the Conference at the annual Modern Language Association Convention; and 2) to publish a type of Newsletter, under the aegis of this Conference of the Modern Language Association, and Loyola University of Chicago.

The Conference devoted to 17th and 18th century drama and theatre has not been held for the past two years, but the publication, which began as a Newsletter centered around the Conference, and which quickly passed beyond this stage to become a journal devoted primarily to Restoration and 18th century theatre research, has just completed its seventh year. The title which, for the first two issues, May and November, 1962, was 17th and 18th Century Theatre Research became, with the third number, May, 1963, Restoration and 18th Century Theatre Research.

One of the permanent features which I planned for the publication was an annual annotated bibliography devoted to all phases of research in Restoration and 18th century theatre. I felt that neither the annual bibliography in PMLA, or in Philological Quarterly covered the field in a manner that would be of instant assistance to scholars and students of Restoration and 18th century theatre and drama. Entries were scattered throughout the annual bibliography, so that much time would be wasted in attempting to learn what had appeared in the previous year. Further, only Philological Quarterly annotated its entries. Finally, I felt that if the person preparing the bibliography confined the search to matters relevant to the theatre he would probably locate more material than to be found in either PMLA or Philological Quarterly. Indeed we do average at least thirty percent more entries than the other two journals.

To help in the preparation of the initial
bibliography, which appeared in issue No. 2, November, 1962, and covered material published in 1961,
I called upon the assistance of Edmund Napieralski
and Jean Comiskey (later to become Mrs. James
Westbrook), of Loyola University. Because this
feature of the periodical seemed to fill a pressing
need, and because it received favorable comment,
the two compilers agreed to work on the bibliography
as a joint project during the coming years. I
agreed to edit the material, to decide on the subject category under which each entry would appear,
to do the cross-indexing, to prepare the author index, as well as to add any additional entries which
I might locate. This excellent partnership continued through the issue for November, 1966, even
though Dr. Napieralski left Loyola University in
1964, to teach at Georgetown University. After the
November, 1966 issue, however, Mrs. Westbrook felt
that she could not continue, and Dr. Napieralski
consented to compile the bibliography without assistance. How he has succeeded can be seen by comparing
the growth of the bibliography from a total number
of entries, 126 for 1961, to 242 entries for 1967.

The present volume is a compilation of the
bibliography from its beginning, which covered the
year 1961, through 1967. We do hope that the cumu-
lation of the seven bibliographies, within the
covers of one volume, will be of some assistance
to students and scholars.

At this time I would like to express my grati-
tude to Jean Westbrook, and especially to Edmund
Napieralski, for their valued assistance in helping
to make Restoration and 18th Century Theatre Research a continued reality. Further, I also wish
to take this opportunity to thank Loyola University
which has borne all expenses for publishing the
journal from its inception to the present.

Carl J. Stratman, C.S.V.
Loyola University, Chicago
January 12, 1969

A

ABINGTON, See No. 13

1 ACTING
Burner, Sandra A. "A Provincial Strolling Company of
the 1670's." Theatre Notebook, XX (Winter, 1965/
66), 74-78.
Suggests the possibility of a touring company,
a contingent from the Nursery, active in Norwich
and the provinces in the early 1670's.

2 Downer, Alan S. "Nature to Advantage Dressed: Eight-
eenth Century Acting." Restoration Drama: Modern
Essays in Criticism. (A Galaxy Book). Edited by
John Loftis. (New York: Oxford University Press,
1966), 328-371.
Reprinted from PMLA, LVIII (L943), 1002-1037.
A study of four "schools" of acting in the 18th
century: Betterton, Cibber-Booth-Wilks, Macklin-
Garrick, and Kemble.

3 Freehafer, John. "The Formation of the London Patent
Companies in 1660." Theatre Notebook, XX (Autumn,
1965), 6-30.
Studies the struggle of Killigrew and Davenant
to establish their authority over the actors and to
bring their companies to the stage during the
period, July 9 to October 8, 1660, following the
granting of patents by Charles II. Includes also
corrections to previous accounts of the London
acting companies of 1659 and 1660.

4 Golding, Alfred. "The Theory and Practice of Pre-
sentational Acting in the Serious Drama of France,
England, and Germany during the 18th and 19th
Centuries." Ph.D. Columbia University, 1962.
Includes a description of the theory and practice of 18th Century acting through a study of actors'
memoirs and treatises for novice players.

5 Golding, Alfred S. "Theory and Practice of Acting in
the Eighteenth and Nineteenth Centuries in Western
Europe." Ph.D. Columbia University Teachers College. 1961.

6   Henshaw, Nancy Wandalie. "Graphic Sources for a
     Modern Approach to the Acting of Restoration
     Comedy." Ph.D. University of Pittsburgh, 1967.
     (Order No. 68-9743).
          Uses seventeenth-century engravings, hand-
     books of deportment, memoirs, diaries, and satires
     to present guides for the realistic method of
     acting that should be employed in modern product-
     ions of Restoration comedies.

7   Hunt, Hugh. "Restoration Acting." Restoration
     Theatre. Edited by John Russell Brown and Bernard
     Harris. (Stratford-Upon-Avon Studies, 6). (Lon-
     don: Edward Arnold, 1965; New York: St. Martin's
     Press, 1965), 179-192.
          Discusses the introduction of actresses and
     movable scenery to the stage.

8   Jensby, Wesley Joe. "A Historical Study of the
     Characteristics of Acting during the Restoration
     Period in England (1660-1710)." Ph.D. University
     of Southern California, 1963. (Order No. 63-
     6327).
          Examines the characteristics of Restoration
     acting through a study of contemporary remarks and
     criticisms of acting, of the relationship between
     Restoration and Elizabethan acting, and of the
     influence of Restoration acting on eighteenth
     century theatrics.

9   Sorelius, Gunnar. "The Rights of the Restoration
     Theatrical Companies in the Older Drama." Studia
     Neophilologica, XXXVII (1965), 174-189.
          The rights of Davenant's and Killigrew's
     companies to the production of plays written by
     Elizabethan and Jacobean playwrights. Killigrew's
     King's Men enjoyed a virtual monopoly. See Also
     Nos. 996, 1089.

10   Woodbury, Lael J. "Death on the Romantic Stage."
     Quarterly Journal of Speech, XLIX (February, 1963),
     57-61.
          Contrasts 19th century styles of acting with
     those employed in the neo-classical age. The
     eighteenth century "fostered an acting style which
     expressed the ideals of order and ideality then in
     vogue."

2

ACTOR, See Nos. 637, 939

ACTORS

11   Bridges-Adams, W. "When did Respectability Begin?"
       Drama, No. 67 (Winter, 1962), 26-28.
           Actor's position in society. Some notes on
       Restoration and Eighteenth Century performers.

12   Cameron, Kenneth M. "The Monmouth and Portsmouth
       Troupes." Theatre Notebook, XVII (Spring, 1963),
       89-94.
           The importance of John Coysh for the history
       of these companies and for an understanding of the
       nature of provincial Restoration companies.

13   Engel, Glorianne. "The Comic Actor in the Age of
       Garrick: His Style and Craftsmanship." Ph.D.
       University of Pittsburgh, 1967. (Order No. 68-
       7520).
           Discusses the criticism and acting treatises
       of the period and studies the careers of nine comic
       actors in depth: David Garrick, Henry Woodward,
       Edward Shuter, Richard Yates, Kitty Clive, Peg
       Woffington, Mrs. Abington, Samuel Foote, and Thomas
       Weston.

14   Highfill, Philip H., Jr. "A Biographical Dictionary
       of Performers, 1660-1801." 17th and 18th Century
       Theatre Research, I (May, 1962), 20-22.
           Announcement concerning the editors, future
       publication, and contents of the dictionary.

15   --"Charles Surface in Regency Retirement: Some
       Letters from Gentleman Smith." Essays in English
       Literature of the Classical Period Presented to
       Dougald MacMillan. Edited by Daniel W. Patterson
       and Albrecht B. Strauss. Studies in Philology,
       (Extra Series, January, 1967), 135-166.
           Letters in the Folger Shakespeare Library
       from William "Gentleman" Smith (1730-1819),
       Garrick's contemporary and sometime protege, to
       banker Thomas Coutts contribute to an under-
       standing of the changing status of the acting
       profession.

16   --"Extra." Theatre Notebook, XVII (Spring, 1963),
       103-104.

The term 'Extra' in Theatre jargon was in
familiar use by 1781 according to BM. Add 40, 166
which gives salary regulations for the Manchester
and Liverpool Theatres.

17   Stone, George Winchester. "The Poet and the Players."
        Proceedings of the American Philosophical Society,
        CVI (1962), 412-421.
                Interpretations of Shakespeare by various
        actors, including Garrick.

18   Wagenknecht, Edward. Merely Players. Norman: Univ-
        ersity of Oklahoma Press, 1966. 270 pp.
                Biographies of David Garrick, Edmund Kean,
        William Charles Macready, Edwin Forrest, Edwin
        Booth, Sir Henry Irving, Joseph Jefferson, and
        Richard Mansfield. See Also Nos. 92, 556, 603,
        605, 630, 631, 632, 950, 1153

19   Wilson, John Harold. "Biographical Notes on Some
        Restoration Actresses." Theatre Notebook, XVIII
        (Winter, 1963/64), 43-47.
                Corrections and supplement to the author's
        All the King's Ladies, 1958, Appendix A, The Act-
        resses, 1660-1689. Notes on Katherine Corey, Mrs.
        Knepp, the two Mrs. Prices, Elizabeth Roche, the
        two Mrs. Knights and others.

20   --"The Duchess of Portsmouth's Players." Notes and
        Queries, New Series, X (1963), 106-107.
                Argues that the Duchess of Portsmouth Players
        never existed. The Indian Emperor was produced
        by a group of amateurs before September 30, 1675.

21   --"Players' Lists in the Lord Chamberlain's registers."
        Theatre Notebook, XVIII (Autumn, 1963), 25-30.
                Reprint of Players' Lists from October 6, 1660
        to November 14, 1698. The names of Thomas Better-
        ton, Colley Cibber, Nathaniel Lee, and other play-
        wrights are found among the actors' names.

ACTORS, See Nos. 102, 106, 434, 439, 544, 545, 548, 570

ACTORS AND ACTRESSES
22   Marinacci, Barbara. Leading Ladies, a Gallery of
        Famous Actresses. New York: Dodd, Mead, & Co., 1961.
        xiii, 306 pp.

4

23   Reed, Sally Lou. "The Advent of Actresses on the
       English Public Stage and Subsequent Effects on the
       Female Role in Restoration Drama." M.A. Univer-
       sity of Southern California. 1961. See Also Nos.
       37, 45, 196, 874

ACTRESS, See Nos. 7, 30, 600, 1119

ADDISON
24   Elioseff, Lee Andrew. The Cultural Milieu of Addi-
       son's Literary Criticism. Austin: University of
       Texas Press, 1963. 252 pp.
              A thorough investigation of Addison's debt to
       18th century culture. Addison's literary criti-
       cism was moulded by the period's "political and
       national loyalties, literary and theatrical pract-
       ices and shifts in taste...." Important chapters
       on tragedy and the Italian opera. See Also No.
       805

25   Kelsall, M. M. "The Meaning of Addison's Cato."
       Review of English Studies, XVII (1966), 149-162.
              Addison's intention was to give a pre-eminent
       example of "Roman virtue' and also an example of
       the virtues of Roman republican liberty.

26   Kenny, Shirley Strum. "Two Scenes by Addison in
       Steele's Tender Husband." Studies in Bibliography:
       Papers of the Bibliographical Society of the Univ-
       ersity of Virginia, XIX (1966), 217-226.
              Addison wrote parts of III, i and V, i.

27   Litto, Fredric M. "Addison's Cato in the Colonies."
       William and Mary Quarterly, XXIII (1966), 431-449.
              The many editions and performances of the play
       in 18th century America demonstrate that the work
       was considered a classic. Its most meaningful
       popularity occurred when it was used as an instru-
       ment of political propaganda.

28   Stratman, Carl J., C. S. V. "Unrecorded Editions of
       Addison's Cato, Published before 1756." Theatre
       Notebook, XV (Spring, 1961), 102.
              Eleven unrecorded eighteenth century editions.

ADDISON, See Also Nos. 194, 507, 568, 571, 760, 782,
       1122

5

AESTHETIC DISTANCE, See No. 153

ALLINGHAM, See No. 249

AMERICA, See Nos. 27, 92, 796, 819, 1104, 1105, 1138

ARCHTYPE, See No. 390

ARISTOPHANES, See No. 139

ARISTOTLE, See No. 741

ARNE, See Nos. 236, 834, 953

ARROWSMITH

29   Love, Harold. "A Lost Comedy by Joseph Arrowsmith."
      Notes and Queries, XIV (1967), 217-218.
          Arrowsmith probably wrote a play performed
      before Charles II on October 4, 1671 in Cambridge
      and The Reformation, a comedy attacking the heroic
      play.

ATKYNS

30   Tisdall, E. E. P. Mrs. 'Pimpernel' Atkyns: The
      Strange Story of a Drury Lane Actress Who Was the
      Only Heroine of the French Revolution. London:
      Jarrolds, 1965. 290 pp.
          A popular biography dealing for the most part
      with the revolutionary activities of Charlotte Wal-
      pole Atkyns (1758-1836). Chapter two concerns her
      acting career in London and her relationship to
      Sheridan and Garrick.

AUDIENCE

31   Avery, Emmett L. "The Restoration Audience." Phil-
      ological Quarterly, XLV (1966), 54-61.
          A study of some known spectators reveals the
      wide social and intellectual range of the Restora-
      tion audience.

32   Kinsley, William Benton. "Satiric Audiences in the
      Augustan Age." Ph.D. Yale University, 1965 (Order
      No. 65-14, 684).
          "The Subtlety and complexity of much Augustan
      satire gave its audiences an important, and some-
      times crucial, role in determining its meaning in
      social contexts."

33   Love, Harold. "The Myth of the Restoration Audience."
      Komos, I (1967), 49-56

34   Pedicord, Harry William. "White Gloves at Five"
      Fraternal Patronage of London Theatres in the Eight-
      eenth Century." Philological Quarterly, XLV (1966),
      270-288
              Freemasons attended performances as a group,
      encouraged the arts, supported actors, and re-
      flected in their behavior Augustan ideals of de-
      cency, decorum, and sentiment.

AUDIENCE, See Also No. 434

AUGUSTANISM, See No. 532

B

BALLAD OPERA
35   Gagey, Edmond. Ballad Opera. New York: Benjamin
      Blom, 1964. 259 pp.
              A reprint of the 1937 edition, the book pro-
      vides a comprehensive description and catalog of
      the types of ballad opera that developed between
      1728 and 1750. See also No. 920.

BALLAD OPERA, See Also Nos. 500, 503, 504, 505, 920

BANKS
36   Devlin, James J. "The Dramatis Personae and the
      Dating of John Banks's The Albion Queens." Notes
      and Queries, New Series, X (1963), 213-215.
              Corrects the list of actors for the 1704
      production at Drury Lane. Additional remarks on
      the date of publication.

BARRY
37   Hook, Lucyle. "Portraits of Elizabeth Barry and Anne
      Bracegirdle." Theatre Notebook, XV (Summer, 1961),
      129-137.
              The two actresses, identified as Britannia

7

and Flora in Kneller's large Equestrian Picture of
William III, now in Hampton Court. Traces source
of engravings in The Biographical Mirrour.

BEAUMONT AND FLETCHER

38   Sprague, Arthur Colby. Beaumont and Fletcher on the
Restoration Stage. New York: Benjamin Blom, 1965.
229 pp.
    A reprint of the 1926 edition, the book concerns
the chronological stage history of the plays between 1660 and 1710 and the alteration and adaptation of the texts for performances.

39   Wilson, John Harold. The Influence of Beaumont and
Fletcher on Restoration Drama. New York: Benjamin
Blom, 1967. 162 pp.
    Reprint of the 1928 edition.

BEHN

40   Behn, Aphra. The Rover. Edited by Frederick M.
Link. (Regents Restoration Drama Series). Lincoln: University of Nebraska Press, 1967.
    Includes introduction, notes and chronology.

41   --The Works of Aphra Behn. Edited by Montague Summers. 6 vols. New York: Phaeton Press, 1967.
    Facsimile of 1915 edition. See also No. 775.

42   Andrew, Richard H. "Social Themes in the Plays of
Aphra Behn." M.A. Bowling Green State University,
1965.

43   Barrett, Alberta Gregg. "Plot, Characterization,
and Theme in the Plays of Aphra Behn." Ph.D.
University of Pennsylvania, 1965. (Order No. 66-
4599).
    Analyzes the works of Aphra Behn from the
standpoint of their dramatic potentiality, ability
to portray human nature, and satiric import.

44   Hargreaves, Henry Allen. "The Life and Plays of Mrs.
Aphra Behn." Ph.D. Duke University. 1961.
    Examines Mrs. Behn's plays, in order to de-
termine some of the characteristics which make them
successful in the Restoration theatre.

BEHN, See Also No. 877

BELLAMY
45   Sewell, Rev. Brocard, O. Carm. "George Anne Bel-
        lamy." Wiseman Review, CCXXXV (1961), 56-59.
            A brief biography of the eighteenth century
        London actress George Anne Bellamy.

BENEFIT PERFORMANCES
46   McKenty, David Edward. "The Benefit System in Augus-
        tan Drama." Ph.D. University of Pennsylvania,
        1966. (Order No. 66-10, 643).
            Augustan poets and performers were paid not
        with cash but with the opportunity to risk capital
        in hope of great gain. The effects of this "bene-
        fit system" on the playwrights, actors, and the
        selection of plays are studied.

BENTLEY, See No. 1121

BETTERTON
47   Bowers, Fredson. "A Bibliographical History of the
        Fletcher-Betterton Play, The Prophetess, 1690."
        Library, 5th Series, XVI (1961), 169-175.
            A bibliographical study of the first and
        second edition, together with the issues, of
        Thomas Betterton's opera, based on Fletcher's
        Prophetess, and published by Jacob Tonson in 1690.

48   Schmunk, Thomas W. "The Acting Style of Thomas Bet-
        terton." M.A. Tufts University, 1964. See also
        No. 965.

BETTERTON, See Also Nos. 2, 21, 228, 238, 941, 966, 971,
        991, 992, 1065

BIBLIOGRAPHY
49   Belknap, S. Yancey. Guide to the Performing Arts
        1961. New York: The Scarecrow Press, 1962. 451 pp.
            Valuable reference work for all phases of
        theatre. The reason for including the work is that
        it lists material published in 1961.

50   Bergquist, G. William, editor. Three Centuries of
        English and American Plays: a Checklist. England:
        1500-1800; United States: 1714-1830. New York and
        London: Hafner Publishing Company, 1963. xii, 281
        pp.
            Basically an index of the microprint edition
        of the Three Centuries of English and American

Plays. Reviewed with corrections in <u>Restoration</u>
<u>and Eighteenth Century Theatre Research</u>, III (May,
1964), 50-56.

51   "Bibliography for 1961." <u>17th and 18th Century</u>
<u>Theatre Research</u>, I (November, 1962), 5-26.
      Annotated bibliography of works dealing with
Restoration and Eighteenth Century theatre. Includes items for Nineteenth Century theatre.

52   Bowers, Fredson. "Bibliography and Restoration
Drama." <u>Bibliography: Papers Read at a Clark</u>
<u>Library Seminar, May 7, 1966</u>. Edited by Fredson
Bowers and Lyle H. Wright. (Los Angeles: Clark
Memorial Library, U. C. L. A., 1966), 3-24.
      Reviews bibliographies of Restoration plays
and discusses the contribution methods of bibliography can make to an orderly account of Restoration drama.

53   Brack, O. M., Jr., Charles N. Fifer, Donald T.
Torchiana, and Curt A. Zimansky. "English Literature, 1660-1800: a Current Bibliography." <u>Philo-</u>
<u>logical Quarterly</u>, XLV (1966), 491-602
      A comprehensive bibliography of books, articles,
and reviews published in 1965 which pertain to
Restoration and Augustan literature. Arranged
alphabetically according to author within six major
classifications.

54   --"English Literature, 1660-1800: a Current Bibliography." <u>Philological Quarterly</u>, XLVI (1967),
289-384.
      A comprehensive bibliography of books, articles,
and reviews published in 1966 that pertain to
Restoration and Augustan Literature. Arranged
alphabetically according to author, within six
major classifications.

55   Crane, Ronald S. <u>English Literature, 1660-1800</u>.
<u>A Bibliography of Modern Studies</u>. Vols. III and
IV. Princeton: Princeton University Press, 1962.
1131 pp.
      Bibliography of scholarship, originally com-
piled for the <u>Philological Quarterly</u>. Volume III
covers the years 1951 to 1956; Volume IV, 1957 to
1960, with index for both volumes. Within six major

divisions arranged alphabetically according to author.

56   Fifer, Charles N., Donald T. Torchiana, and Curt
      A. Zimansky. "English Literature, 1660-1800: a
      Current Bibliography." Philological Quarterly,
      XLIV (1965), 289-386.
         A comprehensive bibliography of books, articles,
      and reviews published in 1964 which pertain to
      Restoration and Augustan literature. Arranged
      alphabetically according to author within six major
      classifications.

57   Grieder, Theodore. "Annotated Checklist of British
      Drama, 1789-99." Restoration and Eighteenth
      Century Theatre Research, IV (May, 1965), 21-47.
         492 items compiled for the most part from the
      dramas in the Reader Microprint Series, Three
      Centuries of Drama: English and American. Anno-
      tations provide information on the historical con-
      text and social milieu of the plays.

58   Halsband, Robert. "Recent Studies in the Restoration
      and Eighteenth Century." Studies in English Liter-
      ature, 1500-1900, III (1963), 433-447.
         Discusses important recent studies on Dryden,
      Fielding, Johnson, and others.

59   Hamer, Philip M., ed. A Guide to Archives and Man-
      uscripts in the United States. Compiled for the
      National Historical Publications Commission. New
      Haven: Yale University Press, 1961. xxiii, 775 pp.
         Invaluable reference tool. The index lists
      twenty-five libraries in the United States with
      theatre manuscript holdings. Some 1300 deposi-
      tories in the 50 States appear in the work.

60   Harbage, Alfred. Annals of English Drama, 975-1700.
      Revised by S. Schoenbaum. London: Methuen, 1964.
      321 pp.
         This revised edition of Harbage's 1940 comp-
      ilation of dramatic pieces written for the English
      stage lists adaptations, translations, works com-
      posed in foreign languages, as well as descriptions
      of royal entertainments. Arranged chronologically
      and indexed according to playwright, title, and

11

dramatic company. Several appendices note doctoral dissertation editions, the location of extant play manuscripts, and the names of theatres in operation during the period.

61   Hilles, Frederick W. "Recent Studies in the Restoration and Eighteenth Century." Studies in English Literature, 1500-1900, VI (1966), 599-628.
        A review article of major critical works published in 1965-1966 contains information on studies of Gay, Fielding, and Goldsmith.

62   Napieralski, Edmund A. "Restoration and 18th Century Theatre Research Bibliography for 1966." Restoration and Eighteenth Century Theatre Research, VI (November, 1967), 1-36.
        An annotated list of works published in 1966 that deal with Restoration and 18th century theatre. 234 items.

63   Napieralski, Edmund A., and Jean E. Westbrook. "Restoration and 18th Century Theatre Research Bibliography for 1962." Restoration and 18th Century Theatre Research, II (November, 1963), 3-19.
        An annotated compilation of books and articles published in 1962, dealing with Restoration and 18th Century Theatre. 126 items.

64   --"Restoration and 18th Century Theatre Research Bibliography for 1963." Restoration and 18th Century Theatre Research, III (November, 1964), 3-24.
        An annotated list of works published in 1963 which deal with Restoration and 18th Century theatre. 151 entries.

65   --"Restoration and 18th Century Theatre Research Bibliography for 1964." Restoration and Eighteenth Century Theatre Research, IV (November, 1965), 11-38.
        An annotated list of works published in 1965 that deal with Restoration and 18th Century theatre. 166 items.

66   --"Restoration and 18th Century Theatre Research

Bibliography for 1965." Restoration and 18th
Century Theatre Research, V (November, 1966), 27-
55.
    An annotated list of works published in 1965
that deal with Restoration and 18th Century theatre.
182 items.

67   Paulson, Ronald H. "Recent Studies in the Restora-
       tion and Eighteenth Century." Studies in English
       Literature, 1500-1900, VII (1967), 531-558.
           A review article of major critical works
       published in 1966-67 contains information on
       studies of Behn, Cibber, Congreve, Dryden, Gay,
       Fielding, Farquhar, Lillo, Shadwell, Murphy, Steele,
       and Wycherley.

68   Price, Martin. "Recent Studies in the Restoration
       and Eighteenth Century." Studies in English Liter-
       ature, 1500-1900, V (1965), 553-574.

           This review article of major critical works
       published in 1964-65 contains references to studies
       on Dryden, Fielding, and Wycherley.

69   Robinson, John. "Revision of Lowe's Bibliography."
       Restoration and 18th Century Theatre Research, II
       (May, 1963), 8-12
           Editor Robinson lists four types of revisions:
       addition of unknown entries, extension of biblio-
       graphy to 1900, more detailed bibliographical des-
       criptions, and corrections of Lowe's notes.

70   Scouten, Arthur H. The London Stage 1660-1800. A
       Calendar of Plays, Entertainments, and Afterpieces.
       Together with Casts, Box-Receipts and Contemporary
       Comment. Compiled from the Playbills, Newspapers
       and Theatrical Diaries of the Period. Part 3:
       1729-1747. Carbondale, Illinois: Southern Illinois
       University Press, 1961. 2 vols. paged continuously.
       1315 pp. Index at end of each volume.
           The Introduction discusses the Playhouses,
       Licensing Act, Theatrical Accomodations and Prac-
       tices, Administration and Management, Advertising,
       The Benefit Performance, Costumes, Scenery, Actors
       and Acting, Repertory, Dancing, Music, Singing,
       Specialty Acts, the Audience, and Production. Very
       valuable work.

71   Spacks, Patricia M. "Recent Studies in the Restora-
        tion and Eighteenth Century." Studies in English
        Literature, 1500-1900, IV (1964), 497-517.
                Reviews important scholarly books and articles
        on Dryden, Garrick, and Murphy.

72   Stone, George Winchester, Jr., ed. The London Stage,
        1660-1800: a Calendar of Plays, Entertainments and
        Afterpieces, Together with Casts, Box-Receipts, and
        Contemporary Comment...Part 4: 1747-1776. Carbon-
        dale: Southern Illinois University Press, 1962.
        3 vols.
                A day by day listing of the plays staged at
        the London theatres, together with the names of the
        actors in each piece. A valuable Introduction
        discusses such matters as topical references, play-
        houses, theatrical financing, management and oper-
        ation, advertising, make-up of the theatrical
        company, actors and acting, the benefit performance,
        costume and scenery, theatrical music.

73   Stratman, Carl J., C. S. V., Compiler and Editor.
        Bibliography of English Printed Tragedy, 1565-
        1900. Carbondale and Edwardsville: Southern
        Illinois University Press; London and Amsterdam:
        Feffer and Simons, 1966. 843 pp.
                6852 numbered entries include 1483 English
        tragedies published from 1565 to 1900. Entries are
        arranged in alphabetical order according to author.
        Each entry gives the author's name, the complete
        title of the play, the imprint, the major pagina-
        tion, and the library symbols.

74   --Dramatic Play Lists: 1591-1963. New York: The New
        York Public Library, 1966. 44 pp.

75   --"Problems in The Prompter, A Guide to Plays."
        Papers of the Bibliographical Society of America,
        LV (1961), 36-40.
                An attempt to solve the problems in The Prompt-
        er, which is a bibliography of plays, having some
        5,107 entries for English drama from the beginnings
        to 1813.

76   --"Theses and Dissertations in Restoration and 18th
        Century Theatre." Restoration and 18th Century
        Theatre Research, II (November, 1963), 20-45.

Lists 352 theses and dissertations written
between 1897 and 1962. Arranged alphabetically by
subject.

77   Tobin, J. E. Eighteenth Century English Literature
      and its Cultural Background: a Bibliography. New
      York: Biblo and Tannen, 1967.
          A reprint of the 1939 edition. Chapter VIII
      of Part I is devoted to works dealing with the cul-
      tural and critical backgrounds of 18th century
      drama; Part II contains bibliographies of critical
      works on individual authors.

78   Van Lennep, William, editor. The London Stage, 1660-
      1800. Part 1: 1660-1700. Critical Introduction by
      Emmett L. Avery and Arthur H. Scouten. Carbondale:
      Southern Illinois University Press, 1965. 532 pp.
          The eighth volume of this invaluable calendar
      lists plays performed during the Restoration. A
      fine Introduction is devoted to a discussion of
      theatrical financing and production, playhouse
      construction, and audience response.

79   --"Plays on the English Stage, 1669-1672." Theatre
      Notebook, XVI (Autumn, 1961), 12-20.
          Five play lists recently acquired by the Har-
      vard Theatre Collection. Provides a supplement to
      Nicoll's History of the Restoration Drama (1952).

80   --"Plays on the English Stage 1669-1672." Theatre
      Notebook, XVI (Autumn, 1961), 12-20.
          An examination of Harvard University's recent-
      ly acquired five warrants by the Lord Chamberlain,
      ordering payment to the Duke of York's Company of
      Players for bills submitted for plays given at the
      Duke's Theatre in Lincoln's-Inn-Fields.

81   Vernon, P. F. "Theses and Dissertations in Restora-
      tion and 18th Century Theatre: Addenda." Restora-
      tion and Eighteenth Century Theatre Research, VI
      (May, 1967), 55-56.
          Twenty-two theses and dissertations in the
      University of London Library. The list is an
      addendum to the list published by Carl J. Strat-
      man, C. S. V., in Restoration and Eighteenth Cent-
      ury Theatre Research, II (November, 1963), 20-45.
      See also Nos. 330, 698

82   Watson, George. The Concise Bibliography of English
       Literature, 600-1950. Second Edition. New York:
       Cambridge University Press, 1965. 270 pp.
              Complete revision of the 1958 text. Contains
       both primary and secondard material for the period
       1660-1800. See also No. 733

83   Wilson, Stuart. "Restoration and 18th Century Theatre
       Research Bibliography for 1935-1939." Restoration
       and 18th Century Theatre Research, V (May, 1966),
       40-58.
              A list of works published from 1935 to 1939
       that deal with Restoration and 18th Century theatre.
       345 items. See also Nos. 291, 682

84   Wolf, Erwin. "Englische Literatur in 18 Jahrhund-
       ert: Ein Forschungsbericht (1950-1960)." Deutsche
       Vierteljahrsschrift fur Literaturwissenschaft und
       Geitesgeschichte, XXXV, Heft 3 (1961), 280-297.
              Includes a brief glimpse at a few of the
       leading books on eighteenth century drama published
       between 1950 and 1960.

BIRKHEAD
85   Wagner, Bernard M. "Annals of English Drama."
       Times Literary Supplement (22 October, 1964),
       p. 966.
              Corrects an error in Harbage's work. Attri-
       butes The Female Rebellion to Henry Birkhead who
       founded by endowment the Professorship of Poetry
       at Oxford.

BOSWELL
86   Lustig, Irma S. "Boswell's Literary Criticism in
       The Life of Johnson." Studies in English Litera-
       ture, 1500-1900, VI (1966), 529-541.

A review of Boswell's occasional literary
opinions in The Life includes his observations on
Othello and on Gay's Beggar's Opera.

87   Tillinghast, A. J. "Boswell Playing a Part." Renaissance and Modern Studies (University of Notting-
ham, IX (1965), 86-97.

BOSWELL, See Also No. 94

BOYLE
88   Lynch, Kathleen M. Roger Boyle, First Earl of Orrery. Knoxville: University of Tennessee Press,
1965. 308 pp.
       A full-length biography of Boyle, tracing his
career as soldier, politician, pamphleteer, and
dramatist. Orrery's heroic plays "offer a val-
uable sidelight" on his character and his relationship with the Crown.

BRACEGIRDLE, See No. 181

BRIETZCKE
89   Hailey, Elma. "Charles Brietzcke's Diary. (1764)."
Notes and Queries, New Series, VIII (January, 1961),
9-14; (February, 1961), 61-63; (March, 1961), 83-
86; (April, 1961), 144-147; (May, 1961), 191-193;
(June, 1961), 210-214; (July, 1961), 258-262;
(August, 1961), 302-307, 320; (September, 1961),
335-339; (October, 1961), 391-395; (November, 1961),
433-434, 437; (December, 1961), 452-561.
       Lists the various theatrical functions which
he attended.

BRISTOL
90   Barker, Kathleen. The Theatre Royal, Bristol: The
First Seventy Years. (Historical Association,
Bristol Branch, Local History Pamphlets, 3).
c/o Bristol University: Historical Association,
1961. [2], 19 pp. 4 plates.
       Concerns the period 1766-1833.

BRISTOL, See Also Nos. 1088, 1089, 1103

BROOKE
91   Needham, Gwendolyn B. "Mrs. Frances Brooke: Dramatic

17

Critic." Theatre Notebook, XV (1961), 47-55.
Her criticism in The Old Maid, 1755 and 1756.

BROWNSMITH, See No. 1111

BRUNTON
92   Doty, Gresdna. "Anne Brunton in Bath and London."
      Theatre Survey, VIII (1967), 53-65.
           Examines Anne Brunton's English provincial
      background, her London debut (as Horatia in The
      Roman Father at Covent Garden on October 17,
      1785), and her successful reception in America.

BUCKINGHAM, See Nos. 146, 351, 933, 1010

BURLESQUE, See No. 395

BURLETTA
93   Byrnes, Edward T. "The English Burletta, 1730-1800."
      Ph.D. New York University, 1967. (Order No. 68-
      6046).
           The English burletta existed only temporarily,
      from 1764 to 1780, as a definable genre. After
      1779 the term was extended to include hybrid forms.
      Special attention is given to Kane O'Hara's Midas
      and The Golden Pippin.

BURNEY
94   Hemlow, Joyce. A Catalogue of the Burney Family
      Correspondence, 1749-1878. New York Public Library
      and McGill University Press, 1967.
           A catalogue of the correspondence of Dr.
      Charles Burney and daughter Fanny Burney with
      prominent persons includes letters to and replies
      from David Garrick, Horace Walpole, James Boswell,
      and Samuel Johnson.

C

CALDERON, See Nos. 329, 358

CAMOENS, See No. 329

CAPELL, See No. 940

CAREY
95   Dane, Henry James. "The Life and Works of Henry
Carey." Ph.D. University of Pennsylvania, 1967.
(Order No. 67-12, 739).
     Emphasizes the central role music played in
Carey's life (1687-1743). Carey's best works were
two dramatic burlesques, Chrononhotontho logos
(1734) and The Dragon of Wantley.

CAREY, See Also No. 146

CARYLL
96   Cameron, Kenneth M. "Strolling with Coysh." Theatre
Notebook, XVII (Autumn, 1962), 12-16.
     Copy of John Caryll's Sir Salomon, or The
Cautious Cox-Comb (London, 1671) at the University
of Chicago, contains annotations made by a member
of the audience to its cast of characters.

CELESIA, See No. 546

CENTLIVRE
97   Hoor, Henry ten. "A Re-Examination of Susanna
Centlivre as a Comic Dramatist." Ed.D. The
University of Michigan, 1963. (Order No. 64-8214)
     A scholarly investigation of seven comedies
reveals that the basis of Mrs. Centlivre's comedy
is man's inability to distinguish appearance from
reality.

98   Stathas, Thalia. "A Critical Edition of Three Plays
by Susanna Centlivre." Ph.D. Stanford University,
1965. (Order No. 66-2621).
     Modern editions of The Busie Body (1709),
The Wonder (1714), and A Bold Stroke for a Wife
(1718). Includes textual commentary and notes.

99   Strozier, Robert. "A Short View of Some of Mrs.
Centlivre's Celebrat'd Plays, Including a Close
Accounting of the Plots, Subplots, Asides, Soli-
loquies, Etcetera, Contain'd Therein." Discourse,
VII (Winter, 1964), 62-80.
     The development of Mrs. Centlivre's talent
in The Perjur'd Husband, The Beaux's Duel, The

The Man's Bewitch'd, The Perplex'd Lovers, The
Stolen Heiress, The Busy Body, and The Wonder.
See also No. 101.

CENTLIVRE, See Also Nos. 249, 775, 852, 1114

CERVANTES, See No.

CHAMPION, See No. 445

CHAPMAN
100   Barber, C. L. "The Ambivalence of Bussy D'Ambois."
       A Review of English Literature, II (October, 1961),
       38-44.
              Discusses the reasons for the popularity of
       the play on the Restoration stage.

CHARACTERIZATION, See Nos. 43, 166, 694, 955, 960, 985

CHARACTERS
101   Bennett, Gilbert. "Conventions of the Stage Villain."
       The Anglo-Welsh Review, XIV (1964), 92-102.
              Cites Otway, Congreve, Mrs. Centlivre, Theo-
       bald, Moore, and Mrs. Manley to show the increas-
       ing tendency in eighteenth century drama to use set
       patterns of speech and action to characterize the
       villain.

102   Somers, Charles Norman. "Offspring of Distress:
       The Orphan in Eighteenth Century English Drama."
       Ph.D. University of Maryland, 1964. (Order No.
       65-644).
              Analyzes the orphan's function as victim,
       hero, and villain in 50 representative plays.
       See also No. 170.

CIBBER
103   Cibber, Colley. The Careless Husband. Edited by
       William W. Appleton. (Regents Restoration Drama
       Series). Lincoln: University of Nebraska Press,
       1966.
              Includes critical introduction and notes.

104   --The Rival Queans, With the Humours of Alexander
       the Great. Edited by William M. Peterson. Lake
       Erie College Studies, Vol. V, 1965.

105   Ashley, L. R. "Colley Cibber: a Bibliography."
        Restoration and Eighteenth Century Theatre Research,
        VI (May, 1967), 51-57.
            The most modern and complete listing of
        Cibber's works. The list of books and articles
        about Cibber and his period is selective.

106   Ashley, Leonard R. N. Colley Cibber. New York:
        Twayne Publishers, Inc., 1965.
            Biographical and critical study of Cibber's
        works. Chapter IV, "Drury Lane," Chapter V, "The
        Management," and Chapter VI, "The Theatre and the
        Company," are of particular note. Includes select-
        ed bibliography. See also Nos. 452, 1002.

107   Evans, John Maurice. "A Critical Edition of An
        Apology for the Life of Mr. Colley Cibber,
        Comedian. Ph.D. Yale University, 1966. (Order
        No. 66-14, 974).
            Includes introduction, notes, appendices
        and a facsimile edition of 1760 with the author's
        notes.

108   Fone, Byrne Reginald Spencer. "Colley Cibber's
        Love's Last Shift, Edited with an Introduction and
        Textual Notes." Ph.D. New York University, 1966.
        (Order No. 67-4815).
            Introduction includes commentary on Cibber's
        life to 1696 and material discussing the play's
        contemporary reception, sources, and its importance
        as a sentimental comedy.

109   Gilmore, Thomas B., Jr. "Colley Cibber's Good Nature
        and His Reaction to Pope's Satire." Papers on
        Language and Literature, II (1966), 361-371.
            Contrary to popular belief, Cibber did not
        respond with good nature to Pope's attacks; slowly
        but perceptibly he became more scurrilous and
        abusive.

110   Habbema, D. An Appreciation of Colley Cibber, Actor
        and Dramatist Together with a Reprint of His Play,
        The Careless Husband. New York: Haskell House,
        1967. 190 pp.
            A reprint of the 1928 edition, the first part
        of the work is given to a biography of Cibber as
        actor, theatre manager and playwright, the second

to a critical introduction for an text of Cibber's play. See also Nos. 775, 887.

111   Kalson, Albert E. "The Chronicles in Cibber's Richard III." Studies in English Literature, 1500-1900, III (1963), 253-267.
The indebtedness of Cibber's alteration of Shakespeare's Richard III to the histories of Holinshed, Stow, Speed and Baker.

112   McAleer, John J. "Colley Cibber--Shakespeare's Adopter." Shakespeare Newsletter, XI (December, 1961), 42.
Brief biography.

113   Morley, Malcolm. "No Apology for Colley Cibber." New Rambler (Johnson Society, London), January, 1962, pp. 25-29. See also No. 501.

114   Peavy, Charles D. "Cibber's Crown of Dulness: A Reexamination of the Pope-Cibber Controversy." Ph.D. Tulane University, 1963.
Pope's enthronement of Cibber stems from "the basic antagonism of aesthetic and moral values that underlies the entire Pope-Cibber controversy."

115   --"Pope, Cibber and the Crown of Dulness." The South Central Bulletin, XXVI (1966), 17-27.
Supplement: Studies by members of SCMLA. See also Nos. 2, 867, 991.

116   --"The Pope-Cibber Controversy: a Bibliography." Restoration and 18th Century Theatre Research, III (November, 1964), 51-55.
34 primary sources, annotated and in chronological order. See also Nos. 802, 976.

117   Prosser, Eleanor. "Colley Cibber at San Diego." Shakespeare Quarterly, XIV (1963), 253-261.
Modern adaptation of Shakespeare's Henry IV, Part 2, at San Diego was more in keeping with Shakespeare's intention than the "pure" Shakespearean production at Ashland. Comparison of Director Ball to Colley Cibber. See also Nos. 21, 921, 992, 1065.

COFFEY, See No. 920

COKAIN
118   Cokain, Sir Aston. The Dramatic Works of Aston
       Cokain. Edited by James Maidment and W. H. Logan.
       New York: Benjamin Blom, 1967. 319 pp.
       A reprint of the 1874 edition contains the
       dramatic works of Cokain (1608-1684) including
       the Tragedy of Ovid (1662).

COLEMAN
119   Traylor, Eugene. "Production and Production Book
       of Coleman's Clandestine Marriage." M.F.A. Univer-
       sity of Texas, 1963. See also Nos. 249, 757.

COLLIER
120   Anthony, Sister Rose. The Jeremy Collier Stage
       Controversy, 1698-1726. New York: Benjamin Blom,
       1966. 343 pp.
       A reprint of the 1937 edition. Examines all
       the Collier pamphlets and studies reactions to
       them.

121   Mattauch, Hans. "A Propos du Premier Jugement sur
       Shakespeare en France." Modern Language Notes,
       LXXVIII (1963), 288-300.
       The influence of Jeremy Collier's A Short
       View of the Profaneness and Immorality of the
       British Stage (1698) on eighteenth century French
       criticism of Shakespeare. See also No. 94.

COLLIER, See Also Nos. 145, 426, 1005

COLMAN
122   Preston, Thomas R. "Smollett and the Benevolent
       Misanthrope Type." Publications of the Modern
       Language Association, LXXIX (1964), 51-57.
       Brief comparison of Matt Bramble with the
       hero of George Colman's The English Merchant.

COLMAN, See Also Nos. 133, 613, 764, 850, 1120

COMEDY
123   Bateson, F. W. "L. C. Knights and Restoration
       Comedy," Restoration Drama: Modern Essays in Criti-
       cism. (A Galaxy Book). Edited by John Loftis.
       (New York: Oxford University Press, 1966), 22-31.
       Reprinted from Essays in Criticism, VII (1957),
       56-57. Answers L. C. Knights; attack in "Restora-

tion Comedy: The Realith and the Myth." See below
No. 142. A different and more sympathetic approach
to Restoration comedy is possible.

124   Bennett, Robert A. "Time for Comedy." The English
       Journal, LIII (1964), 248-255.
              Alludes to Johnson's definition of comedy,
       Restoration bawdry, and eighteenth century senti-
       mental drama.

125   Bevan, Allan R. "Restoration Comedy Once Again."
       Dalhousie Review, XLII (Summer, 1962), 248-253.
              Reviews: 1. Norman N. Holland, The First
       Modern Comedies. The Significance of Etherege,
       Wycherley, and Congreve. Cambridge: Harvard Univer-
       sity Press, 1959; 2. John Loftis, Comedy and Society
       from Congreve to Fielding. Stanford: Stanford
       University Press, 1959.

126   Bevis, Richard Wade. "The Comic Tradition on the
       London Stage, 1737-1777." Ph.D. University of
       California, Berkeley, 1965. (Order No. 65-13444).
              In light of the acting copies preserved in
       the Larpent Collection of the Huntington Library,
       which "augment by one-half the previously known
       comedy" of the period 1737-1777, sentimental comedy
       can only be regarded as a "minor feature" of the
       century's theatrical history.

127   Birdsall, Virginia Ogden. "The English Comic Spirit
       on the Restoration Stage." Ph.D. Brown University,
       1967. (Order No. 68-1439).
              The immorality and libertinism of comic pro-
       tagonists are an essential part of their nature and
       relate them to an English comic tradition that
       always takes sides with the individual against the
       group. The study concentrates on Etherege, Wycher-
       ley, and Congreve.

128   Blistein, Elmer M. Comedy in Action. Durham, North
       Carolina: Duke University Press, 1964. 146 pp.
              The author suggests that his book might ade-
       quately be described in eighteenth-century style as
       "A Modest Inquiry into the Nature of the Comic and
       the Laughable, with Some Appreciation for the
       Creators and Actors of Comedy." Although devoted
       to no particular period, the work includes refer-
       ences to Congreve, Dryden, Fielding, Sheridan, and

24

Wycherley.

129   Bridges-Adams, W. "Period, Style and Scale." Drama,
       No. 77 (Summer, 1965), 28-31.
           The plays of Wycherley, Congreve, Vanbrugh,
       and Etherege are essential to an understanding of
       their time. In them are manifested effectively the
       Restoration virtues of height, style, and mascu-
       linity.

130   Cecil, C. D. "Delicate and Indelicate Puns in
       Restoration Comedy." Modern Language Review, LXI
       (1966), 572-578.
           The attitudes of Dryden, Wycherley, and Ether-
       ege toward word-play were complex. Congreve was
       especially impressed by the pun as a vehicle for
       wit.

131   --"Raillery in Restoration Comedy." Huntington
       Library Quarterly, XXIX (1966), 147-159.
           Studies the importance of raillery for the
       energetic manner of Restoration comedy: "Raillery
       is the Augustan mode for clarifying the tenets and
       refining the values of conversational man."

132   --"Une espéce d'eloquence abrégée': The Idealized
       Speech of Restoration Comedy." Etudes Anglaises,
       XIX (1966), 15-25.
           Studies the influence of the classics and
       especially the French on Restoration writers'
       attempts to achieve elegant expression. Examines
       Dancourt, Etherege, Requard, and Congreve.

133   Detisch, Robert John. "High Georgian Comedy: English
       Stage Comedy from 1760 to 1777." Ph.D. University
       of Wisconsin, 1967. (Order No. 67-12, 115).
           Putting aside the conventional labels of
       laughing and sentimental comedy, the study attempts
       to demonstrate that there is a high proportion of
       genuine comedy, naturalness, vitality, and satire
       in most of the full-length comedies written be-
       tween 1760 and 1777, a span that encompasses the
       significant work of Murphy, Colman, Cumberland,
       Kelly, Mrs. Sheridan, Mrs. Griffith, Whitehead, and
       Kenrick.

134   Drake, Robert.   "Manners Anyone? Or Who Killed the
        Butler?" South Atlantic Quarterly, LXIII (1964),
        75-84.
                Restoration and Twentieth century comedy of
        manners are both animated by the contrast between
        the sophisticated, aristocratic world and the
        pseudo-sophisticated, pseudo-aristocratic one.
        Restoration lewdness and bawdry are acceptable be-
        cause they servie an artistic function.

135   Falle, G. G., editor.   Three Restoration Comedies.
        New York: St. Martin's Press, 1964.   342 pp.
                Student edition with notes and bibliography
        of The Country Wife, The Way of the World, and The
        Rehearsal.

136   Gibb, Carson. "Figurative Structure in Restoration
        Comedy." Ph.D. University of Pennsylvania, 1962.
        (Order No. 63-4153).
                Figurative structure results from the juxta-
        position of apparently unrelated actions in selected
        plays of Dryden, Etherege, and Wycherley.

137   Harris, Bernard. "The Dialect of Those Fanatic
        Times." Restoration Theatre. Edited by John
        Russell Brown and Bernard Harris. (Stratford-Upon-
        Avon Studies, 6). (London: Edward Arnold, 1965;
        New York: St. Martin's Press, 1965), 11-40.
                Traces the language of comedy from Etherege
        to Vanbrugh. Comic language had for its object
        "not so much clarity of analysis as substantial
        human mimicry."

138   Hayman, John Griffiths. "Raillery during the Restor-
        ation Period and Early Eighteenth Century." Ph.D.
        Northwestern University, 1964. (Order No. 64-
        12,288).
                Chapter IV examines "the raillery engaged in
        by the wits and the women of Restoration comedy."

139   Hines, Samuel Philip, Jr.   "English Translations of
        Aristophanes' Comedies, 1655-1742." Ph.D. Univer-
        sity of North Carolina, 1967. (Order No. 68-
        2196).
                Studies Thomas Stanley's Clouds (1655), Henry
        Burnell's Plutus (1659), Lewis Theobald's Plutus
        and Clouds (1715), and Henry Fielding and William

Young's _Plutus_ (1742).

140   Hofstad, Lois Valborg. "The Comic Use of Family
       Relationships, 1760-1779." Ph.D. Case Western
       Reserve University, 1967. (Order No. 68-3312).
       Comic playwrights from 1760 to 1779 were
       generally unable to produce authentic comedies
       because they were unable to create a vigorous
       family conflict. Examines sixty-three comedies,
       eighty-five percent of which were acted for the
       first time from 1760 to 1779 at the Drury Lane,
       Covent Garden, and Haymarket Theatres.

141   Hoy, Cyrus. The Hyacinth Room: an Investigation
       into the Nature of Comedy, Tragedy, and Tragi-
       Comedy. New York: Alfred A. Knopf, 1964.
       Chapter Six deals with Restoration comedy.

142   Knights, L. C. "Restoration Comedy: The Reality
       and the Myth." Restoration Drama: Modern Essays in
       Criticism. (A Galaxy Book). Edited by John Loftis.
       (New York: Oxford University Press, 1966), 3-21.
       Reprinted from Exploration: Essays in Criti-
       cism Mainly on the Literature of the Seventeenth
       Century (London: Chatto and Windus, 1946), pp. 131-
       149. "The criticism that defenders of Restora-
       tion comedy need to answer is not that the comedies
       are 'immoral,' but that they are trivial, gross
       and dull."

143   Legouis, P., et al. "Les voies de la critique
       récente: Comment elle étudie la comédie de la
       restauration." Etudes Anglaises, XIX (1966), 412-
       423.

144   Lott, James David. "Restoration Comedy: The Critical
       View, 1913-1965." Ph.D. University of Wisconsin,
       1967. (Order No. 67-10, 639).
       Summarizes 20th century critical works, cate-
       gorizes the various critical approaches, and comments
       on the effectiveness of each approach.

145   McDonald, Charles O. "Restoration Comedy as Drama of
       Satire: an Investigation into Seventeenth-Century
       Aesthetics." Studies in Philology, LXI (1964),
       522-544.

Restoration comedy is the "most complexly and
consciously moral comedy, avoiding the sentimental
conception of the 'hero' in its presentation of a
satiric scale of ridicule in protagonists and anta-
gonists (knaves and foils) and basing its humor-
ous effects on the Hobbesian idea of laughter
through superiority to the things ridiculed."
Includes references to Collier, Congreve, Dennis,
Dryden, Etherege, Farquhar, and Wycherley.

146   Macey, Samuel Lawson. "Theatrical Satire as a Re-
       flection of Changing Tastes." Ph.D. University of
       Washington, 1966. (Order No. 67-2179).
              Theatrical satire is a valuable tool for
       gauging the changes of taste and standards that
       derive from the middle-class ascendancy which came
       to dominate literature and life. The study is
       chiefly concerned with the works of Buckingham,
       Duffet, Gay, Carey, Fielding, Foote, Murphy,
       Goldsmith, and Sheridan.

147   McLaughlin, John Joseph. "Cruelty in the Comic:
       a Study of Aggression in Drama." Ph.D. University
       of California, Los Angeles, 1966 (Order No. 66-
       9318).
              The Freudian theory of comedy serves to ex-
       plain the presence of aggression, hostility and
       cruelty in comedy. Congreve's The Way of the World
       and Wycherley's The Country Wife are used to study
       Restoration comedy in which the aggressive urge is
       centered on sex.

148   MacMillan, Dougald. "The Rise of Social Comedy in
       the Eighteenth Century." Philological Quarterly,
       XLI (1962), 330-338.
              The decline of tragedy and rise of comedy
       which presented contemporary life and social prob-
       lems of the century. The place of social comedy
       in the history of English drama.

149   Mercier, Vivian. "From Myth to Idea dn Back." Ideas
       in the Drama: Selected Papers from the English
       Institute, ed. John Gassner. (New York: Columbia
       University Press, 1964), 42-70.
              Restoration comedy cannot be considered a part
       of the drama of ideas since it lacks "a fair con-
       frontation of ideals." Its "onesidedness" is best

illustrated in the anti-orthodoxy of Wycherley's
The Country Wife.

150   Mohanty, Harendra Prasad. "Restoration Comedy: a
       Revaluation." *Literary Criterion*, VII, ii (1966),
       21-27.
              Restoration comedy has little intellectual
       quality; its wit is only verbal.

151   Montgomery, Guy. "The Challenge of Restoration
       Comedy." *Restoration Drama: Modern Essays in Crit-*
       icism. (A Galaxy Book). Edited by John Loftis.
       (New York: Oxford University Press, 1966), 32-43.
              Reprinted from *University of California Publi-*
       cations in English, I (University of California
       Press, 1929), 133-151. Discusses the contemporary
       system of ideas that illuminates the backgrounds
       of Restoration comedy.

152   Morrissey, LeRoy John. "The Erotic Pursuit: Changing
       Fashions in Eroticism in Early Eighteenth Century
       English Comic Drama." Ph.D. University of Pennsyl-
       vania, 1964. (Order No. 64-10,409).
              The early writers of "sentimental" comedy not
       only abandoned the erotic patterns popularized at
       the beginning of the century, but found substitutes
       for them. "Mere titillation or sentimental erotic
       expectation or weeping woman eroticism replaced the
       erotic pursuit."

153   Nelson, David Arthur. "The Laughing Comedy of the
       Eighteenth Century." Ph.D. Cornell University,
       1965. (Order No. 65-14711).
              The comic techniques and situations of Van-
       brugh, Farquhar, Goldsmith, and Sheridan are equi-
       valent in terms of their ability to create and main-
       tain aesthetic distance between play-goer and
       character.

154   Nevo, Ruth. "Toward a Theory of Comedy." *Journal of*
       Aesthetics and Art Criticism, XXI (1963), 327-332.
              Slight references to Dryden and the Restora-
       tion theories of comedy.

155   Norell, Lemuel N. "The Cuckold in Restoration Comedy."
       Ph.D. The Florida State University, 1962. (Order
       No. 63-1823).

29

The meaning of "cuckold." Various characteristics of cuckolds in Restoration drama.

156   Porte, Michael Sheldon. "The Servant in Restora-
       tion Comedy." Ph.D. Northwestern University,
       1961.
           Examines the sociological position of the
       domestic servant in Restoration England, and com-
       pares servants in seven Restoration adaptations
       with their prototypes. Relates these findings
       to some sixty Restoration comedies.

157   Riddell, James Allen. "The Evolution of the Humours
       Character in Seventeenth-Century English Comedy."
       Ph.D. University of Southern California, 1966.
       (Order No. 66-8796).
           Traces the development of the humours char-
       acter from Jonson to Farquhar. Jonsonian humour
       characters did not appear in Restoration comedy
       when "humour" took on the meaning of any kind of
       odd or eccentric behavior. Widely differing atti-
       tudes towards humour characterization were held by
       Etherege, Wycherley, Congreve, Vanbrugh, and
       Farquhar.

158   Schutz, Walter Stanley. "The Nature of Farce: Defin-
       ition and Devices." Ph.D. Michigan State Univer-
       sity, 1967. (Order No. 68-4211).
           A definition and analysis of the form in-
       cludes an examination of Nahum Tate's preface to
       A Duke and No Duke (1693) and other Restoration
       plays.

159   Scouten, A. H. "Notes Toward a History of Restora-
       tion Comedy." Philological Quarterly, XLV (1966),
       62-70.
           A history of Restoration comedy should take
       into account more than a few plays of the best
       dramatists. The Restoration volume of The London
       Stage shows that the comedy of manners appeared in
       two distinct and separate periods, that it was
       not the only type of current drama, and that it
       was not the first new type to appear at the Rest-
       oration.

160   Sharma, R. C. "Convention of Speech in the Restora-
       tion Comedy of Manners." Indian Journal of English

Studies, II (1961), 23-38.

161   Sharma, Ram Chandra. Themes and Conventions in the
       Comedy of Manners. New York: Asia Publishing
       House, 1965. 354 pp.
          Studies the plays and playwrights against the
       background of the age, particularly the fashion-
       able world around the court of Charles II.

162   Sharrock, Roger. "Modes of Satire " Restoration
       Theatre. Edited by John Russell Brown and Bernard
       Harris. (Stratford-Upon-Avon Studies, 6). (Lon-
       don: Edward Arnold, 1965; New York: St. Martin's
       Press, 1965), 109-132.
          Studies the relationship of non-dramatic
       satire to Restoration comedy. The business of satire
       was not only to rail at the permanent vices of man-
       kind and to demolish reputations but also to help
       define the ethos of a new elite.

163   Simon, Irene. "Restoration Comedy and the Critics."
       Revue des langues vivantes, XXIX (1963), 397-430.

164   Suckling, Norman. "Molière and English Restoration
       Comedy." Restoration Theatre. Edited by John Rus-
       sell Brown and Bernard Harris. (Stratford-Upon-
       Avon Studies,6). (London: Edward Arnold, 1965;
       New York: St. Martin's Press, 1965), 93-107.
          A reassessment of Molière's contributions
       that emphasizes the difference between his comedy
       and the Restoration comedy of England.

165   Tatum, Nancy R. "Attitudes Toward the Country in the
       Restoration Comedy, 1660-1728." Ph.D. Bryn Mawr,
       1961. 134 pp. (L. C. Card No. Mic. 60-2302).
          Stresses that the charges leveled at the country
       in Restoration comedy are related to its unchanged
       pattern of life and isolation. Country education,
       business, diversions, clothing, speech and manners
       are thoroughly criticized in the comedy.

166   Taylor, Charlene Mae. "Aspects of Social Criticism
       in Restoration Comedy." Ph.D. University of Illi-
       nois, 1965. (Order No. 66-4308).
          Changes in the characterization of the "social
       climber" from Dryden to Farquhar would suggest that
       Restoration comedy consciously reflected the social,

31

political, and economic pressures of the age. See also Nos. 251, 334, 421, 424, 456, 539, 770, 813, 1146, 1176.

167   Tiedje, Egon. Die Tradition Ben Jonsons in der Restaurationskomodie. (Britannica et Americana, Band 11), Hamburg: Cram, de Gruyster and Company, 1963. 168 pp.
        An examination of comedy written after 1660 reveals the influence of Jonson on Restoration theory and practice. Several chapters are concerned primarily with similarities in technique, theme, characterization, satire, and realism.

168   Traugott, John. "The Rake's Progress from Court to Comedy: a Study in Comic Form." Studies in English Literature, 1500-1900, VI (1966), 381-407.
        Studies the efforts of Restoration playwrights to find a comic form suitable for the rake as a representative of the society's values and as the center of a legitimate comedy. See also Nos. 198, 217, 412, 1056.

169   Vernon, P. F. "Marriage of Convenience and Moral Code of Restoration Comedy." Essays in Criticism, XII (1962), 370-387.
        In opposition to former criticism, contends that "Restoration comedy presupposes a wholly consistent moral standpoint."

170   Wall, Donald Clark. "The Restoration Rake in Life and Comedy." Ph.D. The Florida State University, 1963. (Order No. 64-7588).
        Compares the history and comedies of Charles II's reign in order to determine to what extent Restoration comedy portrayed the attitudes of the Restoration libertine.

171   Wilcox, John. The Relation of Molière to the Restoration Comedy. New York: Benjamin Blom, 1964. 240 pp.
        Reprint of Wilcox's 1940 text. Demonstrates the nature and extent of Restoration borrowings from Molière, Vanbrugh, and Farquhar are treated in detail.

172   Wilkinson, D. R. M. The Comedy of Habit: an Essay
on the Use of Courtesy Literature in a Study of
Restoration Comic Drama. (Leidse Germanistische
en Anglistiche Reehs von de Ryksuniversiteit
Leiden, 4). The Hague: Martinus Nijhoff, 1964.
190 pp.
       Uses Frances Osborne's Advice to a Son (1656-
1658) and other contemporary courtesy literature
to examine the wit and characterization of the
gallant, particularly in the plays of Etherege
and Wycherley.

COMEDY OF MANNERS, See Nos. 161, 412, 431

COMMAND PERFORMANCE, See No. 793

COMMEDIA DELL' ARTE, See No. 757

COMPARATIVE DRAMA
173   Simmons, Robert W., Jr. "Comparative Drama in the
17th Century." Restoration and 18th Century
Theatre Research, II (May, 1963), 13-18.
       Reasons for the dearth of scholarship on
Russian, Polish, and German dramas written before
1800. Suggests areas of comparative study for
the student of English literature.

CONCORDANCE, See Nos. 339, 984

CONGREVE
174   Congreve, William. The Complete Plays of William
Congreve. Edited by Herbert Davis. Chicago:
University of Chicago Press, 1967. 503 pp.
       The text is based on the first printed
quartos of the single plays. A general introduction
concerns Congreve's work as a dramatist and his
life before 1700. A short account of the composition and sources, the first performances and subsequent reputation of each play precedes the text.

175   --Incognita and The Way of the World. Edited by A.
Norman Jeffares. (Arnold's English Texts). London: Edward Arnold, 1966.
       Includes introduction, notes, and bibliography.

176   --Love for Love. Edited by Emmett L. Avery. (Regents
Restoration Drama Series). Lincoln: University of

33

Nebraska Press, 1966.
Includes introduction, notes, and chronology.

177   --Love for Love. Edited by A. Norman Jeffares. London: Macmillan; New York: St. Martin's Press, 1967.
Includes general introduction, notes, critical extracts, and select bibliography.

178   --The Way of the World. Edited by Kathleen M. Lynch. (Regents Restoration Drama Series). Lincoln: University of Nebraska Press, 1965.
Includes critical introduction, notes, and bibliography.

179   --The Way of the World. Edited by Gerald Weales. San Francisco: Chandler Publishing Co., 1966.

180   Banhatti, G. S. William Congreve (With a Detailed Study and Text of The Way of the World). (Masters of English Literature Series, 4). Allahabad and Calcutta: Kitab Mahal Pvt. Ltd., 1962.

181   Barnard, John. "Did Congreve Write A Satyr Against Love?" Bulletin of the New York Public Library, LXVIII (1964), 308-322.
Takes issue with the view that the satire was "an expression of feelings experienced by Congreve when Anne Bracegirdle rejected him." Outlines the internal evidence against Congreve's authorship of the piece.

182   Barraclough, Elmer D. "A Production Study and Text of William Congreve's The Way of the World as Presented at Catholic University." M.F.A. Catholic University of America, 1964.

183   Beatty, Max A. "A Project in Design and Execution of a Stage Setting for a Production of William Congreve's The Way of the World." M.A. Indiana University, 1964.

184   De Ment, Joseph Willia, Jr. "The Ironic Image: Metaphoric Structure and Texture in the Comedies of William Congreve." Ph.D. Indiana University, 1965. (Order No. 65-10815).
The metaphorical image patterns and lines of action in Congreve's comedies underscore the con-

flict between the age's theoretical Christian
outlook and its practical Machiavellian ethics.
See also Nos. 129, 135.

185   Dobree, Bonamy. "Congreve." Restoration Drama:
       Modern Essays in Criticism. (A Galaxy Book).
       Edited by John Loftis. (New York: Oxford Univer-
       sity Press, 1966), 97-121.
            Reprinted from Restoration Comedy (Oxford:
       Oxford University Press, 1924), pp. 121-150. A
       survey of Congreve's development and accomplish-
       ments as a dramatist.

186   --William Congreve. New York: Longman's, Green
       and Company (for the British Council and the Nation-
       al Book League), 1963. 35 pp.
            Brief account of Congreve's life and art with
       special emphasis on his comedies and the comedy
       of manners as a literary type.

187   Downer, Alan S. "Mr. Congreve Comes to Judgment."
       Humanities Association Bulletin, XVII (1966), 5-12.

188   "An Early Theatre Ticket." Theatre Notebook, XVIII
       (Winter, 1963/64), 42.
            Notes on ticket to Congreve's The Old Batche-
       lour. Includes illustration.

189   Fujiki, Hakuho. "The Use of Conjunctions in Con-
       greve's Works." Anglica (Osaka), V, i (1962),
       63-97.
            Article in Japanese. See pp. 93-97 for a
       summary in English.

190   Fujimura, Thomas H. "Congreve's Last Play." Rest-
       oration Dramatists: A Collection of Critical
       Essays. (Twentieth Century Views). Edited by
       Earl Miner. (Englewood Cliffs, N. J.: Prentice-
       Hall, Inc., 1966), 165-174.
            Reprinted from The Restoration Comedy of Wit
       (Princeton: Princeton University Press, 1952).
       The Way of the World is not as good a comedy of
       wit as The Man of Mode or Love for Love because
       "it lacks not only a strong naturalistic substratum
       but sceptical and sexual wit, comic wit that is
       easily grasped, and a consistent attitude toward
       life."

191   Gagen, Jean. "Congreve's Mirabell and the
       Ideal of the Gentleman." Publications of
       the Modern Language Association. LXXIX
       (1964), 422-427.
            Common misinterpretations of Mirabell's
       character result from the failure to dis-
       tinguish between the gentleman and rake or
       libertine of the Restoration period. The
       hero of The Way of the World represents the
       ideal of the gentleman current in Congreve's
       time.

192   Gosse, Anthony. "The Omitted Scene in Congreve's
       Love for Love." Modern Philology, LXI (1963),
       40-42.
            Congreve omitted scene ii of Act III
       of Love for Love as unnecessary to the charac-
       terization of Foresight.

193   Gosse, Anthony Cabot. "Dramatic Theory and
       Practice in the Comedies of William Congreve."
       Ph.D. Columbia University, 1962. (Order No.
       62-4232).
            The hitherto ignored technical skill of
       Congreve. Thematic and logical unity evident
       in most of his plays.

194   Hodges, John C., editor. William Congreve:
       Letters and Documents. New York: Harcourt,
       Brace, and World, 1964. 295 pp.
            157 letters and documents illuminate
       Congreve's personal life, business, and
       literary career. Includes his correspondence
       with Joseph Keally, Dryden, Tonson, Dennis,
       Addison, and Pope. Subject index.

195   Holland, Norman N. "Love for Love." Restoration
       Dramatists: A Collection of Critical Essays.
       (Twentieth Century Views). Edited by Earl
       Miner. (Englewood Cliffs, N.J.: Prentice-Hall,
       Inc., 1966), 151-164.
            Reprinted from The First Modern Comedies.
       (Cambridge, Mass.: Harvard University Press,
       1959). Congreve's third comedy concerns
       three different kinds of knowledge, three
       different ways of life: "presocial, social,
       suprasocial."

196   Howarth, R. C.   "Congreve and Anne Bracegirdle."
        English Studies in Africa, IV (1961), 159-161.
                Criticism of John C. Hodges' account
        of the relationship. No evidence that Brace-
        girdle was Congreve's mistress.

197   Juengel, Joyce J.   "A Project in Design and
        Construction of Costumes for a Production
        of The Way of the World, by William Congreve."
        M.A. Indiana University, 1963.

198   Klaus, Carl Hanna.   "The Scenic Art of William
        Congreve: An Approach to Restoration Comedy."
        Ph.D. Cornell University, 1966. (Order No.
        66-10, 272).
                A study of Congreve's plays that focuses
        on the substance, construction, and disposi-
        tion of scenes, particularly in The Old
        Batchelor, The Double Dealer, Love for Love,
        and The Way of the World.

199   Leech, Clifford.   "Congreve and the Century's
        End." Philological Quarterly, XLI (1962),
        275-293.
                Congreve's important place in Restora-
        tion drama. "Congreve brings the diverse
        and often conflicting elements of Restoration
        comedy into a unity."

200   "Congreve and the Century's End." Restoration
        Drama: Modern Essays in Criticism. (A Galaxy
        Book). Edited by John Loftis. (New York:
        Oxford University Press, 1966), 122-143.
                Reprinted from Philological Quarterly,
        XLI (1962), 275-293. With his successful
        work at the end of the century, "Congreve
        brings the diverse and often conflicting
        elements of Restoration comedy into a unity."

201   Lincoln, Stoddard. "Eccles and Congreve: Music
        and Drama on the Restoration Stage." Theatre
        Notebook, XVIII (Autumn, 1963), 7-18.
                The importance of Eccles's music for the
        interpretation and appreciation of Congreve's
        The Way of the World, The Judgment of Paris,
        The Ode for St. Cecilia's Day, and Semele.

37

202   --"The First Setting of Congreve's Semele."
        Music and Letters, XLIV (1963), 103-117.
                The collaboration of John Eccles and
        Congreve in the composition of Semele (1707).
        Eccles's attempt was the first by an English
        composer to produce a completely sung opera
        in English during this time.

203   Lynch, Kathleen M. A Congreve Gallery. New York:
        Octagon Books, 1967. 196 pp.
                A reprint of the 1951 edition. A study
        of Congreve's personality, background and
        times with emphasis on the friends of his
        youth.

204   Lyons, Charles R. "Congreve's Miracle of
        Love." Criticism, VI (1964). 331-348.
                In Love for Love, Congreve's attitude
        toward love is neither insouciant nor morally
        ambiguous. In the actions of Valentine
        and Angelica, Congreve affirms the value of
        an honest and faithful relationship in
        marriage. See also Nos. 101, 128, 145, 171.

205   Maurocordato, Alexandre. Ainsi Va le Monde:
        Etude sur la Structure d'une "Comedy of
        Manners." Paris: Lettres Modernes, 1967.
        55 pp.

206   Muir, Kenneth. "The Comedies of William Con-
        greve." Restoration Theatre. Edited by
        John Russell Brown and Bernard Harris.
        (Stratford-Upon-Avon Studies, 6). (London:
        Edward Arnold, 1965; New York: St. Martin's
        Press, 1965), 221-237.
                Congreve's success with the matter
        and form of the comedy of manners makes
        him "the best writer of comedy between
        Shakespeare and Shaw."

207   Nolan, Paul T. "Congreve's Lovers: Art and
        the Critic." Drama Survey, I (Winter, 1962),
        330-339.
                Concept of morality in The Old Bachelor,
        The Mourning Bride, and The Way of the World.

208   Taylor, D. C. William Congreve. New York:
       Russell and Russell, 1963. See also No. 780

209   Van Voris, W. H. The Cultivated Stance:
       The Designs of Congreve's Plays. Dublin:
       Dolmen Press, 1965; London: Oxford University
       Press, 1965. 186 pp.
            Examines Congreve's assumptions in the
       structures of his four comedies and his
       tragedy. The last chapter studies the dia-
       logue of the plays. See also Nos. 130, 132,
       147, 150, 159, 161

210   Weales, Gerald. "The Shadow on Congreve's
       Surface." Educational Theatre Journal,
       XIX (1967), 30-32.
            Analyzes Vainlove's unconventional
       attitudes toward sex in The Old Bachelor.
       See also Nos. 127, 571, 761, 1108

CONVENTION, See Nos. 161, 437

COSTUME
211   Cunnington, C. Willett, and Phillis Cunnington.
       Handbook of English Costume in the 18th
       Century. Second Edition. London: Faber
       and Faber, 1964. 443 pp.
            Reprint of the 1957 text on 18th cen-
       tury fashion. Many details cited in the
       work are drawn from the dramatic writings
       and theatrical journals of the day. 150
       illustrations. See also No. 527

212   Omary, Jeanne Kay. "An Historical Analysis
       of Eighteenth Century Costume." M.S. Univer-
       sity of Wisconsin, 1963.

213   Pentzell, Raymond Joseph. "New Dress'd in the
       Ancient Manner: The Rise of Historical
       Realism in Costuming the Serious Drama of
       England and France in the Eighteenth Cen-
       tury." Ph.D. Yale University, 1967. (Order
       No. 67-8407).
            Traces the revolution in stage costuming
       from operatic fantasy and conventionality
       to the acceptance of archeological verisi-
       militude.

39

214   Stephenson, Mary Amanda. "The Costume of the Hero of Restoration Tragedy." M.A. University of Florida, 1963. See Also No. 197

COSTUME, See Also No. 975

COSTUMES
215   Ferrar, Eleanor Barbara. "The Costuming of Harlequin in British Satirical Prints, 1740-1820." M.A. Ohio State University, 1961.
    Attempts to trace the evolution of the Harlequin costume, from 1740-1820, to discover how much effect contemporary fashions had upon the costume.

COTE'S WEEKLY JOURNAL, See No. 454

COVENT GARDEN
216   Highfill, Philip H., Jr. "Some Covent Garden Scenes." Theatre Notebook, XV (Spring, 1961), 88.
    Gives a transcript of BM Add 33, 218, which contains a list, by the principal Covent Garden painter Nicholas Thomas Dall, of divers "scenes and pieces of painting" which Colman has caused to be made since 9 September, 1768. See Also Nos. 629, 856, 1093

COVENT-GARDEN JOURNAL, See No. 443

COYSH, See No. 12

CRAWFURD
217   Macaree, David. "David Crawfurd (1665-1708?): His Works and Their Relation to Restoration Literature." Ph.D. University of Washington, 1966. (Order No. 66-12, 023).
    A study of Crawfurd's contribution to the literature of his time in short prose fiction, comedy, and Ovidian verse epistles. Crawfurd's comedies, Courtship-a-la-Mode (1700) and Love at First Sight (1704), are set in the tradition of Jonsonian comedy of humours as carried on by Shadwell rather than in that of Restoration comedy of wit.

CRITICAL REVIEW, See No. 783

CRITICISM, See Nos. 251, 539, 577, 733, 771,
    783, 830, 961, 998, 1004

CROWNE
218   Crowne, John. City Politiques. Edited by
       John Harold Wilson. (Regents Restoration
       Drama Series). Lincoln: University of
       Nebraska Press, 1967.
           Includes introduction, notes, and
       chronology.

219   --The Dramatic Works of John Crowne. Edited
       by J. Maidment and W. H. Logan. 4 vols.
       New York: Benjamin Blom, 1967.
           Reprint of the 1874 edition.

220   --Sir Courtly Nice. Edited by Charlotte
       Bradford Hughes. The Hague: Mouton and
       Co., 1966.
           Includes biography of Crowne, the
       stage history of the play, notes and bibli-
       ography.

221   Capwell, Richard Leonard. "A Biographical
       and Critical Study of John Crowne". Ph.D.
       Duke University, 1964. (Order No. 64-11,
       204).
           A chronological examination of Crowne's
       development as a dramatist. Each play is
       studied in relation to its sources, to con-
       temporary events, to the drama of the age,
       and as a popular stage production.

CROWNE, See Also No. 924

CUMBERLAND, See Nos. 133, 546, 921

CURLL, See No. 545

41

DATING
222   Anderson, Donald K., Jr. "The Date and Hand-
writing of a Manuscript Copy of Ford's
'Perkin Warbeck.'" Notes and Queries, New
Ser., X (1963), 340-341.
    There is evidence that a manuscript of
Ford's play was written in 1745 for the
December 19 production at Goodman's Fields.

223   Langhans, Edward A. "Theatrical References
in the Greenwich Hospital Newsletters."
Notes and Queries, New Ser., XI (1964),
338.
    Information helps date four play per-
formances in January, 1682: The Tempest
(probably Shadwell's version), Crowne's
Destruction of Jerusalem, Otway's Caius
Marius, and Davenant's Circe.

224   Wilson, James. "A Note on the Dating of
Restoration Plays." 17th and 18th Century
Theatre Research, I (May, 1962), 18-19.
    Problems to be considered in establish-
ing dates of publication and performance.

225   Wilson, John Harold. "The Duke's Theatre in
March, 1680." Notes and Queries, New Ser.,
IX (1962), 385-386.
    Evidence that King Charles did not
attend plays listed in the Lord Chamberlain's
list, particularly Otway's Souldier's
Fortune, and Dryden's Spanish Friar. Dates
of plays presented by the Duke of York's
Company.

226   --"Six Restoration Play Dates." Notes and
Queries, New Ser., IX (1962), 221-223.
    Dryden's (?) The Mistaken Husband,
Chamberlayne's Wits Led by the Nose, Dryden
and Lee's Oedipus, Crowne's Thyestes, and
Henry the Sixth, The First Part, and Banks'
The Unhappy Favourite.
    Dates are established for their produc-
tion.

227   D'Avenant, William. The Works of Sir William
       D'Avenant. 2 vols. New York: Benjamin
       Blom, 1967.
            A reprint of the 1673 edition which
       contains all of the plays as well as selec-
       tions of prose and poetry.

228   Bartholomeusz, Dennis. "The Davenant-
       Betterton Macbeth." Komos, I (1967), 41-48.

229   Feil, J. P. "Davenant Exonerated." Modern
       Language Review, LVIII (1963), 335-342.
            There is evidence that Davenant the
       playwright was not involved in the murder
       of Thomas Warren in 1633, that a second
       William Davenant, a resident of Essex, was
       responsible for Warren's death.

230   Nethercot, Arthur H. Sir William D'Avenant:
       Poet Laureate and Playwright-Manager. New
       York: Russell and Russell, 1967, 488 pp.
            A reissue of the 1938 edition with
       additional notes.

231   Palmer, Paulina. "Carew: An Unnoticed Allu-
       sion to Davenant's Illegitimacy." Notes
       and Queries, New Ser., X (1963), 61-62.
            A reference to bastardy in Carew's
       "To Will. Davenant My Friend," recalls Dave-
       nant's insistence that he was Shakespeare's
       illegitimate son.

232   Spencer, Christopher. Davenant's Macbeth
       from the Yale Manuscript: An Edition, with a
       Discussion of the Relation of Davenant's
       Text to Shakespeare's. New Haven: Yale
       University Press, 1961. 226 pp. (Yale
       Studies in English, Vol. 146).
            Presents a text of Davenant's play,
       which has been reproduced only twice since
       1710. Improves on previous editions by the
       addition of line numbers and by the inclusion
       of the Yale MS, which seems to have been
       used in preparing the promptbook.

233   Spencer, T.J.B., Stanley Wells, et al., editors.
       A Book of Masques: In Honour of Allardyce

Nicoll. Cambridge: Cambridge University
Press, 1967, 448 pp.
   Fourteen masques, each edited with an
introduction, textual essay and commentary
by a different scholar. Includes Davenant's
Salmacida Spolia (1640) edited by T. J. B.
Spencer.

234   Squier, Charles L. "Davenant's Comic Assault
on Preciosité: The Platonic Lovers." University of Colorado Studies (Series in Language
and Literature, 10). Edited by J. K. Emery.
(Boulder: University of Colorado Press,
1966), pp. 57-72. See Also No. 551

235   Squier, Charles LaBarge. "The Comic Spirit
of Sir William Davenant: A Critical Study
of His Caroline Comedies." Ph.D. University
of Michigan, 1963. (Order No. 63-6958),
   A study of The Just Italian, News from
Plymouth, The Wits, The Platonic Lovers.

DAVENANT, See Also Nos. 3, 9, 223, 832, 965,
   1002, 1058, 1065

DAWSON

236   Burnim, Kalman A. "Here We Go Round the Mulberry Bush'--With Dr. Arne and Nancy Dawson."
Restoration and Eighteenth Century Theatre
Research, IV (November, 1965), 39-48.
   Conjectures that Nancy Dawson's song,
now the famous nursery rhyme, was composed
by Dr. Arne sometime after her initial summer
success at Sadler's Wells.

237   --"Nancy Dawson's Tombstone." Restoration
and 18th Century Theatre Research, V (May,
1966), 59.
   A note on the author's article, "Here
We Go Round the Mulberry Bush'--With Dr.
Arne and Nancy Dawson." Restoration and
18th Century Theatre Research, IV (November,
1965). 39-48. Discusses a problem of the
epitaph on the actress's tombstone in St.
George's Gardens, Bloomsbury.

DE BOISSY, See No. 458

DENNIS
238   Dickens, Louis George. "The Story of Appius
       and Virginia in English Literature." Ph.D.
       The University of Rochester, 1963. (Order
       No. 63-7762).
              Includes a discussion of the dramatic
       versions of Betterton and Dennis. See Also
       No. 805

239   Richeson, Edward, Jr. "John Dennis as a
       Psychological Critic." Ph.D. Boston Univer-
       sity, 1962. (Order No. 62-5537).
              Analysis of Dennis criticism concerning
       the aesthetic creation, the art object, and
       the effect dependent upon the emotions of
       poet and audience. See Also Nos. 145, 194,
       507, 1081, 1121, 1122

DE WILDE, See No. 908

DICTIONARY
240   Bowman, Robert P., and Robert Hamilton Ball.
       Theatre Language: A Dictionary of Terms in
       English of the Drama and Stage from Medieval
       to Modern Times. New York: Theatre Arts
       Books, 1961.

DIDACTIC AESTHETIC, See No. 590

DIRECTOR, See Nos. 117, 773, 1065

DOCUMENTS
241   McCollum, John L., Jr. The Restoration Stage.
       Boston: Houghton, Mifflin Company, 1961.
       X, 236 pp.
              Provides excerpts from twenty-seven
       documents for the teaching of research method.
       Excerpts are from critical and theoretical
       writings, prologues, epilogues, diaries,
       memoirs, essays, apologies, defences, epistles,
       and short views.

DOMESTIC TRAGEDY, See No. 1135

DORSET, See No. 267

DORSET GARDEN, See Nos. 1086, 1087, 1098, 1101

DRAKE, See No. 998

DRAMATIC FORM, See No. 275

DRAMATIC PERIODICALS
242   "Dublin's First Dramatic Periodical." Restora-
        tion and 18th Century Theatre Research, II
        (May, 1963), 32-36.
             A reproduction of The Play-House Journal
        published in Dublin, January 18, 1749-50.

243   Hummert, Paul A. "The Prompter: An Intimate
        Mirror of the Theatre in 1789." Restoration
        and 18th Century Theatre Research, III (May,
        1964). 37-46.
             Detailed examination of the contents of
        The Prompter reveals that the periodical
        "mirrored typical dramatic opinions and cus-
        toms prevailing in the theatre at this time."

244   "Microfilm of British Dramatic Periodicals."
        Restoration and 18th Century Theatre Research,
        II (May, 1963), 20-31.
             Lists 160 British dramatic periodicals
        available on microfilm at Loyola University
        Library, Chicago, Illinois.

245   "Microfilm of British Dramatic Periodicals."
        Restoration and 18th Century Theatre Re-
        search, III (May, 1964), 46-50.
             Continues list of theatrical periodicals
        begun in Restoration and 18th Century Theatre
        Research, II (May, 1963). 84 entries.

246   Stratman, Carl J., C.S.V. A Bibliography of
        British Dramatic Periodicals, 1720-1960.
        New York: New York Public Library, 1962.
        58 pp.
             A list of 674 dramatic periodicals pub-
        lished in England, Scotland, and Ireland.
        Gives complete titles, title changes, edi-
        tors, place of publication, number of volumes
        and issues, dates of first and last issues,
        frequency of issue, libraries where periodi-
        cal may be found.

247 --"Cotes' Weekly Journal; or, The English Stage
  Player." Papers of the Bibliographical Society
  of America, LVI (1962), 104-106.
   The earliest theatrical paper published in
  England from May 11 to July 16, 1734 in nine
  issues.

248 --"Preparing a Bibliography of British Dramatic
  Periodicals, 1720-1960." Bulletin of the New
  York Public Library, LXVI (1962), 405-408.
   Contains a brief consideration of the
  general plan and scope of the bibliography.

249 --"Scotland's First Dramatic Periodical: The
  Edinburgh Theatrical Censor." Theatre Notebook, XVII (Spring, 1963), 83-86.
   An analysis of the Censor's format, type
  of drama criticism, remarks on theatrical
  conditions and acting. Includes a discussion
  of the periodical's criticism of the following
  plays: Douglas, by John Home; Hear Both Sides,
  by Thomas Holcroft; The Inconstant, and The
  Beaux Stratagem, by George Farquhar; Pizarro,
  by R. B. Sheridan; A Bold Stroke for a Wife, by
  Susanna Centlivre; John Bull and The Heir at
  Law, by George Colman; The Way to Keep Him, by
  Arthur Murphy; and The Marriage Promise, by
  J. T. Allingham.

DRAMATIC THEORY
250 Simon, Irene. "Critical Terms in Restoration
  Translation from the French." Revue Belge de
  Philologie et d'Histoire, XLII (1964), 852-879.

251 Maurocordato, Alexandre. La Critique Classique
  en Angleterre de la Restauration a la Mort de
  Joseph Addison. Paris: M. Didier, 1964. 728
  pp.
   An essay comparing French and English
  critical doctrine between 1660 and 1719. Intended to show the indebtedness of English
  critics to their French counterparts, the study
  focuses on theories of tragedy, comedy, satire,
  and ballad and related critical concepts. See
  Also Nos. 275, 590.

DRURY LANE, See Nos. 106, 466, 623, 624, 856, 1039,
  1102

252 Dryden, John. All for Love; or, The World Well
Lost. Edited by John J. Enck. (Crofts Classics).
New York: Appleton-Century-Crofts, 1966.

253 --An Essay of Dramatic Poesy. A Defence of an
Essay of Dramatic Poesy, Preface to the Fables.
Edited by John L. Mahoney. (Library of Liberal
Arts). Indianapolis, Indiana: Bobbs-Merrill,
1965. 119 pp.
  Includes introduction, notes, and selected
bibliography.

254 --Four Comedies. Edited by L. A. Beaurline and
Fredson Bowers. Chicago: University of Chicago
Press, 1967.
  Includes a general introduction as well as
notes and brief introductory comments for each
play: Secret Love, Sir Martin Mar-All, An
Evening's Love, and Marriage-a-la Mode.

255 --Four Tragedies. Edited by L. A. Beaurline and
Fredson Bowers. Chicago: University of Chicago
Press, 1967.
  Includes a general introduction as well as
notes and brief introductory comments for each
play: The Indian Emperour, Aureng-Zebe, All
for Love, and Don Sebastian.

256 --Literary Criticism of John Dryden. Edited by
Arthur C. Kirsch. (Regents Critics Series).
Lincoln: University of Nebraska Press, 1966.
  An edition of Dryden's major works of
criticism. Includes introduction, notes, and
selected bibliography.

257 --Of Dramatic Poesy and Other Critical Essays.
Edited with an Introduction by George Watson.
(Everyman's Library, Nos. 568, 569). London:
Dent; New York: Dutton, 1962. 2 vols.
  Includes notes and select bibliography.

258 --The Works of John Dryden. General Editor: H.
T. Swedenberg, Jr. Textual editor: Vinton A.
Dearing. Vol. VIII: Plays: The Wild Gallant,
The Rival Ladies, The Indian Queen. Editors:
John Harrington Smith, Dougald MacMillan, and

Vinton A. Dearing, in association with Samuel
H. Monk and Earl Miner. Berkeley and Los
Angeles: University of California Press, 1962,
376 pp.
Excellent editions of the three early
plays. Includes textual variations, commentary
and notes for each play, sections on staging
and actors.

259   --The Works of John Dryden. General Editor: H.
T. Swedenberg, Jr. Associate General Editor:
Earl Miner. Textual Editor Vinton A. Dearing.
Vol. IX: Plays: The Indian Emperour, Secret
Love, Sir Martin Mar-All. Editors: John
Loftis and Vinton A. Dearing. Berkley and Los
Angeles: University of California Press, 1966,
451 pp.
Includes textual variations, commentaries,
and notes for each play.

260   Aden, John M., editor. The Critical Opinions
of John Dryden: A Dictionary. Nashville,
Tenn.: Vanderbilt University Press, 1963,
290 pp.
Arranged alphabetically by subject, with
quotations from Dryden's essays, dedications,
prefaces, headnotes, notes and observations,
biographies and letters. Includes index and
chronological list of sources.

261   Allen, Ned Bliss. The Sources of John Dryden's
Comedies. New York: Gordian Press, 1967,
298 pp.
A reprint of the 1935 edition, chapters
discuss The Wild Gallant, The Rival Ladies,
the tragi-comedies, and Dryden's adaptations of
Molière.

262   Alssid, Michael W. "The Design of Dryden's
Aureng-Zebe." Journal of English and Germanic
Philology, LXIV (1965), 452-469.
Examines the structural design, thematic
unity, characterization, patterns of imagery
and metaphor, and Dryden's development of epic
materials in the play.

49

263   --"The Perfect Conquest: a Study of Theme,
       Structure and Characters in Dryden's The
       Indian Emperor." Studies in Philology, LIX
       (1962), 539-559.
            Discusses elements which contribute to
       the play's success and artistic unity.

264   --Shadwell's MacFlecknoe." Studies in English
       Literature, 1500-1900, VII (1967), 387-402.
            In MacFlecknoe Dryden subverted Shad-
       well's critical ideas and dramatic practice
       and "deliberately and ironically metamor-
       phosed Shadwell into a humors character to
       show us a fool who, like the humors of his
       plays, persistently incriminates himself."

265   Archer, Stanley. "Dryden's MacFlecknoe." The
       Explicator, XXVI (December, 1967), Item No.
       37.
            "Aston Hall" in line 48 may refer to
       Santon Hall, Shadwell's birthplace near Nor-
       wich.

266   --"The Persons in An Essay of Dramatic Poesy."
       Papers on Language and Literature, II
       (1966), 305-314.
            Dryden intended the person to represent
       coherent critical positions, but the char-
       acters do more nearly correspond to the
       originals suggested by Malone than recent
       critics and editors acknowledge.

267   Archer, Stanley Louis. "John Dryden and the
       Earl of Dorset." Ph.D. The University of
       Mississippi, 1965. (Order No. 65-6872).
            Analyzes the relationship between
       Dryden and his patron. Attention is directed
       to Dryden's reasons for dedicating the Essay
       of Dramatic Poesy (1668) to the Earl.

268   Banks, Landrum. "The Imagery of Dryden's Rhymed
       Heroic Drama." Ph.D. University of Tennessee,
       1967. (Order No. 68-9790).
            Analyzes the special imagery Dryden
       created for this special genre. Although
       classical analogies and comparisons are

occasionally used to elevate the style, Dryden relies heavily on traditional associations from the common experiences and the everyday world of the ordinary man.

269   Barnard, John. "The Dates of Six Dryden Letters." Philological Quarterly, XLII (1963), 396-403.
       Dryden's references to the delayed production of his son's play, The Husband His Own Cuckold, aid in dating several letters to Tonson.

270   Bately, Janet M. "Dryden and Branded Words." Notes and Queries, New Ser., XII (1965), 134-139.
       Explains vocabulary discrepancies between the first and second editions of the Essay of Dramatic Poesy.

271   --"Dryden's Revisions in the Essay of Dramatic Poesy: The Preposition at the End of the Sentence and the Expression of the Relative." The Review of English Studies, XV (1964), 268-282.
       Corrections made by Dryden for the edition of 1684 evidence his consciousness of "correct" language.

272   Beckson, Karl, editor. Great Theories in Literary Criticism. (Noonday Paperback 241). New York: Farrar, Straus, 1963. 317 pp.
       Anthology of literary criticism from Aristotle to Arnold. Dryden's Essay of Dramatic Poesy included in Chapter 2.

273   Blackwell, Herbert Robinson. "Some Formulary Characteristics of John Dryden's Comedies." Ph. D. University of Virginia, 1967. (Order No. 67-17, 589).
       Studies Dryden's use of farce, stage conventions, stock characters, and rhetoric in the comedies.

274   Boulton, James T., editor. <u>Of Dramtick Poesie,</u>
       <u>an Essay with Sir Robert Howard's Preface to</u>
       <u>the Great Favourite and Dryden's Defence of</u>
       <u>an Essay.</u> London: Oxford University Press,
       1964, 190 pp.
              Student's edition with introduction,
       biographical outline, notes, and select bibli-
       ography.

275   Bradbrook, M. C. <u>English Dramatic Form: A</u>
       <u>History of its Development.</u> London: Chatto
       and Windus, 1965, 205 pp.
              Chapter VI, "Prisoners and Politics:
       The Social Image from Shakespeare to Dryden,"
       contains a discussion of Dryden's heroic
       plays.

276   Bredvold, Louis I. "Dryden, Hobbes, and the
       Royal Society." <u>Essential Articles for the</u>
       <u>Study of John Dryden.</u> (The Essential Articles
       Series). Edited by H. T. Swedenberg, Jr.
       (Hamden, Conn.: Archon Books, 1966), 314-
       340.
              Reprinted from <u>Modern Philology,</u> XXV
       (1928), 417-438. Dryden's sympathetic in-
       terest in the Royal Society and the new
       science. Includes references to <u>The Rival</u>
       <u>Ladies</u> and <u>The Conquest of Granada.</u>

277   --"Political Aspects of Dryden's <u>Amboyna</u> and
       <u>The Spanish Fryar.</u>" <u>Essential Articles for</u>
       <u>the Study of John Dryden.</u> (The Essential
       Articles Series.) Edited by H. T. Sweden-
       berg, Jr. (Hamden, Conn.: Archon Books,
       1966), 300-313.
              Reprinted from <u>University of Michigan</u>
       <u>Publications, Language and Literature,</u>
       VIII (1932), 119-132. A revaluation of his
       supposed political activities and changes
       during the time in which he wrote these plays
       reveals that Dryden was a firm, consistent,
       and loyal Tory.

278   Brower, Reuben Arthur. "Dryden's Epic Manner
       and Virgil." <u>Essential Articles for the Study</u>
       <u>of John Dryden.</u> (The Essential Articles Series).

                            52

Edited by H. T. Swedenberg, Jr. (Hamden, Conn.:
Archon Books, 1966), 466-492.
Reprinted from PMLA, LV (1940), 119-138.
The influence of Virgil's epic style on Dryden's
works. Includes a discussion of the epic tone
in The Conquest of Granada and Aureng-Zebe.

279   Caracciolo, Peter. "Some Unrecorded Variants
       in the First Edition of Dryden's All for Love,
       1678." Book Collector, XIII (1964), 498-500.
       Notes variant readings in the extant
       copies of the first quarto of the play.

280   Cooke, M. G. "The Restoration Ethos of Byron's
       Classical Plays." Publications of the Modern
       Language Association, LXXIX (1964), 569-578.
       Byron's Classicism is the classicism of
       the Restoration. His theories and practice
       of drama are dependent especially on Dryden.
       Includes extensive comparison of Byron's Sar-
       danapalus with Dryden's All for Love, and
       illustrates some of Byron's borrowings from
       Otway's Venice Preserv'd for his Marino
       Faliero.

281   Davies, H. Neville. "Dryden, Hobbes, and the
       Nimble Spaniel." Notes and Queries, New
       Ser., X (1963), 349-350.
       In a reply to George Watson's note (pp.
       230-231), Davies cites a passage from All
       for Love to prove that the source of Dryden's
       spaniel images was Hobbes's Leviathan.

282   --"Dryden's All for Love and Sedley's Antony
       and Cleopatra." Notes and Queries, XIV
       (1967), 221-227.
       Dryden's borrowings from Sedley's
       work show not only that Dryden is the more
       skillful dramatist but also that he was con-
       sciously "working up" promising material from
       Sedley's 1677 play.

283   --"Dryden's All for Love and Thomas May's The
       Tragedie of Cleopatra Queen of Aegypt." Notes

and Queries, New Ser., XII (1965), 139-144.

A review of Dryden's sources for <u>All for Love</u> and a study of his indebtedness to <u>May's</u> play (acted 1626, published 1639 and 1654) for his first act and perhaps also for his conclusion.

284   Day,, Cyrus Lawrence, ed. <u>The Songs of John Dryden</u>. New York: Russell and Russell, 1967, 199 pp.

A reissue of the 1932 edition which includes songs written by Dryden for the plays.

285   Doyle, Anne. "Dryden's Authorship of <u>Notes and Observations on The Empress of Morocco</u> (1674)." <u>Studies in English Literature, 1500-1900</u>, VI (1966), 421-445.

Reviews the dispute over the authorship of the attack on Elkanah Settle's play, and contends that only the Preface and Postscript can be ascribed to Dryden with certainty.

286   Elloway, D. R., editor. <u>Dryden's Satire</u>. London: Macmillan; New York: St. Martin's Press, 1966, 181 pp.

An edition of <u>MacFlecknoe</u>, <u>Absalom and Achitophel</u>, and <u>The Medal</u> with satiric selections from Dryden's other works, including the Epilogue to <u>Tyrannic Love</u> and the Prologue to <u>All for Love</u>, Includes introduction, notes, and select bibliography.

287   Falle, George. "Sir Walter Scott as Editor of Dryden and Swift." <u>University of Toronto Quarterly</u>, XXXVI (1967), 161-180.

Discusses Scott's editorial limitations and virtues and analyzes the editions to show why the Dryden is to be preferred to the <u>Swift</u>.

288   Feder, Lillian. "John Dryden's Use of Classical Rhetoric." <u>Essential Articles for the Study of John Dryden</u>. (The Essential Articles Series).

Edited by H. T. Swedenberg, Jr. (Hamden, Conn.: Archon Books, 1966), 493-518.
Reprinted from PMLA, LXIX (1954), 1258-1278. In his criticism and poetry Dryden adopted principles of classical rhetoric to the needs of his own time and to his talents.

289   Forker, Charles R. "Romeo and Juliet and the 'Cyndus' Speech in Dryden's All for Love." Notes and Queries, New Ser., IX (1962), 382-383.
Discussion of similarities between the characters of Cleopatra (Dryden) and Juliet, as well as other parallels between the two works.

290   Gagen, Jean. "Love and Honor in Dryden's Heroic Plays." Publications of the Modern Language Association, LXXVII (1962), 208-220.
A review of the Renaissance humanist's concept of honor and the concept of Platonic love to show how these affect Dryden's ideas in The Indian Queen, Aureng-Zebe, Tyrannick Love, The Conquest of Granada, The Spanish Fryar, and The Indian Emperour.

291   Gatto, Louis C. "An Annotated Bibliography of Critical Thought Concerning Dryden's Essay of Dramatic Poesy." Restoration and 18th Century Theatre Research, V (May, 1966), 18-29.
Includes 80 entries: 10 for standard editions, 70 for criticism of the Essay.

292   Goggin, L. P. "This Bow of Ulysses." Essays and Studies in Language and Literature (1963), 49-86.
Dryden subscribed to theories other than those expressed by Neander in Of Dramatic Poesy, An Essay (1668). An examination of the theme, plot, characterization and sources of All for Love reveals that the play was developed upon principles enunciated by Crites, Lisideius, and Eugenius in the Essay and by the author in other writings.

293   Golden, Samuel A. "Dryden's 'Cleomenes' and Theophilus Parsons.: Notes and Queries, New Ser.,

XIII (1966), 380.
Theophilus Parsons, author of the prefatory poem to Dryden's Cleomenes (1693) was a first cousin of Nahum Tate.

294   Griffith, Benjamin W.,Jr., ed. All for Love, or, The World Well Lost. Illustrated by Tom Keough. Great Neck, New York: Barron's Educational Series, 1961.

295   Heise, Howard Sherman. "A Comparative Study of Shakespeare's Antony and Cleopatra and Dryden's All for Love." M.A. University of South Dakota, 1963.

296   Hemphill, George. "Dryden's Heroic Line." Essential Articles for the Study of John Dryden. (The Essential Articles Series). Edited by H.T. Swedenberg, Jr. (Hamden, Conn.: Archon Books, 1966), 519-540.
Reprinted from PMLA, LXXII (1957), 863-879. A study of Dryden's prosody includes occasional references to his statements in the Essay on Dramatic Poesy and to his plays.

297   Huntley, Frank Livingstone. "Dryden, Rochester, and the Eighth Satire of Juvenal." Essential Articles for the Study of John Dryden. (The Essential Articles Series). Edited by H. T. Swedenberg, Jr. (Hamden, Conn.: Archon Books, 1966), 91-111.
Reprinted from Philological Quarterly, XVIII (1939), 269-284. The Preface to All for Love is "a piece of epideictic rhetoric devoted to a censure of Rochester" and is more significant as rhetoric than as criticism.

298   --"On the Persons in Dryden's Essay of Dramatic Poesy." Essential Articles for the Study of John Dryden. (The Essential Articles Series). Edited by H.T. Swedenberg, Jr. (Hamden, Conn.: Archon Books, 1966), 83-90.
Reprinted from Modern Language Notes, LXIII (1948), 88-95. Criticizes Malone's identification of Dryden's four speakers and discusses them as embodiments of attitude necessitated by the argument.

299   Illo, John, "Dryden, Sylvester, and the Correspon-
       dence of Melancholy Winter and Cold Age." English
       Language Notes, I (1963), 101-104.
              Discusses a passage on metaphor from the
       Dedication of The Spanish Friar (1681).

300   Irie, Keitaro.   "The Auxiliary 'Do' in John Dry-
       den's Plays."   Angelica (Osaka), V, i (1962),
       1-19.

301   Jackson, Wallace.   "Dryden's Emperor and Lillo"s
       Merchant: the Relevant Bases of Action."
       Modern Language Quarterly, XXVI (1965), 536-544.
              Desires a more closely unified approach
       to the drama of the late seventeenth and early
       eighteenth centuries. A fundamentally similar
       set of assumptions concerning the primacy of
       social contract governs the actions and characters
       of Dryden's All for Love and Lillo's The London
       Merchant.

302   Jefferson, D. W. "'All, all of a piece throughout':
       Thoughts on Dryden's Dramatic Poetry." Restora-
       tion Theatre. Edited by John Russell Brown and
       Bernard Harris. (Stratford-Upon-Avon Studies,
       6). (London: Edward Arnold, 1965; New York:
       St. Martin's Press, 1965), 159-176.
              The repetition of words, images, and themes
       demonstrates the interrelationships of Dryden's
       heroic plays.

303   --"The Significance of Dryden's Heroic Plays."
       Restoration Drama: Modern Essays in Criticism.
       (A Galaxy Book). Edited by John Loftis. (New
       York: Oxford University Press, 1966), 161-179.
       Also in Restoration Dramatists: A Collection
       of Critical Essays. (Twentieth Century Views).
       Edited by Earl Miner. (Englewood Cliffs, N.J.:
       Prentice-Hall, Inc., 1966), 19-35.
              Reprinted from Proceedings of The Leeds
       Philosophical and Literary Society, V (1940),
       125-139. Dryden's "comic" purpose in the
       heroic plays helped to develop the qualities
       which later made him a superb satirist.

304   Jensen, Harvey James. "A Glossary of John Dryden's
       Critical Terms." Ph.D. Cornell University, 1966.
       (Order No. 67-1471).

Definitions of critical terms drawn from
George Watson's Of Dramatic Poesy and Other
Critical Essays and the Scott-Saintsbury edition
of Dryden's Works.

305   Jeune, Simon. "Hamlet d'Otway, Macbeth de Dryden;
       ou Shakespeare en France en 1714." Revue de
       littérature comparée, XXXVI(1962),560-564.

306   Kallich, Martin. "Oedipus: from Man to Archetype."
       Comparative Literature Studies, III(1966),33-46.
              Studies the several meanings of the Oedipus
       myth from Sophocles to Cocteau and discusses
       the unusual sentimental interpretation by Dryden
       and Lee in Oedipus (1678).

307   King, Bruce. "Absalom and Dryden's Earlier Praise
       of Monmouth." English Studies, XLVI (1965),
       332-333.
              Notes an ironic contrast between the dedi-
       cation of Tyrannic Love to Monmouth in 1670
       and Dryden's allusion to it in Absalom and
       Achitophel eleven years later.

308   --"Anti-Whig Satire in The Duke of Guise." English
       Language Notes, II(1965), 190-193.
              Offers three possible sources for the Whig
       propaganda in the play: The anonymous A Letter
       from a Person of Quality to his Friend Concern-
       ing His Majesties late Declaration, Shadwell's
       Epistle to the Tories, and Filmer's Patriarchia.

309   --"Don Sebastian: Dryden's Moral Fable." Sewanee
       Review, LXX(1962), 651-670.
              The play is indicative of Dryden's growth
       toward a fuller dramatic form. Discusses the
       influence of mid-century French neo-classical
       critics in providing Dryden with a moral purpose
       and "thematic organizing principle."

310   --"Dryden, Tillotson, and Tyrannic Love." Review
       of English Studies, XVI(1965), 364-377.
              Parallels between St. Catherine's speeches
       in Tyrannic Love and Tillotson's early sermons,
       especially The Excellency of the Christian
       Religion suggest that, at the time of the play,
       Dryden was a Latitudinarian Anglican and influ-
       enced by Tillotson's attempt to give faith a lo-

316   --"The Significance of Dryden's State of Inno-
       cence." Studies in English Literature, 1500-
       1900, IV, (1964), 371-391.
              Examines The State of Innocence as a
       philosophical work concerned with "the moral
       disobedience which results from the nature of
       man's appetite, pride, and unrest."

317   Kirsch, Arthur C. "Dryden, Corneille, and the
       Heroic Play." Modern Philology, LIX (1962),
       248-264.
              A definition of the heroic code of be-
       havior which demonstrates a relationship be-
       tween Dryden and Corneille.

318   --Dryden's Heroic Drama. Princeton: Princeton
       University Press, 1965, 157 pp.
              The perennial interest in Dryden's plays
       rests in their fluidity. Dryden's theory of
       the heroic play, his concept of the hero, and
       his stage practice were modified frequently to
       meet the demands of a transitional society.

319   --Dryden's Theory and Practice of the Rhymed
       Heroic Play." Ph.D. Princeton University,
       1961, 248 pp. (Order No. 61-4797).
              The first three chapters deal with Dry-
       den's theory; the last two chapters are con-
       cerned principally with his practice. Influences
       upon his theory and practice.

320   --"An Essay on Dramatick Poetry (1681)."
       Huntington Library Quarterly, XXVIII (1964),
       89-91.
              Quotes a brief essay affixed to a trans-
       lation of Madeleine de Scudéry which praises
       Dryden as the leading dramatist of the age.

321   --"The Significance of Dryden's Aureng-Zebe."
       Journal of English Literary History, XXIX
       (1962), 160-174.
              The increased use of sentimental heroes
       and domestic situations and the absence of
       rhyme in Aureng-Zebe are indicative of general
       changes in serious drama during second decade
       of the Restoration.

gical basis.

311   --"Dryden's Ark: The Influence of Filmer."
        Studies in English Literature, 1500-1900,
        VII (1967), 403-414.
             Dryden probably found his favorite image
        for the Restoration, Noah's ark, in the poli-
        tical theories of Sir Robert Filmer. Reference
        to Filmer's theories may be found in several
        plays: The Unhappy Favorite, Oedipus, Don
        Sebastian, and The Spanish Friar.

312   --"Dryden's Intent in All for Love." College
        English, XXIV (1963), 267-271.
             Crucial documents by Dryden before 1678
        qualify his statement in the preface to All
        for Love that he wrote the play "for the ex-
        cellency of the moral."

313   --"Dryden's Marriage a la Mode." Drama Survey,
        IV (1965), 28-37.
             The brilliance of the play derives from
        "an extended comparison between fashionable
        Restoration society and Thomas Hobbes' theory
        that man in his natural state is permanently
        at war to conquer the property of others."

314   --Dryden's Major Plays. Edinburgh and London:
        Oliver and Boyd, 1966, 215 pp.
             An interpretation of the individual plays
        that attempts to demonstrate "how the same
        intelligence that worked through wit and humour
        in the heroic plays was striving to express
        itself in a more serious manner in the later
        moral fables." Also traces the intellectual
        background of Dryden's themes and his approach
        to the literary fashions of his day.

315   --"Heroic and Mock-Heroic Plays." Sewanee Re-
        view, LXX (1962), 514-517.
             Dryden's dramatic satire, its implied
        morality, and attack upon Hobbes' theory of
        natural man.

322   --"The Significance of Dryden's Aureng-Zebe."
        Restoration Drama: Modern Essays in Criticism.
        (A Galaxy Book). Edited by John Loftis. (New
        York: Oxford University Press, 1966), 180-
        194. Also in Restoration Dramatists: A Col-
        lection of Critical Essays. (Twentieth Century
        Views). Edited by Earl Miner. (Englewood
        Cliffs, N.J.: Prentice-Hall, Inc., 1966),
        37-49.
            Reprinted from A Journal of English Liter-
        ary History, XXIX (1962), 160-175. The increased
        use of sentimental heroes and domestic situations
        and the absence of rhyme in Aureng-Zebe are in-
        dicative of general changes in serious drama
        during the second decade of the Restoration.

323   Klima, S. "Some Unrecorded Borrowings from
        Shakespeare in Dryden's All for Love." Notes
        and Queries, New Ser., X (1963), 415-418.
            Lists borrowings from plays other than
        Antony and Cleopatra.

324   Krupp, Kathleen McCoy. "John Dryden on the Func-
        tions of Drama." Ph.D. Florida State University,
        1966. (Order No. 67-298).
            While Dryden accepted the utile and dulci
        ideas of Horace, his critical discussions of
        comedy, tragedy, and the heroic play reveal that
        he was most interested in the pleasurable emo-
        tional effects of plays.

325   Lavine, Anne Rabiner. "The Bow of Ulysses:
        Shakespeare's Troilus and Cressida and Its
        Imitation by Dryden." Ph.D. Bryn Mawr, 1961.
        415 pp. (Order No. 62-1).
            A study of Dryden's imitation in all its
        aspects, with special emphasis on style. Also
        a study of Dryden's criticism in order to deter-
        mine some causes for the Restoration practice
        of adaptation.

326   Leeman, Richard Kendall. "Corneille and Dryden:
        Their Theories of Dramatic Poetry." Ph.D.
        University of Wisconsin, 1961, 445 pp. (Order
        No. 61-3131).

An examination of their theories shows that
they were remarkably alike in their independence
of major neo-Aristotelian dogmas, especially
those concerning dramatic imitation, dramatic
function, and dramatic production.

327   Legouis, Pierre. "Ouvrages recents sur Dryden."
       Etudes Anglaises, XVII (1964), 148-158.
            Reviews six scholarly studies which affirm
       the vitality of Dryden's art.

328   Loftis, John. "Exploration and Enlightenment:
       Dryden's The Indian Emperour and Its Background."
       Philological Quarterly, XLV (1966), 71-84.
            The intellectual dimension of exploration
       presented in the play includes a dramatic
       elucidation of seventeenth century ideas on
       primitivism, religion, and political theory,
       and enables Dryden to expose irrationalities of
       European beliefs.

329   --"The Hispanic Element in Dryden." Emory Univer-
       sity Quarterly, XX (1964), 90-100.
            The influence of Lope de Vega, Camoens, and
       especially of Calderon on Dryden's comedies and
       heroic plays. Reviews previous scholarship on
       the question of Hispanic influence.

330   MacDonald, Hugh. John Dryden: A Bibliography of
       Early Editions and of Drydeniana. London:
       Dawsons of Pall Mall, 1966, 358 pp.
            Facsimile reprint of the 1939 edition.

331   Mace, Dean T. "Dryden's Dialogue on Drama."
       Journal of the Warburg and Courtald Institutes,
       XXV (1962), 87-112.
            On the Essay of Dramatic Poesy. The dispute
       between two aesthetic principles: 1 poetry
       should be founded on historical truth; 2 poetry
       should ignore the history of things and concen-
       trate on emotional and imaginative effectiveness.

332   McFadden, George. "Dryden and the Numbers of His
       Native Tongue, " Essays and Studies in Language
       and Literature, ed. Herbert H. Petit (Pittsburgh:
       Duquesne Press, 1964), 87-109.

On sound patterns in Dryden's dramatic
speeches and songs.

333   --"Dryden's 'Most Barren Period' - and Milton."
      The Huntington Library Quarterly, XXIV (August,
      1961), 283-296.
           Deals with the period of adjustment in
      Dryden's career after 1674. An examination of
      Aureng-Zebe discovers the Miltonic and Ver-
      gilian influence Dryden demonstrates in works
      after this period.

334   McNamara, Peter Lance. "John Dryden's Contribu-
      tion to the English Comic Tradition of Witty
      Love-Play." Ph.D. Tulane University, 1964.
      (Order No. 65-2517).
           Examines Dryden's comedies and subsequent
      reputation as a playwright in light of his
      interest in Fletcher and other comedians in the
      love-play tradition.

335   Martin, Leslie Howard, Jr. "Conventions of the
      French Romances in the Drama of John Dryden."
      Ph.D. Stanford University, 1967. (Order No.
      67-11, 053).
           Examines parallels in epic theory, theme,
      and conventions of action and characterization
      in Dryden's plays and Madeleine de Scudery's
      Ibrahim, Almahide, and Grand Cyrus.

336   Maxwell, J.C. "Dryden's Epilogue to Oedipus, 11,
      5-6." Notes and Queries, New Ser., IX (1962),
      384-385.
           Line 6 shows an indebtedness to Horace's
      Ars Poetica, lines 38-40.

337   Miner, Earl. Dryden's Poetry. Bloomington:
      Indiana University Press, 1967. 354 pp.
           A study of Dryden's major poetry that com-
      bines scholarly and critical approaches.
      Chapter II treats All for Love.

338   Monk, Samuel Holt. "Dryden and the Beginnings of
      Shakespeare Criticism in the Augustan Age,"
      The Persistence of Shakespeare Idolatry: Essays
      in Honor of Robert W. Babcock, ed. Herbert M.

Schueller (Detroit: Wayne State University
Press, 1964), 47-75.
   A reexamination of Dryden's criticism of
Shakespeare. "Dryden's generous praise of
Shakespeare and his honest confronting of what
seemed the faults of the father of the English
stage set the pattern of Shakespeare criticism
for subsequent generations."

339   Montgomery, Guy, compiler. Concordance to the
       Poetical Works of John Dryden. New York: Rus-
       sell and Russell, 1967. 722 pp.
          A reprint of the 1957 edition.

340   Moore, F. H. "The Composition of Sir Martin Mar-All."
       Essays in English Literature of the Classical
       Period Presented to Dougald MacMillan. Edited
       by Daniel W. Patterson and Albrecht B. Strauss.
       Studies in Philology, (Extra Series, January,
       1967), pp. 27-38.
          Discusses the peculiarities of the play
       and how these may be accounted for as traces of
       an imperfectly coordinated collaboration be-
       tween Dryden and the Duke of Newcastle.

341   Moore, Frank Harper. The Nobler Pleasure: Dryden's
       Comedy in Theory and Practice. Chapel Hill:
       University of North Carolina Press, 1963, 264 pp.
          Chronological study of Dryden's comic
       theory, comedies and tragicomedies, and career
       as a comic writer. Includes bibliography and
       notes.

342   Mullin, Joseph Eugene. "The Occasion, Form, Struc-
       ture, and Design of John Dryden's MacFlecknoe:
       A Varronian Satire." Ph.D. Ohio State University,
       1967. (Order No. 68-3036).
          Studies Dryden's use of Varronian satire
       which centers on some single-mindedness, enthu-
       siastic about its own learning, hypnotized by
       its own know-how, excited by its own ambitions
       and lurid fantasies, and crazed by its own hopes
       for glory.

343   Nazareth, Peter. "All for Love: Dryden's Hybrid
       Play." English Studies in Africa, VI (1963),
       154-163.

344   Nicoll, Allardyce. _Dryden and His Poetry._ New
       York: Russell and Russell, 1967. 152 pp.
           A reissue of the 1923 edition. Includes
       commentary on prologues, songs, and epilogues
       from Dryden's plays.

345   Novak, Maximillian E. "The Demonology of Dryden's
       Tyrannick Love and 'Anti-Scot.'" _English Language_
       Notes, IV (1966), 95-98.
           The demonic lovers, Nakar and Damilcar, of
       Dryden's play are traced to _A Discourse Con-_
       cerning the Nature and Substance of Devils and
       Spirits in Reginald Scot's _Discovery of Witch-_
       craft (1665).

346   Novarr, David. "Swift's Relation with Dryden and
       Gulliver's _Annus Mirabilis._" _English Studies,_
       XLVII (1966), 341-354.
           Concerned primarily with the relationship
       between _Gulliver's Travels_ and _Annus Mirabilis_,
       the article makes occasional references to
       Swift's regard for Dryden's playwriting.

347   Osborn, James M. _John Dryden: Some Biographical_
       Facts and Problems. Revised Edition. Gainesville:
       University of Florida Press, 1965, 316 pp.
           A revised edition of the 1940 biography of
       Dryden. Chapter VII surveys Dryden scholarship
       during the past twenty-five years, with particu-
       lar attention to the work of Kinsley, MacDonald
       Ward, Noyes and Young.

348   Palmer, Roderick. "Treatments of _Antony and_
       Cleopatra." _CEA Critic_, XXVII (1965), iv, 8-9.

349   Pendlebury, Bevis John. _Dryden's Heroic Plays: A_
       Study of the Origins. New York: Russell and
       Russell, 1967. 138 pp.
           A reissue of the 1923 edition which examines
       the heroic tradition before Dryden, his dramatic
       theory, and the development of the English heroic
       play.

350   Price, Martin. _To the Palace of Wisdom: Studies_
       in Order and Energy from Dryden to Blake. Gar-
       den City, New York: Doubleday and Company, 1964,
       465 pp.

Chapter II, "Dryden and Dialectic." concerns
Dryden's use of the heroic couplet and his concept of order in the heroic plays.

351   Reichert, John.   "A Note on Buckingham and Dryden."
        Notes and Queries, New Ser., IX (1962), 220.
                Dryden's careless use of letters in Marriage
        a la Mode led Buckingham to satirize the play
        in The Rehearsal.

352   Ringler, Richard N.   "Two Sources for Dryden's
        The Indian Emperour."   Philological Quarterly,
        XLII (1963), 423-429.
                Evidence of borrowings from Donne's First
        Anniversarie, and Spenser's The Fairie Queene
        suggests the breadth of Dryden's literary imagi-
        nation.

353   Roper, Alan.   Dryden's Poetic Kingdoms.   New York:
        Barnes and Noble, Inc., 1965.
                Fundamentally a study of Absalom and Achi-
        tophel, one chapter, "The Kingdom of Letters,"
        refers to Dryden's drama and to his correspondence
        with fellow playwrights.

354   Rostvig, Maren-Sofie, and others.   The Hidden
        Sense and Other Essays.   (Norwegian Studies in
        English, No. 9).   Oslo: Universitetsverlaget;
        New York: Humanities Press, 1963. 226 pp.
                Contains an essay on Dryden's All for Love,
        by Otto Reinert.

355   Schilling, Bernard N., editor.   Dryden: A Collec-
        tion of Critical Essays.   Englewood Cliffs, N.J.:
        Prentice-Hall, 1963.   186 pp.
                Reprints various and significant essays on
        Dryden scholarship in the twentieth century.
        For Dryden's drama, R. J. Kaufmann's "On the
        Poetics of Terminal Tragedy: Dryden's All for
        Love," and Moody E. Prior's "Tragedy and the
        Heroic Play."

356   Schulz, Max F.   "Coleridge's 'Debt' to Dryden and
        Johnson."   Notes and Queries, New Ser., X (1963),
        189-191.

Discusses the relationship of Coleridge's
Biographia Literaria to Dryden's An Essay of
Dramatic Poesy.

357   Scott, Sir Walter. The Life of John Dryden.
       Edited with an introduction by Bernard Kreiss-
       man. Lincoln, Nebraska: University of
       Nebraska Press, 1963, 471 pp.
              Reproduction of the 1834 edition. Includes
       notes.

358   Shergold, N.D. and Peter Ure. "Dryden and Calderon:
       A New Spanish Source for 'The Indian Emperor,'"
       Modern Language Review, LXI (1966), 369-383.
              The influence of Calderon's El principe
       constante on the plot, dialogue, and heroic
       themes of Dryden's play.

359   Sherwood, John C. "Dryden and the Critical
       Theories of Tasso." Comparative Literature,
       XVIII (1966), 351-359.
              Dryden was influenced by Tasso for his
       conception of the heroic play and for his
       approach to the problem of reconciling native
       and classical traditions in drama.

360   Sherwood, Margaret. Dryden's Dramatic Theory and
       Practice. New York: Russell and Russell, 1966.
       110 pp.
              A reissue of the work first published in
       1898. One chapter discusses Dryden's theories;
       three succeeding chapters then apply the theories
       to his comedies, heroic plays and tragedies.

361   Simon, Irene. "Dryden's Revision of the Essay of
       Dramatic Poesy." Review of English Studies, XIV
       (1963), 132-141.
              Comparison of the revised Essay with the
       earlier edition. Dryden's alterations make the
       work more formal and polished than the first
       version.

362   Sivgh, Sarup. "Dryden and the Unities." Indian
       Journal of English Studies, II (1961), 78-90.

363   Smith, David Nichol. <u>John Dryden</u>. Hamden, Conn.:
        Archon Books, 1966, 93 pp.
                A reprint of the original edition of 1950,
        the book contains four lectures on Dryden's
        works delivered at Cambridge in 1948. Chapter
        two deals with Dryden's plays.

364   Starnes, D. T. "Imitation of Shakespeare in Dry-
        den's <u>All for Love</u>." <u>Texas Studies in Literature
        and Language</u>, VI (1964), 39-46.
                Contends that Dryden's imitation is not re-
        stricted solely to <u>Antony and Cleopatra</u>. Passages
        in <u>All for Love</u> may be traced to <u>The Merchant
        of Venice</u>, <u>Julius Caesar</u>, <u>As You Like It</u>, and
        <u>Macbeth</u>. Moreover, some of the play's imagery
        is derived from <u>Othello</u>, and its scene iii is a
        lengthy imitation of <u>Coriolanus</u>, V, iii. See
        Also Nos. 128, 145, 171, 194, 561, 782

365   Staves, Sarah Susan. "Studies in the Comedy of
        John Dryden." Ph.D. University of Virginia,
        1967. (Order No. 67-17, 624).
                A doubleness of mind is reflected in the
        structure of the comedies: Dryden affirms
        traditional values but is too interested in
        the new science and new philosophy to let
        scepticism alone.

366   Stratman, Carl J., C.S.V. "John Dryden's <u>All
        for Love</u>; Unrecorded Editions." <u>Papers of the
        Bibliographical Society of America</u>, LVII
        (1963), 77-79.
                Lists fifteen previously unrecorded editions
        of the play between 1710 and 1792.

367   Swedenberg, H.T., Jr. "Dryden's Obsessive Concern
        With the Heroic." <u>Essays in English Literature
        of the Classical Period Presented to Dougald
        MacMillan</u>. Edited by Daniel W. Patterson and
        Albrecht B. Strauss. <u>Studies in Philology</u>,
        (Extra Series, January, 1967), pp. 12-26.
                An analysis of Dryden's interest in the
        heroic begins with a study of <u>An Essay of
        Dramatic Poesy</u>.

368   Taylor, Aline Mackenzie. "Dryden's 'Enchanted
       Isle' and Shadwell's 'Dominion.'" Essays in
       English Literature of the Classical Period
       Presented to Dougald MacMillan. Edited by
       Daniel W. Patterson and Albrecht B. Strauss.
       Studies in Philology, (Extra Series, January,
       1967), pp. 39-53.
            Explains Dryden's reference to Barbados
       in 1.140 of MacFlecknoe as part of his angry
       reaction to Shadwell's successful operatic re-
       vision of The Tempest.

369   Teeter, Louis. "The Dramatic Use of Hobbes's
       Political Ideas." Essential Articles for the
       Study of John Dryden. (The Essential Articles
       Series). Edited by H. T. Swedenberg, Jr.
       (Hamden, Conn.: Archon Books, 1966), 341-373.
            Reprinted from English Literary History,
       III (1936), 140-169. The influence of Hobbes's
       political ideas on the Restoration drama was,
       like Machiavelli's on the Elizabethan, almost
       completely theatrical.

370   Thale, Mary. "Dryden's Critical Vocabulary: The
       Imitation of Nature." Papers on Language and
       Literature, II (1966), 315-326.
            Examines the phrase's origin, significations,
       functions, and frequency of occurrence to
       illuminate Dryden's argumentative techniques
       and critical ideas. The concept is the princi-
       pal means by which Dryden achieves the recon-
       ciliation of ancients and moderns, foreign and
       domestic, poetry and painting, art and science.

371   --"Dryden's Dramatic Criticism: Polestar of the
       Ancients." Comparative Literature, XVIII (1966),
       36-54.
            In his approach to the Ancients for his
       criticism of modern dramatic theory and prac-
       tice Dryden supplemented and reinterpreted
       classical dramatic theory, appealed to classical
       nondramatic sources, and emphasized a concept
       of the imitation of nature.

372   Trowbridge, Hoyt. "The Place of Rules in Dryden's
       Criticism." Essential Articles for the Study of

John Dryden. (The Essential Articles Series).
Edited by H. T. Swedenberg, Jr. (Hamden, Conn.:
Archon Books, 1966), 112-134.
Reprinted from Modern Philology, XLIV
(1946), 84-96. For Dryden literary criticism
was a process of national judgment, which de-
termined the merit of works and writers by the
application of the probable rules."

373   Verrall, A. W. Lectures on Dryden. New York: Russell and Russell, 1963.

374   Waith, Eugene M. "All for Love." Restoration
Dramatists: A Collection of Critical Essays.
(Twentieth Century Views). Edited by Earl
Miner. (Englewood Cliffs, N.J.: Prentice-
Hall, Inc., 1966), 51-62.
From the Herculean Hero (New York:
Columbia University Press, 1962). The resem-
blances that bind All for Love to its prede-
cessors, The Conquest of Granada and Aureng-
Zebe, are very strong.

375   --The Herculean Hero in Marlowe, Shakespeare,
and Dryden. London: Chatto and Windus; New
York: Columbia University Press, 1962, 224 pp.
Includes chapters on Conquest of Granada,
Aureng-Zebe, and All for Love.

376   --"The Voice of Mr. Bayes." Studies in English
Literature, 1500-1900, III (1963), 335-343.
Investigates Dryden's attitude toward his
protagonists, patrons, and audience. The voice
of Bayes in The Rehearsal is a part of Dryden's
rhetorical strategy.

377   Wallerstein, Ruth. "Dryden and the Analysis of
SShakespeare's Techniques." Essential Articles
for the Study of John Dryden. (The Essential
Articles Series). Edited by H. T. Swedenberg,
Jr. (Hamden, Conn.: Archon Books, 1966), 551-
575.
Reprinted from Review of English Studies,
XIX (1943), 165-185. Analyzes Dryden's concep-
tion of poetry as it is defined in his "imitation"
of Shakespeare in All for Love.

378   Ward, Charles E. The Life of John Dryden. Raleigh,
       North Carolina: University of North Carolina
       Press, 1961. ix, 380 pp.
              Scholarly work. Each of Dryden's plays
       receives consideration, as do his theories of
       drama.

379   Ward, Charles E. and H. T. Swedenberg. John
       Dryden: Papers Read at a Clark Library Seminar,
       February 25, 1967. Introduction by John Loftis.
       Los Angeles: Clark Memorial Library, 1967.
              Charles E. Ward discusses "Challenges to
       Dryden's Biographer"; H. T. Swedenberg, "Chal-
       lenges to Dryden's Editor."

380   Wasserman, George R. John Dryden. New York:
       Twayne Publishers, Inc., 1964.
              Biographical and critical study of Dryden's
       life and works. Chapter III, "Essays on Dramatic
       and Heroic Poetry," and Chapter IV, "Comedy and
       Tragedy," are of special interest. Includes
       selected bibliography.

381   Watson, George. "Dryden's First Answer to Rymer."
       Review of English Studies, XIV (1963), 17-23.
              One of Dryden's most "rewarding"statements
       on drama.Tonson's text of the "Heads of an
       Answer to Rymer" is "the one critical document
       in English between the Restoration and Johnson's
       Shakespeare in which the Poetics of Aristotle
       are attacked frontally and without qualification."

382   --The Literary Critics: A Study of English Descrip-
       tive Criticism. (Pelican Books, A553). Harmonds-
       worth and Baltimore: Penguin Books, 1962, 249 pp.
              Evaluates the critical principles of both
       John Dryden and Johnson.

383   Weinbrot, Howard D. "Alexas in All for Love: His
       Genealogy and Function." Studies in Philology,
       LXIV (1967), 625-639.
              Dryden borrowed the eunuch from several
       earlier plays and Roman histories, but only in
       All for Love does the character contribute to a
       vividly felt contest of good and evil and
       demonstrate the greater nobility of the protagon-
       ists.

384   --"Robert Gould: Some Borrowings from Dryden."
       English Language Notes, III (1965), 36-40.
              Cites passages in Gould's 'The Playhouse'
       which manifest an indebtedness to Dryden's All
       for Love, The Conquest of Granada, and Essay
       of Dramatick Poesy.

385   Welle, J. A. van der. Dryden and Holland. Gron-
       ingen: J. B. Walters, 1962, 153 pp.

386   Williamson, George. "Dryden's View of Milton."
       Milton and Others (London, 1965), 103-121.
              A compilation of Dryden's statements on
       the limitations of the Miltonic epic form; its
       inferiority to the heroic play in certain
       dramatic respects.

387   --"The Occasion of An Essay of Dramatic Poesy."
       Essential Articles for the Study of John Dryden.
       (The Essential Articles Series). Edited by
       H. T. Swedenberg, Jr. (Hamden, Conn.: Archon
       Books, 1966), 65-82.
              Reprinted from Modern Philology, XLIV
       (1946), 1-9. Studies the relationship of Samuel
       Sorbiere and Thomas Sprat to Dryden's Essay.

388   Winterbottom, John A. "The Place of Hobbesian
       Ideas in Dryden's Tragedies." Essential Articles
       for the Study of John Dryden.(The Essential
       Articles Series). Edited by H. T. Swedenberg,
       Jr. (Hamden, Conn.: Archon Books, 1966), 374-
       394.
              Reprinted from Journal of English and Ger-
       manic Philology, LVII (1958), 665-683. Although
       Hobbesian ideas are present in the tragedies,
       they are not espoused by Dryden himself; other
       lines of thought provide a more plausible philo-
       sophical basis for the plays. See Also Nos. 130,
       551, 930, 986, 1121

389   --"Stoicism in Dryden's Tragedies." Journal of
       English and Germanic Philology, LXI (1962),
       868-883.
              Dryden's application of the stoic philosophy
       tempered by Christianity in his plays. See Also
       Nos. 136, 225, 226

72

390   Zebouni, Selma Assir. <u>Dryden: A Study in Heroic
       Characterization</u>. Baton Rouge: Louisiana State
       University Press, 1965. 111 pp.
            The protagonist of a Dryden heroic tragedy
       is not, as has been previously thought, an ego-
       tist possessing superhuman courage and an all-
       consuming desire for power. He is rather an
       archetypal figure embodying "common sense and
       order." A product of the cultural milieu and
       Dryden's own psychological development, he shares
       certain characteristics with the Cornelian hero.
       See Also Nos. 68, 765, 947, 969, 1005, 1009, 1075

391   --"The Hero in Dryden's Heroic Tragedy: A Re-
       valuation." Ph.D. Louisiana State University,
       1963. (Order No. 64-169).
            A definition of Dryden's heroes in relation
       to the contemporary intellectual and historical
       milieu and to Dryden's own psychological evolu-
       tion demonstrates that heroic tragedy is not
       outside the main course of English literature,
       but rather an important link in the evolution
       of English drama. See Also Nos. 20, 58, 154,
       756, 780, 924, 934, 1065

392   Zesmer, David. <u>Dryden: Poems, Plays and Essays</u>.
       (Bantam Classics). New York: Bantam Books, 1967.
       529 pp.
            Includes prologues, epilogues and songs by
       Dryden as well as <u>All for Love</u> and <u>An Essay of
       Dramatic Poesy</u>. See Also Nos. 550, 571, 761,
       767, 775, 1008

       DUBLIN
393   Stewart, John Hall. "The French Revolution on the
       Dublin Stage, 1790-1794." <u>Journal of the Royal
       Society of Antiquaries of Ireland</u>, XC(1961),
       183-192.
            The Revolution depicted in plays produced
       by Philip and John Astley of London. Reflections
       of the Revolution and these performances in
       the Dublin Press. See Also No. 1074

       DUFFETT
394   Cameron, Kenneth M. "Duffett's New Poems and
       Vacation Plays." <u>Theatre Survey</u>, V(1964),64-70.

Thomas Duffett's New Poems, Songs, Prologues
and Epilogues (London, 1676) not only provides
a record of the so-called Duchess of Portsmouth's
company, but also gives information on the
vacation performances by the hirelings of the
Theatre Royal.

395   Lewis, Peter Elvet. "The Three Dramatic Burles-
       ques of Thomas Duffett." Durham University
       Journal, LVIII (1966), 149-156.
           Duffett's plays were "burlesques of specific
       dramatic productions rather than satires of a
       particular mode of writing." See Also Nos. 146,
       1008, 1010

D'URFEY
396   D'Urfey, Thomas. Wonders in the Sun; or, The
       Kingdom of the Birds (1706). With an Introduc-
       tion by William W. Appleton. Los Angeles:
       Clark Memorial Library, University of California,
       Los Angeles, 1964. 71 pp.
           A facsimile reproduction of the Tonson
       edition of the comic opera. (No. 104 in the
       Augustan Reprint series).

397   Carpenter, William E., Jr. "An Edition of Thomas
       D'Urfey's The Virtuous Wife." Ph.D. University
       of Kansas, 1967. (Order No. 68-571).
           The Virtuous Wife, first produced in 1679,
       is one of D'Urfey's better plays and provides a
       lively presentation of his themes and techniques.

398   Vaughan, Jack A. "A D'Urfey Play Dated." Modern
       Philology, LXIV (1967), 322-323.
           A Fond Husband was first printed in the
       summer of 1677, shortly after its premier per-
       formance at Dorset Gardens in May of that year.

399   --"'Persevering, Unexhausted Bard': Tom D'Urfey."
       Quarterly Journal of Speech, LIII (1967), 342-
       348.
           Reviews the life and works of D'Urfey whose
       plays exhibit a frenetic theatricality and
       vitality and reveal the tastes of the Restoration
       audience.

400   Vaughn, Jack Alfred. "Thomas D'Urfey's A Fond
       Husband: An Edition and Critical Study." Ph.D.
       University of Denver, 1964. (Order No. 64-13,
       176).
            Critical commentary on 32 other dramatic
       works of D'Urfey supplement the general intro-
       duction to The Fond Husband.

                            E

       ECCLES
401   Jackson, Allan S. "The Frontispiece to Eccles's
       Theater Musick, 1699." Theatre Notebook, XIX
       (Winter, 1964-5), 47-49.
            Offers explanations for several errors in
       the print used to illustrate Eccles's three vol-
       ume work. See Also Nos. 201, 202, 832

       EDINBURGH, See Nos. 249, 1090

       EDITIONS, See Nos. 98, 104, 135, 178, 417, 419, 520,
            523, 572, 592, 617, 647, 650, 765, 943, 945,
            1002, 1156

       EDKINS
402   Barker, Kathleen M.D. "Michael Edkins, Painter."
       Theatre Notebook, XVI (Winter, 1961), 39-55.
            An account of his work for the Theatre
       Royal, Bristol, as a painter--based on his
       ledger--from 1768 to 1779.

       ENTERTAINER, See Nos. 822, 823

       EPIC, See No. 262

       EPILOGUE, See Nos. 871, 872, 873

       EROTICISM, See No. 152

       ETHEREGE
403   Etherege, George. The Man of Mode. Edited by W.B.
       Carnochan. (Regents Restoration Drama Series).
       Lincoln: University of Nebraska Press, 1966.

Includes introduction, notes and chronology.

404   Aiken, W. Ralph, Jr.   "Nature to Advantage Dress'd:
       A Study of Sir George Etherege As Playwright."
       Ph.D. Duke University, 1962.   (Order No. 63-859).
             A study of Etherege's development from The
       Comical Revenge; or, Love in a Tub, and She
       Would if She Could, to The Man of Mode; or, Sir
       Fopling Flutter.   See Also Nos. 136, 148

405   Boyette, Purvis E.   "The Songs of George Etherege."
       Studies in English Literature, 1500-1900, VI
       (1966), 409-419.
             Etherege surpassed his fellow playwrights
       in the composition of songs for his plays, and
       believed in the architectonic relationship of
       lyrics to the structure of the play.

406   Bracher, Frederick.   "The Letterbooks of Sir
       George Etherege."   Harvard Library Bulletin,
       XV (1967), 238-245.
             Three letterbooks, (BM add Mss 11513),
       edited as The Letterbook of Sir George Etherege
       by Sybil Rosenfeld in 1927, and Harvard Library's
       fMS Thr. 11 and fMS Thr. 11.1 shed considerable
       light on Etherege's three-year residence at
       Ratisbon.

407   --"Sir George Etherege and His Secretary."   Har-
       vard Library Bulletin, XV (1967), 331-344.
             Etherege's secretary, Hugo Hughes, plotted
       to discredit and replace him as English envoy
       at Ratisbon.   See Also Nos. 127, 760

408   Brett-Smith, H.F.B.   "Sir George Etherege."   Res-
       toration Drama: Modern Essays in Criticism.   (A
       Galaxy Book).   Edited by John Loftis.   (New
       York: Oxford University Press, 1966), 44-56.
             Reprinted from the Introduction to The Works
       of Sir George Etherege (Oxford: Basil Blackwell,
       1927), pp. lxix-lxxxiii.   Etherege's contributions
       to later Restoration comedy.

409   Hymas, Scott Simpson.   "The Satiric Attitude: Re-
       jection in the Comedies of Wycherley and Etherege."
       Ph.D. Western Reserve University, 1964.   (Order
       No. 65-2325).

Seeks to discover that the dramas of
Wycherley and Etherege are "more expressive of
the rejection of the satiric attitude than the
acceptance of the comic."

410   Powell, Jocelyn. "George Etherege and the Form of
        a Comedy." Restoration Theatre. Edited by John
        Russell Brown and Bernard Harris. (Stratford-
        Upon-Avon Studies, 6). (London: Edward Arnold,
        1965; New York: St. Martin's Press, 1965), 43-
        69. Also in Restoration Dramatists: A Collection-
        of Critical Essays. (Twentieth Century Views).
        Edited by Earl Miner. (Englewood Cliffs, N.J.:
        Prentice-Hall, Inc., 1966), 63-85.
            Love in a Tub, She Would if She Could, and
        The Man of Mode show an increasing economy of
        dramatic means and an increasing dissatisfaction
        with comic conventions. Gradually, Etherege
        moves from the "comedy of judgment" to the
        "comedy of experience."

411   Thorpe, James, editor. The Poems of Sir George
        Etherege. Princeton: Princeton University Press,
        1963, 149 pp.
            Includes the principal songs from the plays
        with textual and explanatory notes. See Also
        Nos. 145, 171, 172

412   Underwood, Dale. "The Comic Language." Restora-
        tion Dramatists A Collection of Critical Essays.
        (Twentieth Century Views). Edited by Earl
        Miner. (Englewood Cliffs, N.J.: Prentice-Hall,
        Inc., 1966), 87-103.
            Reprinted from Etherege and the Seventeenth-
        Century Com. of Manners (New Haven: Yale Univer-
        sity Press, 1957). The language of the Restora-
        tion comedy of manners may be divided into two
        distinct sets of literary characteristics, the
        metaphoric and the nonmetaphoric, which have
        distinct rhetorical characters and complicate
        the logical surfaces of the language in somewhat
        different ways.

413   --"The Comic Values--The Man of Mode." Restoration
        Drama Modern Essays in Criticism. (A Galaxy Book).

Edited by John Loftis. (New York: Oxford University Press, 1966), 57-81. Reprinted from Etherege and the Seventeenth-Century Comedy of Manners (New Haven: Yale University Press, 1957), pp. 72-93. The play gives a comprehensive definition to those questions of reality and value which constitute the essential interest of Restoration comedy of manners. See Also Nos. 130, 132, 137, 157, 161, 1075

F

FAMILY, See No. 140

FARCE, See No. 452

FARQUHAR
414   Farquhar, George. The Beaux' Stratagem. Edited by Vincent F. Hopper and Gerald B. Lahey. With a Note on the Staging by George L. Hersey. (Theatre Classics for the Modern Reader). Great Neck, New York: Barron's Educational Series, 1963, 182 pp.
       Includes biographical sketch, critical introduction, notes on staging, and brief bibliography.

415   --"The Beaux' Stratagem." Edited by Eric Rothstein. New York: Appleton-Century Crofts, 1967.
       Includes introduction, notes, and select bibliography.

416   --The Complete Works. Edited by Charles Stonehill, 2 vols. New York: Gordian Press, 1967.
       Reprint of the 1930 edition. Includes general introduction and textual and explanatory notes for the plays. Volume II also contains Farquhar's correspondence, poems, and A Discourse Upon Comedy.

417   --The Recruiting Officer. Edited by Michael Shugrue. (Regents Restoration Drama Series). Lincoln: University of Nebraska Press, 1965.

Includes critical introduction, notes, bibliography, and an appendix on variant passages.

418   --The Recruiting Officer. Edited by Michael
       Shugrue. (Regents Restoration Drama Series).
       London: Edward Arnold, 1966.
       Includes critical introduction, notes,
       bibliography, and an appendix on variant passages.

419   --The Recruiting Officer. Edited by Kenneth Tyman.
       London: Hart-Davis, 1965, 144 pp.

420   --La Ruse des Galants//The Beaux' Stratagem.
       Edited by J. Hamard. Paris: Aubier, 1966.
       382 pp.
       The introduction is a study of Farquhar's
       career and plays.

421   Berman, Ronald. "The Comedy of Reason." Texas
       Studies in Literature and Language, VII (1965),
       161-168.
       An analysis of The Beaux' Stratagem demon-
       strates that "the fundamental verity in the play
       is money; the fundamental metaphor involves
       commerce; the fundamental axiom is that poverty
       is nonexistence."

422   Farmer, A.J. George Farquhar. London and New York:
       Longman, Green and Co., 1966, 40 pp.
       A brief survey of the playwright's life
       and works. Includes select bibliography. See
       Also Nos. 157, 161

423   Hutton, Virgil R. "The Aesthetic Development of
       George Farquhar in His Early Plays." Ph.D.
       University of Michigan, 1966. (Order No.67-8280).
       Analyzes Love and a Bottle, The Constant
       Couple, Sir Harry Wildair, The Inconstant, and
       The Twin-Rivals. Also examines Farquhar's criti-
       cal theories, the moral stance of the plays, and
       the relation of the plays to earlier Restoration
       comic tradition and to the growing sentimental
       tradition.

424   James, Eugene Nelson. "The Burlesque of Restoration
       Comedy in Love and a Bottle." Studies in English

79

<u>Literature, 1500-1900</u>,V (1965), 469-490.
The play intentionally satirizes and imi-
tates exaggeratedly the hero of Restoration
comedy, its intrigues, moral, form, wit, humor,
characters, and comic situations. See Also
No. 153

425 Rosenfeld, Sybil. "Notes on <u>The Recruiting Officer.</u>"
<u>Theatre Notebook</u>, XVIII (Winter, 1963-64), 47-48.
Farquhar had definite actors in mind when
he composed the play which was an immediate
success at its first performance on April 8,
1706. A new edition is needed. See Also No. 249.

426 Rothstein, Eric. "Farquhar's <u>Twin Rivals</u> and the
Reform of Comedy." <u>Publications of the Modern
Language Association</u>, LXXIX(1964), 33-41.
Farquhar intended to present the kind of
moral comedy Collier and other abolitionists
claimed to favor. The failure of the play indi-
cated that the New Comedy would not be structured
on Collier's principles. See Also Nos. 145, 171

427 Rothstein, Eric. <u>George Farquhar</u>. New York:
Twayne Publishers, Inc., 1967. 206 pp.
Biographical and critical study of Farqu-
har. Separate chapters are given to discussions
of <u>The Recruiting Officer</u> and <u>The Beaux'
Stratagem</u>. Includes selected bibliography.

FAUST, See No. 781

FICINO, See No. 688

FIELDING
428 Fielding, Henry. <u>The Author's Farce</u> (Original
Version). Edited by Charles B. Woods. (Regents
Restoration Drama Series). Lincoln: University of Nebraska Press, 1966.
Includes introduction, notes, bibliography,
and appendices concerning the revision of the
play, the individuals represented, and the tunes
of the play.

429 --<u>The Complete Works of Henry Fielding, Esq.</u> With
an Essay on the Life, Genius and Achievement of
the Author by William Ernest Henley. 16 vols.

New York: Barnes and Noble, 1967.
A reprint of the 1902-03 edition with
Fielding's plays and poems contained in five
volumes.

430   --The Historical Register for the Year 1736 and
       Eurydice Hissed. Edited by William A. Appleton.
       (Regents Restoration Drama Series). Lincoln"
       University of Nebraska Press, 1967.
            Includes introduction, notes and chrono-
       logy.

431   Amory, Hugh. "Henry Fielding's Epistles to Wal-
       pole: A Reexamination." Philological Quarterly,
       XLVI (1967), 236-247.
            Studies the relationship of the Epistles
       to Fielding's attacks on Walpole and includes
       references to Tom Thumb and The Grub-Street
       Opera.

432   Baker, Sheridan. "Political Allusion in Field-
       ing's Author's Farce, Mock Doctor, and Tumble-
       Down Dick." Publications of the Modern Language
       Association, LXXVII, (1962), 221-231.
            Baker illustrates Fielding's anti-Walpole
       satire in three plays composed between 1730-
       1736, and demonstrates also how the satire is
       leveled at Cibber, Dr. John Misaubin, and John
       Rich respectively, so that Fielding simultaneous-
       ly supported the opposition as well as good
       theatre in his attacks.

433   Battestin, Martin C. "Fielding and 'Master Punch'
       in Panton Street." Philological Quarterly,
       XLV (1966), 191-208.
            For one season in 1748 Fielding owned and
       operated his own puppet theatre in Panton Street
       under the name of "Madame de la Nash."

434   Chaudbury, Awadhesh. "Henry Fielding: His Atti-
       tude Towards the Contemporary Stage." Ph. D.
       The University of Michigan, 1963. (Order No.
       64-6664).
            A detailed study of Fielding's novels and
       prefaces reveals his desire to expose and correct
       the decadent taste of 18th century playwrights,
       actors and spectators.

435   Coley, W. B.   "Henry Fielding and the Two Walpoles."
       Philological Quarterly, XLV (1966), 157-178.
              The writings of Horace Walpole give valu-
       able information on the relationship of Field-
       ing to Robert Walpole and on Fielding's political
       disillusionment.

436   Coley, William B.   "Fielding and the Two Covent-
       Garden Journals." Modern Language Review, LVII
       (1962), 386-387. His relation to the journals
       of 1749 and 1752.

437   Dircks, Richard J. "The Perils of Heartfree: A
       Sociological Review of Fielding's Adaptation
       of Dramatic Convention." Texas Studies in
       Literature and Language, VII (1966), 5-13.
              For purposes of social criticism in
       Jonathan Wild Fielding reflects, directly and
       by contrast, ideas found in the drama of sen-
       sibility and adopts the techniques of the
       sentimental dramatist in his characterization
       and manipulation of plot.

438   Dudden, Frederick Homes. Henry Fielding:His Life
       Works, and Times, Hamden, Conn.: Archon Books
       1966, 582 pp.
              A reissue of the work first published in
       1952. Chapters I-VIII deal with Fielding's
       career as a playwright.

439   Ferguson, Oliver W."Partridge's Vile Encomium:
       Fielding and Honest Billy Mills." Philological
       Quarterly, (1964), 73-78.
              In Book XVI, Chapter V of Tom Jones,
       Partridge's praise for the actor playing Claudius
       to Garrick's Hamlet is a reference to William
       Mills, the Claudius at Drury Lane.

440   Hatfield, Glenn W. "Quacks, Pettyfoggers, and Par-
       sons: Fielding's Case Against the Learned Pro-
       fessions." Texas Studies in Literature and
       Language, IX (1967), 69-83.
              Examines Fielding's "responsible" satire
       in the plays and novels. Fielding had a clear
       conception of the ideal standard of these
       professions and a respect for them.

441 --"The Serpent and the Dove: Fielding's Irony and
the Prudence Theme in Tom Jones,: Modern Philology, LXV (1967), 17-32.
Studies Fielding's interest in the clear
meaning of words. Fielding exhibits this interest
not only in his fiction but also in The Covent
Garden Journal, in his comedies which can be read
as dramatic definitions of abstract social and
moral virtues, and in his theatrical burlesques
and satires that include attacks on debasers of
language.

442 Irwin, Michael. Henry Fielding: The Tentative
Realist. Oxford: Clarendon Press, 1967, 147 pp.
Emphasizes Fielding's didactic intentions
in the novels but also considers the plays as
vehicles for Fielding's didacticism.

443 Jensen, Gerard Edward, editor. The Covent-Garden
Journal. 2 vols. New York: Russell and Russell,
1964, 368, 293 pp.
A scholarly edition of Fielding's contri-
butions to his Covent-Garden Journal. The origin
of the periodical, its format, general character,
program of reform, and theatrical criticism are
discussed in detail in the Introduction. Includes
Notes and Index.

444 Kinder, Marsha. "Henry Fielding's Dramatic Experi-
mentation: A Preface to His Fiction." Ph. D.
U.C.L.A., 1967 (Order No. 67-9652).
Examines the general decline of the drama
and the rise of the novel in the eighteenth
century by studying the relationships between
Fielding's plays and novels. Emphasis is given
to the most experimental plays: The Author's
Farce, The Tragedy of Tragedies, Pasquin, and
The Historical Register. See Also Nos. 870,
887, 1137

445 Levine, George R. "Henry Fielding's 'Defense' of
the Stage Licensing Act. "English Language Notes
II (1965), 193-196.
In The Champion of December 10, 1739-40,
Fielding assumes a persona which typifies the
elements of society held accountable for the
Licensing Act.

446   Roberts, Edgar V. "Eighteenth-Century Ballad Opera:
       The Contribution of Henry Fielding." Drama Sur-
       vey, I (1961), 77-85.

447   --"Fielding's Ballad Opera The Lottery (1732), and
       the English State Lottery of 1731." Huntington
       Library Quarterly, XXVII (November, 1963), 39-52.
              Supplies pertinent information about lotteries
       prior to 1732 as a background for an understanding
       of Fielding's play. See Also Nos. 58, 884

448   --"Henry Fielding and Richard Leveridge: Authorship
       of The Roast Beef of Old England." Huntington
       Library Quarterly, XXVII (1964), 175-181.
              Concerns the authorship of 'The Mighty
       Roast Beef' in Fielding's The Grub-Street Opera
       (1731) and Don Quixote in England (1734). Evidence
       from songbooks and miscellany collections of
       the period proves that Fielding's version anti-
       cipated that of Leveridge.

449   --"Henry Fielding's Lost Play, Deborah; or, A Wife
       For You All (1733): Consisting Partly of Facts
       and Partly of Observations Upon Them." Bulletin
       of the New York Public Library, LXVI (1962),
       576-588.
              Discussion of existing facts concerning the
       lost play. Concludes that Deborah "was a brief
       entertainment based upon a farcial trial scene
       handled in his usual way" and contained a con-
       demnation of the English judicial structure.

450   --"Possible Additions to Airs 6 and 7 of Henry
       Fielding's Ballad Opera, The Lottery." Notes and
       Queries, New Ser., IX (1962), 455-456.
              There is evidence that stanzas of Airs 6
       and 7 of The Lottery may have been written by
       Fielding, that they were suppressed when the
       play was performed and published.

451   Smith, J. Oates. "Masquerade and Marriage: Field-
       ing's Comedies of Identity." Ball State Univer-
       sity Forum, VI, iii (1965), 10-21.
              Studies the development of the masquerade
       motif in Fielding's dramas and novels. Fielding
       skillfully treats the struggle of the individual

                              84

for virtue and self-identity in a hypocritical
world. See Also Nos. 61, 146, 509, 867

452   Woods, Charles. "Cibber in Fielding's Author's
Farce: Three Notes." Philological Quarterly,
XLIV (1965), 145-151.
      Fielding's satirical representation of Cib-
ber as Mr. Keyber, Marplay, and Sir Farcical
Comic.

453   --"Theobald and Fielding's Don Tragedio." English
Language Notes, II (1965), 266-271.
      Identifies Lewis Theobald as the source of
Fielding's Satirical Characterization of Don
Tragedio.

454   Woods, Charles B. "The Folio Text of Fielding's
The Miser." Huntington Library Quarterly,XXVIII
(1964), 59-61.
      The folio Miser was probably published in
1734 as a supplement to the fifth number of
Cotes's Weekly Journal: or, The English Stage-
Player.

455   --"The 'Miss Lucy' Plays of Fielding and Garrick."
Philological Quarterly, XLI (1962), 294-310.
      The relationship of Fielding's The Virgin
Unmask'd and Miss Lucy in Town to Garrick's
Lethe.

456   Wright, Andrew. Henry Fielding: Mask and Feast.
London: Chatto and Windus, 1965, 214 pp.
      The comic structure, characterizations,
and dramatic tableaux of Tom Jones, Joseph
Andrews, and Amelia offer ample proof that
Fielding's dramatic career was responsible
for many of the artistic devices employed in
his novels. See Also Nos. 68, 1010

457   Wright, Kenneth D. "Henry Fielding and the
Theatres Act of 1737. "Quarterly Journal of
Speech, L (1964), 252-258.
      Studies the actual passing of the Licen-
sing Act through Parliament and Fielding's
participation in events leading to its passage.

Testimony by Fielding's contemporaries, especially Colley Cibber and Benjamin Victor, confirms
his responsibility for passage of the Act. See
Also No. 128

FILMER, See No. 311

FLETCHER, See No. 334

FOOTE

458   Berveiller, Michel. "Anglais et Francais de
       comédie chez Louis de Boissy et Samuel Foote."
       Comparative Literature Studies, II (1965), 259-
       269.
            A comparison of the comic techniques of
       Louis de Boissy and Samuel Foote, especially
       in their treatment of displaced persons.

459   Bogorad, Samuel N. "Samuel Foote: the Prospects
       for a Life and Works." Restoration and Eighteenth
       Century Theatre Research, VI (May, 1967), 11-13.
            Reviews the most important scholarly work
       on Foote's life and plays and explains the need
       for a documented biography and critical edition
       of the works. Suggests available resources.

460   Byrnes, Joseph Alfred. "Four Plays of Samuel
       Foote: The Knights, The Minor, The Lyar, The
       Mayor of Garratt: An Edition with Commentary."
       Ph.D. New York University, 1963. (Order No.
       63-7210).
            General introduction places Foote in the
       theatrical history of the eighteenth century;
       introductions to individual plays provide infor-
       mation about the targets of Foote's satire.

461   Trefman, Simon. "Sam. Foote, Comedian, 1720-1777."
       Ph.D. New York University, 1967. (Order No. 68-
       10, 099).
            Foote's comedies, despite their topicality,
       are a sure and lively guide to the temper of
       mid-eighteenth century life. See Also No. 13.

462   Wharton, Robert V. "The Divided Sensibility of
       Samuel Foote." Educational Theatre Journal,
       XVII (1965), 31-37.

86

A strange mingling of sentimentalism and
satire pervades the comedies of Samuel Foote.
It stems from Foote's inability to reconcile his
Hobbesian temperament with the period's Shaftes-
buryean climate. See Also Nos. 146, 824

FORD
463   Leech, Clifford. "A Projected Restoration Perfor-
mance of Ford's The Lover's Melancholy." Modern
Language Review. LVI (July, 1961), 378-381.
A study of a copy of the Quarto of Ford's
The Lover's Melancholy (1629), at the Folger
Library, which has been extensively worked for
abridgement, to determine if this is done for a
projected Restoration performance. See Also
No. 222

FORGERY, See No. 569

FORREST, See No. 18

FRANCE, See No. 251

FREEMAN, See No. 34

FREEMASONS, See No. 34

FRENCH INFLUENCE, See No. 132

                              G

GARRICK
464   Boulton, James T. "David Garrick (1717-1779)."
Burke Newsletter, IV (1962), 171-174.
Burke's correspondence reveals Garrick as
generous, kind and affable.

465   Burnim, Kalman. David Garrick: Director. Pittsburgh:
University of Pittsburgh Press, 1961. 234 pp.
A detailed study of the actor's work as
manager of the Drury Lane Theatre, with a close
analysis of four Garrick prompt-books of Shakespearean tragedies and a Vanbrugh comedy. Most

87

complete treatment of mid-eighteenth century
production techniques that has appeared.

466   Burnim, Kalman A. "The Theatrical Career of
       Guiseppe Galli-Bibiena." Theatre Survey, VI
       (1965), 32-53.
             Includes brief reference to Garrick's
       use of transparent back scenes at Drury Lane
       for a production of Harlequin's Invasion, 1759.

466a   --"David Garrick's Early Will." Theatre Research,
       VII (1965), 26-44.
             Publishes the text of a will discovered in
       the Harvard Theatre Collection which was drawn
       up by Garrick on March 23, 1767.

467   Deelman, Christian. "Garrick at Edial." Johnson-
       ian News Letter, XXI (September, 1961), 12.
             Discusses Garrick's Lethe and the question
       of Garrick's debt to Lucian.

468   --The Great Shakespeare Jubilee. New York: The
       Viking Press, 1964. 326 pp.
             Full-length study of the Jubilee of 1769,
       beginning with a review of Shakespeare's
       reputation to 1741. Examines the elaborate and
       confused preparations, progress, close, and
       aftermath of the festival with which "Garrick
       chose to stage the worship of his god." In-
       cludes illustrations, notes, bibliography and
       index.

469   England, Martha Winburn. "Garrick and Stratford."
       Bulletin of the New York Public Library, LXVI
       (1962), 73-92, 178-204, 261-272.
             Garrick's Shakespeare jubilee in 1769.
       "The combination of Garrick and Stratford formed
       a catalyst that precipitated the concepts of
       romanticism."

470   --Garrick and Stratford. New York: The New York
       Public Library, 1962. 72 pp.
             Garrick's Shakespeare Jubilee in 1769. A
       reprint with additions and illustrations of Miss
       England's "Garrick and Stratford" in the Bulletin
       of the New York Public Library, LXVI (1962).

88

73-92; 178-204; 261-272.

471   --Garrick's Jubilee. Columbus: Ohio State Univer-
        sity Press, 1964. 273 pp.
            A more extensive study of the Jubilee by
        the author of Garrick and Stratford (New York
        Public Librory, 1962). Includes two appendices
        containing a list of some persons who attended
        the Jubilee and Garrick's Ode to Shakespeare.

472   Gottesman, Lillian. "Garrick's Institution of the
        Garter." Restoration and Eighteenth Century
        Theatre Research VI (November, 1967), 37-43.
            A discussion of Garrick's play produced at
        Drury Lane for at least twenty-six performances.
        "Its historical value lies in that it is the
        only obtainable dramatic work on the subject of
        this supposed Arthurian society, that it is a
        patriotic interpretation and glorification of a
        theme associated with Arthurian tradition, and
        that it embodies the Elizabethan concept of the
        divine guidance of monarchs."

473   Hafter, Ronald. "Garrick and Tristram Shandy."
        Studies in English Literature, 1500-1900, VII
        (1967), 475-489.
            Sterne's adaptation of Garrick's stage
        technique to the purpose of prose fiction gives
        Tristram Shandy much of its unique coloration.

474   Highfill, Philip H. "A Real 'Bill of Mortality."
        Theatre Notebook, XVI (Spring, 1962), 107-108.
            Copy of a Drury Lane Bill for January 19,
        1779, at Huntington Library. Bill contains
        note by William Hopkins, Drury Lane prompter,
        which refers to cancellation of performance due
        to Garrick's death.

475   Jennings, John. "David Garrick and Nicholas Nip-
        close." Educational Theatre Journal, XVI (1964),
        270-275.
            A reexamination of those portions of Nip-
        close's The Theatres; a Poetical Dissection
        which are directed at Garrick. Includes critical
        response to the piece.

89

476   Kahrl, George M. "Garrick, Johnson, and Litch-
       field." New Rambler, Serial No. C.I. (June,
       1966), 15-28.
              Describes the social and economic dispari-
       ties that separated the Johnson and Garrick
       families in Lichfield and discusses the relation-
       ship of the two men there and in London.

477   Knight, Donald. "The Technique of Nature in the
       Age of Garrick." M.F.A. Yale University, 1965.

478   Little, David M., and George M. Kahrl, editors.
       The Letters of David Garrick. Associate Editor
       Phoebe de K. Wilson. Cambridge: Belknap Press
       of Harvard University Press, 1963. 3 vols.
       1418 pp.
              Chronological arrangement of Garrick's
       correspondence. Valuable introduction on the
       actor-producer's life provides an excellent
       background for the 1300 letters. Includes an
       index and seven appendices. See Also Nos. 757,
       884, 992, 993, 1059

479   Little, David Mason. Pineapples of Finest Flavour
       or A Selection of Sundry Unpublished Letters of
       the English Roscius, David Garrick, New York:
       Russell and Russell, 1967, 101 pp.
              A reissue of the 1930 edition contains 44
       letters by Garrick to friends, colleagues and
       members of his family.

480   Lloyd-Evans, Gareth. "Garrick and the 18th-Century
       Theatre." Transactions of the Johnson Society
       (December, 1965), 17-27.
              David Garrick influenced the whole of 18th
       century theatre by his "naturalistic" acting,
       use of contemporary material, unique staging
       techniques, and magnetic personality.

481   Loose, Dorothy Loretta. "The Theatrical Opinions
       and Policies of David Garrick as Expressed in
       His Private Correspondence, 1747-1779." M.A.
       University of Nebraska, 1961.

482   McAleer, John J. "Garrick--'High-Priest of Avon's
       Oracle.'" The Shakespeare Newsletter, XIV

(1964), 6.
Brief review of Garrick's productions of
Shakespeare.

483   McNamara, Brooks. "The Stratford Jubilee: Dram
to Garrick's Vanity." Educational Theatre
Journal, XIV (1962), 135-140.
Story of Garrick's Stratford Jubilee of
1769. The three-day festival, though a failure
to Garrick himself, was indicative of Shakespeare idolatry in the later Eighteenth Century.
See Also No. 455

484   Pritchett, V.S. "Unfrogged Frenchman." New
Statesman, LXVII (January 31, 1964), 167-168.
The popular allegation that Garrick owed
his acting genius to his French blood is denied
by Garrick in his letters. Comments also on
Garrick's personality and dramatic ability as
revealed in his formal and informal correspondence.

485   Sawyer, Paul. "Garrick, Joseph Reed, and Dido."
Restoration and Eighteenth Century Theatre Re-
search, VI (November, 1967), 44-50.
Studies the tireless efforts of Joseph
Reed (1723-1787) to persuade Garrick to produce
Dido at Drury Lane.

486   Stein, Elizabeth. David Garrick, Dramatist. (MLA
Revolving Fund Ser. 7). New York: Benjamin Blom,
1967,   315 pp.
A reprint of the 1938 edition, the book
examines Garrick's plays to determine their merit,
to assess Garrick's contribution to the dramatic
literature of the period, and to discover Garrick's own position in the history of drama.

487   --ed. Three Plays by David Garrick. New York:
Benjamin Blom, 1967.
A reprint of the 1926 edition includes
texts, introductions and notes for Harlequin's
Invasion, The Jubilee, and The Meeting of the
Company. See Also Nos. 13, 18, 94, 764, 950,
1078

91

488   Stockholm, Johanne M. Garrick's Folly: The Shake-
        speare Jubilee of 1769 at Stratford and Drury
        Lane. London: Methuen, 1964, 178 pp.
                A study of the Jubilee's failure at Strat-
        ford, its success at Drury Lane, and its influence
        on the literary and theatrical world. See Also
        Nos. 599, 802, 959, 965, 1048

489   Stone, George Winchester, Jr. "Garrick and Othello."
        Philological Quarterly, XLV (1966), 304-320.
                A history of Garrick's experience with
        Othello in which he played Iago twice as many
        times as he played the hero. Considers contem-
        porary comment on his performances, the probable
        text used by Garrick, and the impact of the play
        on Garrick personally. See Also Nos. 2, 30,
        624, 821, 966, 991

490   Wolfit, Donald. "Little Davy." Drama, No. 72
        (Spring, 1964), 37-39.
                Review of Little and Kahrl's edition of
        David Garrick's letters. The "vivid picture
        (which the letters) give of the life of the
        theatre spanning the middle of the 18th century
        from Quin to Sheridan" makes them unique in
        English literature. See Also Nos. 613, 623, 941

        GAY
491   Gay, John. The Beggar's Opera. A Faithful Repro-
        duction of the 1729 Edition, Which Includes the
        Words and Music of All the Airs, As Well as the
        Score for the Overture. With Commentaries by
        Louis Kronenberger and Max Goberman on the
        Literary and Musical Background and with the
        Original Words of All the Airs that John Gay
        Adapted for this Work. Larchmont, New York:
        Arganaut Books, 1961. viii, 60 pp. (text
        facsimile); 46 pp. (music facsimile); xxv-
        liv pp.

492   --The Beggar's Opera and Companion Pieces. Edited
        by C.F. Burgess. (Crofts Classics). New York:
        Appleton-Century-Crofts, 1966.
                Besides introduction, notes, and bibliography,
        the edition also provides related materials such

as "Newgate's Garland" and selections from <u>Trivia</u> and Gay's letters.

493 Armens, Sven M. <u>John Gay, Social Critic</u>. New York: Octagon Books, 1966, 262 pp.
  A reprint of the book first published in 1954. Chapter II concerns Gay's social criticism in <u>The Beggar's Opera</u>.

494 Bronson, Bertrand H. "The Beggar's Opera." <u>Restoration Drama: Modern Essays in Criticism</u>. (A Galaxy Book). Edited by John Loftis. (New York: Oxford University Press, 1966), 298-327.
  Reprinted from <u>Studies in the Comic</u> (Berkeley: University of California Press, 1941), pp. 197-231. An analysis of the ballad opera explains its popularity as its original production and even today.

495 --"The True Proportions of Gay's <u>Acis and Galatea</u>." <u>Publications of the Modern Language Association</u>, LXXX (1965), 325-331.
  Critics have slighted the achievement of Gay and Handel in <u>Acis and Galatea</u>, a supreme masterpiece in its genre. "It can only be truly apprehended as a <u>pastoral opera</u>, words and music inseparably united."

496 Burgess, C.F. "The Genesis of <u>The Beggar's Opera</u>." <u>Cithara</u>, II (1962), 6-12.
  Gay was concerned with the subject matter of <u>The Beggar's Opera</u> before Swift's suggestion for a "Newgate pastoral."

497 --"John Gay's 'Happy Vein': the Ambivalent Point of View." Ph.D. University of Notre Dame, 1962. (Order No. 62-4405).
  Gay's "happy vein" consists in the union of satiric and sympathetic attitudes demonstrated in <u>The Shepherd's Week</u>, <u>The What D' Ye Call It</u>, <u>Trivia</u>, and <u>The Beggar's Opera</u>.

498 --<u>The Letters of John Gay</u>. Oxford: Clarendon Press, 1966, 142 pp.

Edition of 81 letters written by Gay from
1705 to 1732. Includes introduction, notes,
and index.

499 --"Political Satire: John Gay's The Beggar's
Opera." The Midwest Quarterly, VI (1965), 265-
276.
The motives, nature, and the immediate
impact of Gay's satire on Walpole, Gay, and the
Tory party.

500 Forsgren, Adina. John Gay, Poet "of a Lower Order":
Comments on his Rural Poems and Other Early
Writings. Stockholm: Natur och kultur, 1964,
249 pp.
A critical and historical study of Gay's
early writings as typical of his mature work.
Includes references to Gay's plays and ballad
operas.

501 Fuller, John. "Cibber, The Rehearsal at Goatham
and the Suppression of Polly." Review of English
Studies, XIII (1962), 125-134.
The Rehearsal at Goatham hints that Gay
believed Cibber to have been influential in the
suppression of Polly.

502 Griffith, Benjamin W., Jr., ed. The Beggar's
Opera. Great Neck, New York: Barron's, 1962.
Includes music.

503 Hogarth, William. The Beggar's Opera. A port-
folio compiled by Wilmarth Sheldon Lewis and
Philip Hafer. Cambridge, Harvard University
Press, New Haven, Yale University Press, 1965.
11 plates reproduce Hogarth and Blake's
illustrations of Gay's ballad opera.

504 Hohne, H. "John Gays Beggar's Opera und Polly,
Teil I." Zeitschrift fur Anglestik und Ameri-
kanistik, XIII (1965), 232-260.
A philological and aesthetic analysis of
The Beggar's Opera and Polly reveal them to be
a reliable key to the age's Weltanschauung.

505   --"John Gays Beggar's Opera und Polly, Teil II."
        Zeitschrift fur Anglistik und Amerikanistik,
        XIII (1965), 341-359.
            Gay's use of irony, wit, satire, and humor
        in his two masterpieces.

506   Höhne, Horst. "John Gay's Bühneneverke in Ver-
        hältnis zum zeitgenössischen Dramenschaffen."
        Wissenschaftliche Zeitschrift der Humboldt-
        Universität zu Berlin, XI (1962), 150.

507   Lewis, Peter Elvet. "Gay's Burlesque Method in
        The What D'Ye Call It." Durham University
        Journal, LX (1967), 13-25.
            The play attacks the mixed forms that
        were being produced at the time. "Although Gay's
        satire is directed against several dramatic
        and poetic modes as the title indicates, his
        principal targets are undoubtedly the main
        tragedians of the previous forty years, Otway,
        Lee, Dennis, Rowe, Philips, and Addison."

508   Noble, Yvonne. "John Gay, The Beggar's Opera:
        A Critical Edition." Ph.D. Yale University,
        1966. (Order No. 66-13, 922).
            Provides a text for both dialogue and
        music, examines in a critical introduction
        pertinent historical phenomena, and supplies
        the sources of airs in this work and in its
        sequel, Polly.

509   Preston, John. "The Ironic Mode: A Comparison of
        Jonathan Wild and The Beggar's Opera." Essays
        in Criticism, XVI, (1966) 268-280.
            Studies the rhetorical and structural
        function of irony in the two works. For Field-
        ing irony is a stylistic device, for Gay a
        means of articulating and organizing his know-
        ledge of life.

510   Rees, John O., Jr. "'A Great Man in Distress':
        Macheath as Hercules." University of Colorado
        Studies. (Series in Language and Literature, 10).
        Edited by J. K. Emelry. (Boulder: University
        of Colorado Press, 1966), 73-77. See Also Nos.
        61, 86, 146

511   Schultz, William Eben. Gay's Beggar's Opera:
        Its Content, History and Influence. New York:
        Russell and Russell, 1967,   407 pp.
                A reissue of the 1923 edition. See Also
        Nos. 571, 862, 1072, 1147

512   Siegmund-Schultze, Dorothea. "Betrachtungen zur
        satirisch-polemischen Tendenz in John Gays
        Beggar's Opera." Wissenschaftliche Zeitschrift
        der Martin-Luther Universitat Halle-Wittenberg.
        Gesellschafts-und- Sprachwissenschaftliche
        Reihe, XII (1963), 1001-1014.

513   Spacks, Patricia Meyer. John Gay. New York:
        Twayne Publishers, Inc., 1965.
                Biographical and critical study of Gay's
        life and works. Chapter V, "The Poet's
        Plays" and Chapter VI, "The Begger's Triumph,"
        are of special interest. Includes selected
        bibliography.

514   Thompson, Keith Maybin. "Honest John Gay, A
        Re-Estimate of the Man and His Works." Ph.D.
        New York University, 1961. (Order No. 62-
        3337).
                A reexamination of the crosscurrents in
        his writings, with a view to the re-evaluation
        of the author as, probably, belonging in the
        continuum of British "romantic" tradition, rather
        than to the school of his great contemporaries,
        Pope, Swift, Arbuthnot, and Addison. Examines
        the songs in The Beggar's Opera.

515   Warner, Oliver. John Gay. New York: Longman's,
        Green, and Company (for the British Council and
        the National Book League), 1964, 40 pp.
                Short introduction to Gay as a man of
        letters. Significant sections on The Beggar's
        Opera, Polly and Achilles. See Also No. 815

    GAY, POPE ARBUTHNOT
516   Gay, John, Alexander Pope, and John Arbuthnot.
        Three Hours After Marriage. Edited by Richard
        Morton and William M. Peterson. Painesville,
        Ohio, 1961. xvi, 111 pp. (Lake Erie College
        Studies, Vol. I).

Prints the 1717 edition, noting it in both
corrected and uncorrected state. Also gives sub-
stantive variants in all editions of any authority
later.

517   Gay, John, Alexander Pope, and John Arbuthnot.
       Three Hours After Marriage. Edited, with an
       Introduction by John Harrington Smith. Los
       Angeles: Clark Memorial Library, University of
       California, 1961. 14, vi, 139-222 pp.(Augustan
       Reprint Society. Publication Nos. 91-92).
           Uses as a text the second edition of the
       Dublin Supplement to the Works of Alexander
       Pope (1758).

GENTLEMAN'S MAGAZINE, See No. 783

GEORGIAN, See No. 538

GERMAN DRAMA
518   Grieder, Theodore. "The German Drama in England,
       1790-1800." Restoration and 18th Century Theatre
       Research, III(November, 1964), 39-50.
           Studies the popularity of German drama in
       England from Holcroft's The German Hotel (1790).
       The low quality of the English plays and the
       emotionalism of the times accounted for its popu-
       larity; weak translations, English nationalism,
       and charges of social and political immorality
       contributed to its decline.

519   Milburn, Douglas Lafayette. "German Drama in
       England: 1750-1850, With a List of German Plays
       Published and Performed." Ph.D. Rice University,
       1964. (Order No. 64-10, 185).
           The changing attitudes toward German drama
       in Great Britain between the middle of the 18th
       century and the middle of the 19th century can
       be attributed to political and historical con-
       siderations rather than to objective criticism
       of the works translated.

GERMANY, See Nos. 943, 946, 947

GOLDSMITH

520   Goldsmith, Oliver. <u>She Stoops to Conquer</u>. Edited
with an introduction by A. Norman Jeffares.
London: Macmillan, 1965, 100 pp.

521   --<u>She Stoops to Conquer</u>. Edited by H. A. Kresner,
Sydney, Australia: Horwitz, 1963. See Also Nos.
780, 815

522   --<u>She Stoops to Conquer</u> and Sheridan, Richard
Brinsley. <u>The School for Scandal</u>. (Bantam
Pathfinder Editions). New York: Bantam Books,
Inc., 1966.
With brief introduction and notes.

523   --<u>The Vicar of Wakefield</u> and <u>She Stoops to Conquer</u>.
With an Introduction by R.H.W. Dillard. (Harper
Perennial Classics). New York: Harper and Row
Publishers, 1965, 265 pp.
Includes biographical notes, bibliography
and Goldsmith's "On the Theatre."

524   Baer, Joel H. "Revival of the Comic Spirit: Goldsmith's <u>She Stoops to Conquer</u>." <u>Setting the
Stage</u>. Minnesota Theatre Company Publication,
1967.

525   Butzier, Kenneth G. "An Evaluation of Technical
Problems Encountered in a Period Revival at
State College High School, Cedar Falls, Iowa,
of Oliver Goldsmith's <u>She Stoops to Conquer</u>."
M.S. University of Wisconsin, 1963.

526   Coulter, John Knox, Jr. "Oliver Goldsmith's
Literary Reputation, 1757-1801." Ph.D. Indiana
University, 1965. (Order No. 65-10, 814).
Considers the reaction of contemporary
critics to Goldsmith's works and suggests that
both <u>The Good-Natured Man</u> and <u>She Stoops to
Conquer</u> represent an attack upon sentimental
comedy and the author's attempt to revive a
comic tradition unhindered by false illusions
about man's goodness.

527   De Haas, Jeanne Marie. "The Design and Execution
       of Costumes for Oliver Goldsmith's She Stoops
       to Conquer." M.F.A. Ohio University, 1965.

528   Ferguson, Oliver W. "Goldsmith." South Atlantic
       Quarterly, LXIV (1967), 465-472.
           A general review of Goldsmith's achieve-
       ments and character.

529   --"The Materials of History: Goldsmith's Life
       of Nash." Publications of the Modern Language
       Association, LXXX (1965), 372-386.
           Information about Goldsmith's success,
       particularly from George Scott, for his The
       Life of Richard Nash, Esq.

530   Friedman, Arthur, editor. The Collected Works
       of Oliver Goldsmith, 5 vols. Oxford: Clarendon
       Press, 1966.
           Volume V includes the plays with introduc-
       tions and notes.

531   Garrod, H.W. The Study of Good Letters. Edited
       by John Jones. Oxford: Clarendon Press, 1963,
       211 pp.
           An essay on Goldsmith's achievement (origi-
       nally published in 1924 as part of the Nelson's
       Poets series) stresses the humanistic value of
       The Good-Natured Man and She Stoops to Conquer.

532   Griffin, Robert Julian. "Goldsmith's Augustanism:
       A Study of his Literary Works." Ph.D. Univer-
       sity of California, Berkeley, 1965. (Order No.
       65-13497).
           Considers The Good Natured Man and She
       Stoops to Conquer as efforts to correct the
       age's one-sided "sentimental" view.

533   Gutting, John G. "Humour Humbled and Exalted:
       Oliver Goldsmith and the Theatre of Comedy."
       M.A. Xavier University, 1967.

534   Jeffares, A. Norman. A Critical Commentary on
       Goldsmith's 'She Stoops to Conquer'. (Mac-
       millan Critical Commentaries). London: Mac-
       millan, 1966, 40 pp.

Besides an analysis of the play's plot,
characters, and significance, the work provides
a brief biography, a description of the contemporary stage, and a selected bibliography.

535   Joel, Helmuth Wulf, Jr. "The Theme of Education
in the Works of Oliver Goldsmith." Ph.D. University of Pennsylvania, 1967. (Order No. 67-12,
761).
       Studies Goldsmith's approach to the problems
attendant upon bringing up the young to survive
in a hostile world. Includes discussion of The
Good Natured Man and She Stoops to Conquer.

536   Kirk, Clara M. Oliver Goldsmith. New York: Twayne
Publishers, 1967, 202 pp.
       Biographical and critical study of Gold-
smith's major works. Chapter IV, "Two Laughing
Comedies," is of particular note. Includes
selected bibliography.

537   Quintana, Ricardo. Oliver Goldsmith: A Georgian
Study. (Masters of World Literature Series).
New York: Macmillan Co., 1937, 213 pp.
       A biographical and critical study of
Goldsmith's works. Chapter VIII. "Comedy for
the Theatre," is of special interest. See
Also No. 767

538   --"Goldsmith's Achievement as Dramatist." University of Toronto Quarterly, XXXIV (1965), 159-177.
       Occupies itself with such questions as the
relationship between Goldsmith's earlier works
and his dramas, the influence of Georgian
comedy upon his dramatic career, and the nature
of his comic disposition.

539   --"Oliver Goldsmith as a Critic of the Drama."
Studies in English Literature, 1500-1900, V
(1965), 435-454.
       Goldsmith's criticism of his own plays,
of comedy, and of contemporary dramatists reveals "a truly sophisticated poetic of the
drama."

100

540   Reed, Duane E. "A Project in Design and Execution
       of Costumes for a Production of Goldsmith's She
       Stoops to Conquer." M.A. Indiana University,
       1962.

541   Rodway, Allan. "Goldsmith and Sheridan: Satirists
       of Sentiment." Renaissance and Modern Essays.
       Edited by G. R. Hibbard. (London: Routledge
       and Kegan Paul, 1966), 65-72.
            The anti-sentimental plays of Goldsmith
       and Sheridan are themselves affected by the
       "usurping Genteel or Sentimental Mode they
       purported to attack." See Also Nos. 61, 146

542   Schenk, William Murrel. "A Development of the
       Scenic Designs for the Ohio State University
       Production of She Stoops to Conquer." M. A.
       Ohio State University, 1965. See Also No. 153

543   Sherwin, Oscar. Goldy: The Life and Times of
       Oliver Goldsmith. New York: Twayne Publishers,
       1961, 367 pp.
            Popular life, "based on fact...and...
       artistic imagination." Goldsmith's relations
       to the theatre are mentioned. Some contemporary
       documents used. See Also No. 802

       GOODMAN
544   Wilson, John Harold. Mr. Goodman the Player.
       Pittsburgh: University of Pittsburgh Press, 1964,
       153 pp.
            Studies Goodman's colorful career particu-
       larly in his association with the King's Company
       of Comedians from 1673 to 1682.

GOULD, See No. 384

GRAMMAR, See No. 666

GRANVILLE, See No. 1002

GREENWICH HOSPITAL NEWSLETTERS, See No. 223

GREENWOOD, See No. 913

GREVILLE, See No. 1039

GRIFFITH, See No. 133

GWYNN
545   Moncpda, Ernest J. "The Source of an Epigraph
Attributed to Rochester." Notes and Queries,
New Ser., XI (1964), 95-96.
        Ascribes to James Howell the authorship
of an obscene poem written under the portrait
of Nell Gwynn in Curll's The Works of the Earl
of Rochester, Roscommon, and Dorset. (1718)

H

HAMMER, See No. 952

HAMPDEN-LIBRARY, See No. 857

HARBAGE, See No. 133

HARLEQUIN, See No. 215

HARVARD LIBRARY, See No. 812

HAWKESWORTH
546   Eddy, Donald O. "John Hawkesworth: Book Reviewer
in the Gentleman's Magazine." Philological
Quarterly, XLIII (1964), 223-238.
        Contemporary reviews of plays by Hawkes-
worth in the Monthly Review and Gentleman's
Magazine. Table of entries includes reviews of
Wit's Last Stand by T. King; Fatal Discovery
by J. Home; The Sister by Mrs. C. Lennox; The
West Indian by R. Cumberland; Almida by D.
Celisia and D. Garrick; A Word to the Wise by
H. Kelly; and 'Tis Well It's No Worse by I.
Bickerstaffe.

HAYDN
547   Shepard, Brooks, Jr. "A Haydn Opera at Yale."
Yale University Library Gazette, XXXVI (1962),
184-187.
        A copy of Philemon and Baucis under the
title of "Die Feuerbrunst" at Yale.

HAYMARKET, See No. 856

HAYWOOD
548   Elwood, John R. "The Stage Career of Eliza Haywood."
       Theatre Survey, V(1964), 107-116.
            Biographical notes on the novelist-play-
       wright-actress whose stage career extended at
       least from 1715 to 1737.

HENDERSON, See Nos. 857, 951

HERO, See Nos. 318, 424, 550, 729, 730, 955, 1176

HEROIC
549   Newman, Robert Stanley. "The Tragedy of Wit:
       the Development of Heroic Drama from Dryden to
       Addison." Ph.D. University of California, Los
       Angeles, 1964. (Order No. 65-2556).
            Argues that "heroic artifice was not a
       reflection of literary history but rather of
       political and psychological malaise, and that
       its idealizing quality was always associated
       with a skeptical and satiric wit identical in
       attitude to that of Restoration comedy." See
       Also Nos. 88, 268, 275, 349, 350, 367, 380,
       386, 390, 550

HEROIC PLAY, See No. 319

HEROIC TRAGEDY
550   Biddle, Evelyn Q. "A Critical Study of the In-
       fluence of the Classical and Christian Traditions
       Upon the Character of the Hero as Revealed
       Through Concepts of 'Love' and 'Honor' in Three
       Restoration Heroic Tragedies." Ph.D. University
       of Southern California, 1967. (Order No. 67-6491).
            Considers Orrery's Henry V, Dryden's The
       Conquest of Granada, and Settle's The Empress of
       Morocco.
551   Rasco, Kay Frances Dilworth. "Super-naturalism in
       the Heroic Play." Ph.D. Northwestern University,
       1966. (Order No. 67-4261).
            Studies Restoration attitudes toward the
       appropriateness and function of supernatural ele-
       ments in the heroic play, and considers the

relevance of supernatural elements to various Restoration dramas. Concerned especially with the works of Davenant, Dryden, Orrery, Otway, and Lee. See Also Nos. 302, 303

HILL

552   Hill, Aaron and William Popple. The Prompter: A Theatrical Paper (1734-1736). Edited by William A. Appleton and Kalmin A. Burnim. New York: Benjamin Blom, 1965.
      Contemporary reviews of plays and essays on the art of acting.

553   Bergman, Gosta M. "Aaron Hill: Ein englischer Regisseur des 18. Jahrhunderts." Maske und Kothurn (Graz-Wein), VIII(1962), 295-340.

554   Burnim, Kalman A. "Aaron Hill's The Prompter: An Eighteenth-Century Theatrical Paper." Educational Theatre Journal, XIII (May 1961), 73-81.
      An analysis of The Prompter, and Hill's purposes. The Prompter is valuable for reconstructing acting styles.

555   Burns, Landon C. "Three Views of King Henry V." Drama Survey, I (Winter, 1962), 278-300.
      Includes a discussion of Aaron Hill's adaptation of Henry V, written in 1723.

556   Eddison, Robert. "Topless in Jerusalem." Theatre Notebook, XXII (Autumn, 1967), 24-27.
      Discusses the success of Hill's Zara, produced at Drury Lane in 1736 and a drawing depicting Susannah Cibber in the title role. See Also No. 887

HOBBES

557   Nigh, Douglas J. "Hobbes' Relevance to Dramatic Theory." Xavier University Studies, V (1966),
      See Also Nos. 276, 313, 369, 388, 1079

HOFMANNSTHAL, See No. 842

HOGARTH, See No. 503

HOLCROFT
558   Ter-Abramova, V.G.   "Roman Tomasa Xolkrofta
       Anna Sent-Iv." Filologiceskie Nauki, VII (1964),
       iv, 93-108. See Also Nos. 249, 518, 797

HOME
559   Emslie, Mac Donald,   "Home's Douglas and Wully
       Shakespeare." Studies in Scottish Literature,
       II (1964), 128-129. See Also No. 1120

560   Parker, Gerald Douglas. "Edition of John Home's
       Douglas: A Tragedy (1757)." Ph.D. University
       of Toronto, 1967.
              Includes discussion of the editorial con-
       troversy surrounding the two "first" editions
       and an account of the play's stage history.
       See Also Nos. 249, 546

HOPKINS, See No. 474

HOWARD
561   Sutherland, James R.   "The Date of James Howard's
       All Mistaken, or, The Mad Couple." Notes and
       Queries, New Ser., XI (1964), 339-340.
              Fixes the date of Howard's comedy at 1665
       and posits the theory that Dryden's Secret Love;
       or, the Maiden Queen was substantially derived
       from it. See Also No. 274

562   Oliver, H. J.   Sir Robert Howard (1626-1698): A
       Critical Biography. Durham, North Carolina:
       Duke University Press, 1963. 346 pp.
              Treats extensively Howard's literary re-
       lationship with Dryden. Important discussion
       relating to the authorship of The Indian Queen.

HUGHES
563   Knapp, J. Merrill. "A Forgotten Chapter in English
       Eighteenth-Century Opera." Music and Letters,
       XLII (1961), 1-16.
              An account of John Hughes' Calypso and
       Telemachus produced 1712, with music by John
       Ernest Galliard.

HUME
564   Cohen, Ralph. "The Transformation of Passion: a
       Study of Hume's Theories of Tragedy." Philologi-
       cal Quarterly, XLI (1962), 450-464.
       A comparison of Hume's theory of sympathy
       in the Treatise of Human Nature and his later
       Four Dissertations. See Also No. 780

HUMOURS, See No. 157

HUNT
565   Fenner, Theodore Lincoln. "Leigh Hunt on Opera:
       The Examiner Years." Ph.D. Columbia University,
       1967. (Order No. 68-8578).
       Chapter I discusses the traditions of
       Italian Opera and "English opera" and describes
       the complex cultural attitudes and conditions
       that affected the state of opera during the
       Examiner years (1808-1822).

HUNTINGTON, See No. 126

                              I

IMAGERY, See Nos. 184, 262, 988

INCHBALD
566   Inchbald, Elizabeth, ed. The Modern Theatre.   10
       vols. New York: Benjamin Blom, 1967.
       A reprint of the 1809 edition includes fifty
       plays by twenty-three playwrights of the late
       eighteenth century.

567   Beer, E. S. de. "Lovers' Vows: 'The Dangerous In-
       significance of the Butler.'" Notes and Queries,
       New Ser., IX (1962), 421-422.
       By altering the part of the butler, Mrs.
       Inchbald has averted the theatrical dangers of
       the character in Kotzebue's Das Kind der Liebe.
       See Also No. 797

INFLUENCE
568   Tumasz, Sister M. Florence, C.S.F.N. "Eighteenth
       Century English Literature and the Polish En-

lightenment." Ph.D. Fordham University, 1963.
(Order No. 64-2411).
Descriptive study of the influence of English letters in Poland between 1764 and 1822. Chapter V is devoted to the reception of 18th century playwrights, especially Moore, Addison, and Sheridan. See Also No. 171

IRELAND, H.
569   Grebanier, Bernard. The Great Shakespeare Forgery.
New York: W.W. Norton, 1965, 308 pp.
Deals with the forgeries of Shakespeare plays and material perpetrated by William Henry Ireland, 1794-1796. 12 chapters and bibliography.

IRELAND (Place)
570   Clark, William Smith. The Irish Stage in the
County Towns: 1720-1800. Oxford: Clarendon Press, 1965, 405 pp.
A "tour" of nine county seats, interspersed with social and political history of the era, provides a significant account of the theatrical activities during the 18th century. Considerable attention is devoted to biographical data on English actors and actresses who performed in Ireland during the period. Two appendixes list Plays and Actors in Ireland outside Dublin, 1720-1800. A comprehensive bibliography of maps, manuscripts, playbills, newspapers, books and articles completes the text.

IRVING, See No. 18

J

JEFFERSON, See No. 18

JOHNSON
571   Johnson, Samuel. Lives of the English Poets,
Edited by George Birkbeck Hill. 3 vols. New York: Octagon Books, 1967.
A reprint of the 1905 edition. Volume I includes Milton, Dryden, and Otway; Volume II Rowe, Addison, Congreve and Gay.

107

572   Barnes, G. "Johnson's Edition of Shakespeare."
       Johnson Society Transactions, 1964, 16-39
              Although Johnson's Preface is a work of
       merit and distinction, the actual edition of
       Shakespeare's plays fall short of Johnson's
       abilities and intentions.

573   Davies, R. T., editor. Samuel Johnson: Selected
       Writings, London: Faber and Faber, 1965, 398 pp.
              This anthology includes the Preface to
       Shakespeare and Notes from the Edition of
       Shakespeare.

574   Eddy, Donald D.   "Samuel Johnson's Editions of
       Shakespeare (1765)." Papers of the Bibliograph-
       ical Society of America, LVI (1962),428-444.
              Presents variations of all the editions of
       Johnson's Shakespeare published in 1765.

575   Findlay, Robert R. "Samuel Johnson: A Transitional
       View of Mixing Tragedy and Comedy." Ohio
       Speech Journal, III (1965), 29-33.

576   Fleischmann, Wolfgang Bernard.   "Shakespeare,
       Johnson, and the Dramatic 'Unities of Time and
       Place." Essays in English Literature of the
       Classical Period Presented to Dougald MacMillan.
       Edited by Daniel W. Patterson and Albrecht B.
       Strauss. Studies in Philology (Extra Series,
       January, 1967), pp. 128-134.

577   Gardner, Helen.   "Johnson on Shakespeare." New
       Rambler, No. B. XVII (1965), 2-12.
              An appreciation of Johnson's Shakespeare
       criticism based on his qualities as a serious
       editor, professional writer, and Christian
       moralist.

578   Griffin, Robert J. "Dr. Johnson and the Drama."
       Discourse, V (Winter, 1961-62), 95-101.
              Discussion of Johnson's idea of the func-
       tion of drama and its relation to nature.

579   Hagstrum, Jean H. Samuel Johnson's Literary
       Criticism. Chicago: University of Chicago
       Press, 1967, 212 pp.

A reissue of the 1952 edition with a new
preface by the author and a bibliography of
studies of Johnson's literary criticism since
1952, this study attempts to define the principles underlying Johnson's criticism of particular works.

580   Hamilton, Harlan W. "Samuel Johnson's Appeal to
       Nature." Western Humanities Review, XXI (1967),
       339-345.
              Examines Johnson's "consuming interest in
       closely ascertained details" in selected works,
       including the Preface to Shakespeare.

581   Hardy, John. "The 'Poet of Nature' and Self-
       Knowledge: One Aspect of Johnson's Moral Reading
       of Shakespeare." University of Toronto Quar-
       terly, XXXVI (1967), 141-160.
              Although Johnson felt that Shakespeare was
       "so much more careful to please than to instruct,"
       his "just representations of general nature"
       were nevertheless able to provide a picture of
       human nature from which all men could learn
       something about themselves.

582   --"The Unities Again: Dr. Johnson and Delusion."
       Notes and Queries, New Ser., IX (1962), 350-
       351.
              Suggests that R. K. Kaul's article on the
       unities can be substantiated further by common
       allusions to Alexander the Great in both Far-
       quhar's and Johnson's writings. Additional
       remarks on Johnson's idea of illusion.

583   Kaul, R. K. "Dr. Johnson on the Emotional Effect
       of Tragedy." Cairo Studies in English, 1963-
       1966, pp. 203-211.
              Collects Johnson's statements on the effects
       of tragedy and discusses their relationship to
       Aristotelian catharsis. See Also Nos.86, 476

584   --"The Unities Again: Dr. Johnson and Delusion."
       Notes and Queries, New Ser., IX (1962), 261-
       264.
              Johnson supports the position of Farquhar
       rather than Lord Kames in his defense of English

drama's failing to adhere to the unities.

585   Kazin, Alfred. "The Imagination of a Man of
       Letters." The American Scholar, XXXIV (1964-5),
       19-27.
           Maintains that Johnson's commentary on
       Shakespeare is the beginning of a tradition of
       criticism by men of letters with imagination.

586   McAdam, E. L. and George Milne, editors. A
       Johnson Reader. New York: Pantheon Books,
       1964,   464 pp.
           Popular anthology of Johnson's writings.
       "Preface to Shakespeare." reprinted with notes.

587   McAleer, John J. "Samuel Johnson and 'The Sove-
       reign of the Drama.'" Shakespeare Newsletter,
       XVII (1967), 28.
           Relates the circumstances leading to
       Johnson's edition of Shakespeare and discusses
       the quality of his criticism.

588   Maxwell, J. C. "Prescriptive." Notes and
       Queries, New Ser., IX (1962), 268.
           The use of "prescriptive" in Johnson's
       Preface to Shakespeare antedates the first
       quotations for it in the OED and in Black-
       stone.

589   Misenheimer, James B.,Jr. "Dr. Johnson's Con-
       cept of Literary Fiction." Modern Language
       Review, LXII (1967), 598-605.
           The phrases "irregular combination of
       fanciful invention" and "the stability of
       truth" in Johnson's Preface to Shakespeare
       point to the two kinds of literary fiction
       Johnson recognized.

590   Misenheimer, James Buford. "Samuel Johnson and
       the Didactic Aesthetic." Ph.D. University of
       Colorado, 1964. (Order No. 65-4261).
           Johnson's ideas on specific literary genres,
       e.g., drama, are founded on his belief in a
       "didactic aesthetic" which demanded a truthful
       portrayal of human nature, moral edification,
       and spiritual enrichment.

591   Sachs, Arieh. "Generality and Particularity in
        Johnson's Thought." Studies in English Litera-
        ture, 1500-1900, V (1965), 491-511.
                Johnson's statements on particularity and
        generality in poetry are related to his moral
        and religious thought. Includes references to
        Johnson's Shakespeare criticism.

592   Sherbo, Arthur. "Johnson as Editor of Shakespeare:
        The Notes," Samuel Johnson: A Collection of
        Critical Essays. Edited by Donald J. Greene.
        (Englewood Cliffs, New Jersey: Prentice-Hall,
        1965), 124-137.
                An abridgement of an earlier article from
        Samuel Johnson, Editor of Shakespeare, with an
        Essay on the Adventurer, published in 1956.
        Examines Johnson's critical principles as re-
        vealed in his textual commentary on Shakespeare.

593   --Johnson on Shakespeare. Intro. by Bertrand Bron-
        son. (The Yale Edition of the Works of Samuel
        Johnson, Vols. VII and VIII). New Haven: Yale
        University Press, 1967.
                Includes the notes of Johnson's first and
        revised edition of Shakespeare, the Preface and
        General Observations, the Miscellaneous Obser-
        vations on the Tragedy of Macbeth, the Preface
        to Mrs. Lennox's Shakespeare Illustrated and the
        Proposals for an edition.

594   Sorelius, Gunnar. "The Unities Again: Dr. Johnson
        and Delusion." Notes and Queries, New Ser., IX
        (1962), 466-467.
                Stresses similarities between passages from
        Dryden's Epistle Dedicatory to Love Triumphant
        and Johnson's Preface to Shakespeare.

595   Sprague, Arthur Colby. "The Alchemist on the Stage."
        Theatre Notebook, XVII (Winter, 1962-63), 46-47.
                Includes information on the play's popu-
        larity from 1721 until the retirement of Garrick
        in 1776.

596   Stock, Robert Douglas. "The Intellectual Background
        of Dr. Johnson's Preface to Shakespeare." Ph.D.
        Princeton University, 1967. (Order No. 68-2522).

Uses an investigation of dramatic critical
theory from 1730 to 1770 to approach the Preface
with something of an eighteenth-century perspective. See Also Nos. 94, 612, 763, 963

597   Sullivan, Gerald Joseph. "Politics and Literature
of Samuel Johnson." Ph.D. The University of
Oklahoma, 1964. (Order No. 64-10, 505).
        The action of Irene "corresponds to John-
son's belief that government can function suc-
cessfully and preserve the peace and order nec-
essary to happiness only if it has the authority
to insure the proper subordination of its
members."

598   Waingrow, Marshall. "The Mighty Moral of Irene."
From Sensibility to Romanticism: Essays Presented
to Frederick A. Pottle, eds. Frederick W. Hilles
and Harold Bloom (New York: Oxford University
Press, 1965), 79-92.
        Argues against the traditional interpreta-
tion that the play's simple moral is a reflection
of poetic justice and of Johnson's subscription
to "the absolute imperatives of the Christian
religion." Irene is the play's heroine who, in
Johnson's words, is "in a kind of equipoise
between good and ill." See Also Nos. 955, 969,
1005, 1120

599   Wolper, Roy S. "Samuel Johnson and the Drama."
Ph.D. University of Pittsburgh, 1964. (Order No.
65-7950).
        This inquiry into Johnson's activities in
the theatre and his relation to 18th century
drama stresses his friendship with Garrick, his
attendance at theatrical productions, and his
familiarity with world drama. See Also Nos. 58,
124, 356, 382, 756, 782, 956, 999

JONSON, See No. 167

JORDAN
600   Fothergill, Brian. Mrs. Jordan: Portrait of an
Actress. London: Faber and Faber, 1965, 334 pp.
        Biographical study of the 18th century
comic actress Dorothy Jordan.

JOURNALS, See Nos. 946, 947

K

KEAN, See No. 18

KELLY
601   O'Leary, Thomas Kenneth. "Hugh Kelly: Contribu-
       tions Toward a Critical Biography." Ph. D.
       Fordham University, 1965, (Order No. 65-920).
          The life and writings of dramatist Hugh
       Kelly provide an excellent guide to the taste
       and goals of the 18th century.

602   Rawson, C.J. "Some Remarks in Eighteenth Century
       'Delicacy,' with a Note on Hugh Kelly's False
       Delicacy (1768)." Journal of English and Ger-
       manic Philology, LXI (1962), 1-13.
          Definition of "delicacy." Its spiritual and
       physical attributes.

KELLY, See Also Nos. 133, 546

KEMBLE
603   Donohue, Joseph W., Jr. "Kemble and Mrs. Siddons
       in Macbeth: The Romantic Approach to Tragic
       Character." Theatre Notebook, XXII (Winter,
       1967-8), 65-86.
          Examines the Kembles' approach to their
       roles in several performances to determine how
       "theatrical performance faithfully mirrors an
       age."

604   --"Kemble's Production of Macbeth (1794)."
       Theatre Notebook, XXI (Winter, 1966-7), 63-74.
          Discusses the specific contributions of
       individual painters, the scenic effects and
       costumes of the production at the new Drury
       Lane on April 21, 1794. See Also Nos. 2, 951

605   McAleer, John J. "John Kemble--Shakespeare's
       First Great Producer." Shakespeare Newsletter,
       XVII (1967), 17.

A brief biography that concentrates on
Kemble's relationship to Sheridan and his Shakespeare revivals, twenty-five productions between
1788 and 1817.

KENRICK, See No. 133

KILLIGREW
606   Killigrew, Thomas. Comedies and Tragedies
       Written by Thomas Killigrew. New York: Benjamin
       Blom, 1967, 656 pp.
               Reprint of the 1664 edition.

607   Harbage, Alfred. Thomas Killigrew, Cavalier
       Dramatist 1612-83. New York: Benjamin Blom,
       1967, 256 pp.
               A reprint of the 1930 biography. See
       Also No. 775

KILLIGREW, See Also Nos. 3, 9

KING, See Nos. 546, 951

KING'S COMPANY, See No. 544

KING'S MEN, See No. 9

KOTZEBUE, See No. 909

                         L

LACY
608   Lacy, John. The Dramatic Works of John Lacy,
       Comedian. Edited by James Maidment and W. H.
       Logan. New York: Benjamin Blom, 1967, 416
       pp.
               A reprint of the 1874 edition includes
       five plays by Lacy.

LAMB
609   Schwarz, John Henry, Jr. "Charles Lamb on the
       Drama." Ph.D. Duke University, 1967, (Order
       No. 68-5244).

                        114

Chapter IV considers Lamb's critical
judgments of Restoration and 18th century playwrights and studies his "On the Artificial
Comedy of the Last Century."

LANGBAINE, See No. 970

LANGUAGE, See No. 412

LARPENT, See No. 126

LAWES, See No. 663

LEE
610   Lee, Nathaniel. Lucius Junius Brutus, edited by
       John Loftis. (Regents Restoration Drama Series).
       Lincoln: University of Nebraska Press, 1967.
              Includes introduction, notes and chronology.
       See Also No. 507

611   McLeod, A.L. "A Nathaniel Lee Bibliography, 1670-
       1960." 17th and 18th Century Theatre Research,
       I (November, 1962), 27-39.
              Includes listings of Lee's collected works,
       individual plays, occasional poems, and books
       and articles concerning Lee. See Also Nos. 21,
       306, 308, 551

LENNOX
612   Isles, Duncan. "Johnson and Charlotte Lennox."
       The New Rambler, Serial No. C. III (June, 1967),
       34-48.
              A discussion of the financial and literary
       assistance given to Mrs. Lennox by Johnson in-
       cludes mention of her three dramas and her
       Shakespeare Illustrated, a work on the sources
       of the plays. See Also No. 546

LENNOX COLLECTION
613   Isler, Duncan E. "Other Letters in the Lennox
       Collection." Times Literary Supplement, (5
       August 1965), p. 685.
              Includes letters by Garrick and Colman to
       Mrs. Charlotte Lennox.

LETTERS, See Nos. 490, 1039

LEVERIDGE, See Nos. 448, 832

LEWIS

614   Guthke, Karl S. "F.L. Schroder, J.F. Regnard, and
      M.G. Lewis." Huntington Library Quarterly,
      XXVII (November, 1963), 79-82.
            Detailed comparison of Lewis's The Twins
      with its source, F. L. Schroder's adaptation
      of J.F. Regnard's Les Ménechmes, ou les Jumeaux.

615   --"M.G. Lewis' The Twins." Huntington Library
      Quarterly, XXV (1962), 189-223.
            "The only hitherto unpublished manuscript
      known to be by Lewis." Includes criticism,
      possible sources, and complete text of play.

LIBERTINE, See No. 770

LICENSING ACT, See No. 445

LIGHTING, See No. 1063

LILLO

616   Lillo, George. Fatal Curiosity. Edited by William
      H. H. McBurney. (Regents Restoration Drama
      Series). Lincoln: University of Nebraska Press,
      1966.
            Includes introduction, notes, and appendices
      for variant and additional passages and for the
      source of the play.

617   --The London Merchant. Edited by William H. H.
      McBurney. (Regents Restoration Drama Series).
      Lincoln: University of Nebraska Press, 1965.
            Includes critical introduction, notes,
      bibliography, and appendices with Lillo's ad-
      vertisement and "The Ballad of George Barnwell."

618   Burgess, C.F. "Further Notes for a Biography of
      George Lillo." Philological Quarterly, XLVI
      (1967), 424-428.
            Two recently discovered documents, one an
      entry in the Apprentice Register in Goldsmith's
      Hall, London and the other in the Lambeth Palace
      Library respectively reveal that George Lillo's
      brother James was an apprenticed goldsmith and
      that Lillo's religious orientation was not

Puritan but Anglican. See Also No. 1122

619   Carson, Herbert L. "The Play That Would Not Die:
        George Lillo's The London Merchant." Quarterly
        Journal of Speech, XLIX(1963), 287-294.
            Conditions which favored the composition
        of the play; its weaknesses and influence on
        subsequent drama. See Also Nos. 815, 921

620   Daunicht, Richard. Die Entstehung des Bürger-
        lichen Trauerspiels in Deutschland. (Quellen
        und Forschungen zur Sprach-und-Kulturgeschichte
        der germanischen Völker. Neue Folge, herausge-
        geben von Hermann Kunisch, 8). Berlin: Walter
        de Gruyter and Company, 1963, 309 pp.
            Several chapters of this critical treatise
        are devoted to the influence of English drama
        on German bourgeoise tragedy. Chapter V con-
        tains a history of the first printings and
        performances of The London Merchant in German.

621   De Boer, Fredrik Eugene. "George Lillo." Ph.D.
        The University of Wisconsin, 1965. (Order No.
        65-9232).
            A descriptive history of the life, writings,
        and reputation of Lillo. Lillo's dramatic en-
        deavors are seen as "direct attempts to turn the
        theatre to the service of a specifically Calvin-
        istic morality." A bibliography lists all the
        published editions of Lillo's works. See Also
        Nos. 301, 946, 1120

622   McBurney, William H. "What George Lillo Read: A
        Speculation. Huntington Library Quarterly,
        XXIX (1966), 275-286.
            A partially annotated list of books probably
        owned by Lillo and sold at auction by the booksel-
        ler John Oswald in 1739.

LOCKE, See No. 832

LONDON MAGAZINE, See No. 783

LOPE DE VEGA, See No. 329

117

LOUTHERBOURG
623   Allen, Ralph G. "Topical Scenes for Pantomime."
       Educational Theatre Journal, XVII (1965),
       289-300.
              An examination of five "topical spectacles"
       prepared by P. J. De Loutherbourg during his
       stay at Drury Lane for Garrick and Sheridan.
       See Also Nos. 909, 916

624   Preston, Lillian E. "Loutherbourg's Letters to
       Garrick." Drama Critique, IX (1966), 42-44.
              Reprints two letters from the Forster Col-
       lection at the Victoria and Albert Museum that
       illuminate some of Loutherbourg's early plans
       for the Drury Lane Stage.

625   --"The Noble Savage: Omai; or A Trip Round the
       World." Drama Critique, VIII (1965), 130-132.
              An account of Loutherbourg's realistic
       design for the musical pantomime of 1785-1786.
       See Also No. 907

LUDLOW CASTLE, See No. 647

LUTTRELL, See No. 873

LYCEUM THEATRES, See No. 1112

LYRIC, See Nos. 699, 735, 743, 967

M

MACKENZIE
626   Lindsay, David W. "Henry Mackenzie, Alexander
       Thomson and Dramatic Pieces from the German."
       Studies in Scottish Literature, III (1966),
       253-255.
              Thomson, not Mackenzie, is the translator
       of the work published in Edinburgh in 1792.

627   Quaintance, Richard E., Jr. "Henry Mackenzie's
       Sole Comedy." Huntington Library Quarterly,
       XXVI (1962), 249-251.

Substantiates from manuscript of the play
that False Shame; or, The White Hypocrite is
merely another title for The Force of Fashion,
(1789).

628   Rouch, John S. "Henry Mackenzie: A Re-examination."
        Ph.D. University of Cincinnati, 1961. 271 pp.
        (Order No. 61-5231).
            The analysis given of three of his plays,
        The Prince of Tunis (1773), The Spanish Father
        (1773), and False Shame (1789), shows his moral
        dualism functioning in both tragedy and comedy.

MACKLIN
629   Macklin, Charles. Covent Garden Theatre. With
        an introduction by Jean B. Kern. Los Angeles:
        Clark Memorial Library, University of California,
        Los Angeles, 1965.
            A facsimile reproduction for the Augustan
        Reprint Society. See Also Nos. 941, 951

630   Bartley, J. O. "Charles Macklin: Appearances Out-
        side London." Theatre Notebook, XXII (Autumn,
        1967), 4-5.
            An alphabetical list of 18 plays in which
        Macklin acted. Each item includes the author
        and title of the play, the character played by
        Macklin, and the places and dates of perform-
        ance.

631   Coleman, William S.E. "Post-Restoration Shylocks
        Prior to Macklin." Theatre Survey, VIII (1967),
        17-36.
            Questions the common assumption that a
        comedic approach to Shylock prevailed in the
        early 18th century. Examines the roles of
        Thomas Dogget, Benjamin Griffin, Anthony Boheme,
        John Ogden, Anthony Aston, and John Arthur.

632   Findlay, Robert R. "Charles Macklin and the
        Problem of Natural Acting." Educational Theatre
        Journal, XIX (1967), 33-40.
            Examines all of Macklin's roles to discover
        a distinct pattern among them that does not de-
        mand or even suggest "natural" acting.

119

633   --"Macklin's Legitimate Acting Version of <u>Love a</u>
<u>la Mode</u>." Philological Quarterly, XLV (1966),
749-760.
Disputes W. Matthews' conclusion in "The
Piracies of Macklin's <u>Love a-la-Mode</u>" in <u>Re-</u>
<u>view of English Studies</u>, X (1934), and contends
that Macklin used in performance the text he
authorized for publication in 1793.

634   Findlay, Robert Raymond. "A Critical Study of the
Extant Plays of Charles Macklin." Ph.D. State
University of Iowa, 1964. (Order No. 64-7917).
Examines ten dramatic works of Macklin
as vehicles of satire written to "display his
acting talents." See Also No. 965

635   Maloney, Timothy. "Charles Macklin and 'The Art
and Duty of an Actor." M.A. University of
Delaware, 1966. See Also No. 2

MACREADY
636   Bassett, Abraham Joseph. "The Actor-Manager
Career of William Charles Macready." Ph.D.
Ohio State University, 1962.
The managerial career of Macready is
studied in respect to the staging of the plays
and popular reaction to them.

637   Downer, Alan S. <u>The Eminent Tragedian: William</u>
<u>Charles Macready</u>. Cambridge: Harvard University
Press, 1966, 392 pp.
This biography of Macready includes comments
on his contribution to stagecraft during the
transitional period between the late 18th century and the later reform of Craig, Appia, and
others.

638   Wolfit, Donald. "The Actor's Life Today and Yes-
terday." <u>Drama</u>, No. 69 (Summer, 1963), 26-29.
The life of the actor from Elizabethan
times to the present day. Some references are
made to William Macready in the article. See
Also No. 18

MALONE
639   Walton, J.K. "Edmund Malone: an Irish Shakespeare
scholar." <u>Hermathena</u>, XCIX (1964), 5-26.

Supplies biographical facts about Malone's
Irish origin and education. Briefly indicates
the textual achievements of his 1790 edition of
Shakespeare's works.

MANLEY, See Nos. 101, 776

MANSFIELD, See No. 18

MAPS, See No. 1101

MASQUE, See Nos. 647, 688

MATTHEWS, See No. 856

MAY, See No. 283

MELODRAMA
640   Booth, Michael R. English Melodrama. London: Her-
       bert Jenkins, 1965, 223 pp.
            Concentrating on the period 1790-1900, the
       work discusses melodrama's relationship to
       previous drama and its social and theatrical
       background. Includes index and bibliography.

MENCKE, See No. 947

MERRY
641   Adams, M. Ray. "A Newly Discovered Play of Robert
       Merry, Written in America." Manuscripts, XII
       (1961), 20-26.
            Manuscripts description, plot summary, and
       short criticism of Merry's The Tuscan Tournament,
       a blank verse tragedy, completed on January 2,
       1798. In the Manuscript Division of the Library
       of Congress.

MILLER
642   Esar, Evan. "The Legend of Joe Miller." American
       Book Collector, XIII (October, 1962), 11-26.
            Short history of Joe Miller (1684-1738),
       a comic actor who performed at Drury Lane for
       almost thirty years. The use of his name in
       subsequent jestbooks.

MILTON
643   Milton, John. <u>Arcades and Comus</u>, With Preface by
        Giovanna Foa. Milano: La goliardica, 1964.
        49 pp.

644   Ades, John I. "The Pattern of Temptation in <u>Comus</u>."
        <u>Papers on English Language and Literature</u>, I
        (1965), 265-271.
                <u>Comus</u> might justifiably be regarded as Mil-
        ton's first major work on the theme of redemption.
        Here, as in <u>Paradise Regained</u>, Milton employs a
        three-part structure to symbolize the tempta-
        tions of the world, the flesh and the Devil.

645   Allain, Mathé. "The Humanist's Dilemma: Milton,
        God, and Reason." <u>College English</u>, XXVII
        (1966), 379-384.
                Traces the conflict of humanism and
        Christianity in Milton's major works. The
        peace of <u>Samson Agonistes</u> results from a reso-
        lution: 'man whose essence is rational cannot
        conflict with God who is Reason.'

646   Arai, A. "Milton in <u>Comus</u>." <u>Studies in English</u>
        <u>Literature</u> (The English Literary Society of
        Japan), XLII (1965), 19-31.

647   Barber, C.L. "A Mask Presented at Ludlow Castle:
        The Masque as a Masque," <u>The Lyric and Dramatic</u>
        <u>Milton.</u> Selected Papers from the English Institute.
        Edited with a Foreword by Joseph H. Summers.
        (New York and London: Columbia University Press,
        1965), 35-63.
                Attempts to answer two questions: (1) How
        does Milton succeed "in making a happy work
        which centers, seemingly, on the denial of im-
        pulse, when typically in the Renaissance such
        works involve, in some fashion or other, release
        from restraint?" and (2) How does the form of
        the piece relate to Renaissance comedy and allied
        traditions?

648   Barker, Arthur E. "Structural and Doctrinal Pat-
        terns in Milton's Later Poems." <u>Essays in English</u>
        <u>Literature from the Renaissance to the Victorian</u>
        <u>Age Presented to A. S. P. Woodhouse, 1964</u>, ed.

Millar MacLure and F. W. Watts. (Toronto: University of Toronto Press, 1964), 168-194.
Samson Agonistes, like Paradise Regained, depends upon "the contrast and relation between the Law and the Prophets" for its content and development.

649   Beum, Robert. "The Rhyme in Samson Agonistes." Texas Studies in Literature and Language, IV (1962), 177-182.
A distinct pattern of rhyme is discernible in the work. Milton's use of rhyme enforces climaxes and the role of the chorus.

650   Blondel, Jacques. Le 'Comus' de John Milton, masque neptunien. Publs. de la Faculte des lettres et Sciences Humaines de l'Universite de Clermont-Ferrand, 2^{me}Serie, fasc. XX. Paris: Presses Universitaires de France, 1964.

651   --"The Function of Mythology in Comus." Durham University Journal, LVII (1966), 63-66.
The mythology in Comus has ethical significance; it also serves to magnify the players and to define the contrast between reason and self-indulgence.

652   Broadbent, J.B. Milton: Comus and Samson Agonistes. London: Edward Arnold, Ltd., 1961, 63 pp. (Studies in English Literature Series, ed. David Daiches).
Critical analyses and evaluations intended for university students. Includes biographical and historical materials, select bibliography.

653   Bush, Douglas. John Milton. New York: Macmillan Company, 1964, 224 pp.
Critical and biographical introduction for students. Elucidates the main problems in Comus and Samson Agonistes.

654   Carey, John. "Sea, Snake, Flower, and Flame in Samson Agonistes." Modern Language Review, LXII (1967), 395-399.
The imagery does not merely reinforce the drama's upward arc. "On the contrary, it contributes meaning which threaten to invert this

arc and bring the weak-minded, vengeful hero to
the level of Dalila and the Philistines."

655   Carrithers, Gale H., Jr. "Milton's Ludlow Mask:
       From Chaos to Community." Journal of English
       Literary History, XXXIII (1966), 23-42.
            The work is animated by an ideal of com-
       munity: man finds fulfillment in a loving, God-
       seeking society.

656   Chambers, A.B. "Wisdom and Fortitude in Samson
       Agonistes." Publications of the Modern Language
       Association, LXXVIII (1963), 315-320.
            Milton's use of the sapientia et fortitudo
       tradition demonstrates his concern for the qual-
       ity of his strength and provides the best guide
       to the poem's thematic structure.

657   Cox, Lee Sheridan. "The 'Ev'ning Dragon' in Sam-
       son Agonistes: A Reappraisal." Modern Language
       Notes, LXXVI (November, 1961), 577-584.
            Line 1692 - Interpretation of the phrase.

658   --"Structural and Thematic Imagery in Samson
       Agonistes and Paradise Regained." Ph. D.
       Indiana University, 1962. (Order No. 63-
       3812).
            The contribution of imagery to the frame-
       work of thought, to structure, motive, and theme.
       Reveals Milton's relationship to Elizabethan
       dramatists and to the Metaphysicals.

659   Daniels, Edgar F. "Samson in 'Areopagitica.'"
       Notes and Queries, New Ser., XI (1964), 92-93.
            Interprets the allusion to Samson's restored
       strength in Areopagitica which pictures England
       as "a noble and puissant Nation rousing herself
       like a strong man after sleep, and shaking her
       invincible locks."

660   Daniells, Roy. Milton, Mannerism and Baroque.
       Toronto: University of Toronto Press, 1963,
       229 pp.
            An analysis of Comus reveals that "the
       dislocations are such as to provoke an aesthetic
       response" in the reader, that the techniques

employed are a translation of seventeenth century art theories into appropriate literary
practices.

661   Dawson, S.W. and A.J. Smith. "Two Points of View:
       Samson Agonistes." The Anglo-Welsh Review, XIV
       (1964-5), 92-101.
              The merits and shortcomings of Samson
       Agonistes are juxtaposed to provide a good intro-
       duction to the work.

662   Demaray, John G. "Comus as a Masque." Ph. D.
       Columbia University, 1964. (Order No. 67-10,
       367).
              An attempt to recreate what the first
       performance of Comus was like as a staged
       presentation. Includes a brief review of the
       history of the masque and a study of recent
       Comus criticism.

663   --"Milton's Comus: The Sequel to a Masque of
       Circe." Huntington Library Quarterly, XXIX
       (1966), 245-254.
              Henry Lawes's masquing career and his con-
       tribution to Comus

664   Diekhoff, John S., ed. Milton on Himself:Milton's
       Utterances upon Himself and His works. London:
       Cohen and West, 1965, 307 pp.
              The second edition with a new preface. Ex-
       tracts from Milton's statements grouped by sub-
       ject and arranged within the groups in order of
       composition.

665   Ebbs, John Dale, "Milton's Treatment of Poetic
       Justice in Samson Agonistes." Modern Language
       Quarterly, XXII (December, 1961), 377-389.
              Includes a brief review of past cricitism
       and scholarship for purposes of explication.
       Attempts to clarify Milton's treatment of poetic
       justice, the most significant means by which
       Milton presents the lesson of the poem.

666   Emma, Ronald David. Milton's Grammar. (Studies in
       English Literature, Volume II). The Hague:
       Mouton and Company, 1964, 164 pp.

125

A study of Milton's grammar, its relationship
to the English of his own time and to modern
English. Includes references to <u>Comus</u> and <u>Sam-
son Agonistes</u>.

667   Empson, William. <u>Milton's God</u>. London: Ghatto and
       Windus, 1965. 320 pp.
           A revised edition of Empson's 1961 work.
       Chapter VI concerns Dalilah's role in <u>Samson
       Agonistes</u>.

668   Fixler, Michael. Milton and the Kingdoms of God.
       Evanston, Illinois: Northwestern University
       Press, 1964. 293 pp.
           Milton's approach through poetry, prophecy,
       and politics to the establishment of God's truth
       and the visionary ideal of Puritanism. In-
       cludes references to <u>Comus</u> and <u>Samson Agonistes</u>.

669   Fox, Robert C. "A Source for Milton's <u>Comus</u>."
       <u>Notes and Queries</u>, New Ser., IX (1962), 52-53.
           A figure in Jonson's <u>Poetaster</u> (1601) as
       a possible source for the character of Comus.

670   Frank, Joseph. "The Unharmonious Vision: Milton
       as a Baroque Artist." <u>Comparative Literature
       Studies</u>, III (1966), 95-108.
           Milton's poetry generally becomes more
       Baroque and his theology becomes less assured.
       Includes discussion of <u>Comus</u> and <u>Samson
       Agonistes</u>.

671   Fraser, Russell. "On Milton's Poetry." <u>Yale Re-
       view</u>, LVI (1967), 172-196.
           A study of Milton's attempt to make the
       language of poetry convey the truth with abso-
       lute reality and precision includes a discus-
       sion of <u>Samson Agonistes</u>.

672   Freedman, Morris. "Milton's 'On Shakespeare'
       and Henry Lawes." <u>Shakespeare Quarterly</u>, XIV
       (1963), 279-281.
           Brief account of Milton's relationship
       with Lawes through <u>Comus</u>.

673   Gabrieli, Vittorio. "Milton agonista." Cultura, V
       (1967), 316-334.

674   Gohn, Ernest S. "The Christian Ethic of Paradise
       Lost and Samson Agonistes." Studia Neophilo-
       logica, XXXIV (1962), 243-268.
              Considers the didactic aim and ethics of
       Milton's works in relation to Renaissance
       ethical theory.

675   Goldberg, S.L. "The World, the Flesh, and Comus."
       Melbourne Critical Review, VI (1963), 56-68.
              In Comus the diction and imagery fail to
       provide sufficient support for the philosophi-
       cal ideas. The Lady's view of Comus is not
       convincing.

676   Gossman, Ann. "Milton's Samson as the Tragic Hero
       Purified by Trial." Journal of English and
       Germanic Philology, LXI (1962), 528-541.
              Discusses Samson as a combination of the
       classical and Christian concepts of the hero.

677   --"Samson, Job, and 'The Exercise of Saints."
       English Studies,XLV (1964), 212-224.
              The Book of Job as part of the tradition
       behind Samson Agonistes.

678   Greene, Donald. "The Sin of Pride: A Sketch for
       a Literary Exploration." New Mexico Quarterly,
       XXXIV (Spring, 1964). 8-30.
              Uses Samson Agonistes as an example of
       self-psychoanalysis in literature.

679   Grewe, Eugene Francis. "A History of the Criticism
       of John Milton's Comus. 1637-1941." Ph. D. The
       University of Michigan, 1963.
              Surveys English and American criticism of
       Comus from the comments in the first edition to
       the present day. Three Appendices scrutinize
       the annotations in the editions of Newton. War-
       ton and Todd. A fourth Appendix lists editions
       of Comus from 1637 to 1941.

680   Hall, James Martin. "Milton's Rhetoric in Prose
       and Poetry." Ph.D. Yale University, 1967.(Order

No. 67-7019).
Examines the controversial rhetorical
techniques in Milton's prose to show how they
elucidate certain problems of form, character,
and action in the major poetry. Includes discussion of Comus and Samson Agonistes.

681   Hanford, James Holly. John Milton: Poet and
       Humanist. Foreword by John S. Diekhoff.
       Cleveland: The Press of Western Reserve Univer-
       sity, 1966. 286 pp.
           Reprints eight essays written by Professor
       Hanford between 1910 and 1925. "Samson Agonistes
       and Milton in Old Age," pp. 264-286, is reprinted
       from Studies in Shakespeare, Milton and Donne.
       New York: Macmillan, 1925.

682   --and Charles W. Crupi. Milton. (Goldentree Bibli-
       ographies). New York: Appleton-Century-Crofts,
       1966, 63 pp.
           A selective bibliography of primary and
       secondary materials for the study of Milton.

683   Harris, William O. "Despair and 'Patience as
       the Truest Fortitude' in Samson Agonistes." Journal
       of English Literary History, XXX (1963), 107-120.
           Examines the structural and thematic impor-
       tance of two choral passages (11. 652-666, and
       11. 1268-1296) in Samson Agonistes in light of
       Milton's statements on patience and fortitude.

684   Hill, R. F. "Samson Agonistes." Time and Tide,
       XLIV (4-10 April, 1963), 28.
           Milton's work is a classic of Aristotelian
       Unity but is weak as drama because "the moral
       pattern which circumscribes Samson precludes in-
       tensity of conflict."

685   Hone, Ralph E., editor. John Milton's Samson
       Agonistes: The Poem and Materials for Analysis.
       San Francisco: Changler Publishing Co., 1966,
       284 pp.
           Includes text of the play, previous versions
       of the Samson story in the Bible, criticism of
       the play, and an appendix with suggested topics
       for study and selected bibliography.

128

686   Huntley, John. "A Revaluation of the Chorus' Role
       in Milton's Samson Agonistes." Modern Philology,
       LXIV (1966), 132-145.
              The chorus participates in Samson's regene-
       ration as they gradually experience "a change
       from vanity covered with platitudes to knowledge
       poised for action."

687   Hyman, Lawrence W. "Milton's Samson and the Modern
       Reader." College English, XXVIII (1966), 39-43.
              Not the justification of God's ways but
       Samson's courage in confronting a God whose ways
       are dark to our understanding gives the poem a
       special interest for the modern reader.

688   Jayne, Sears. "The Subject of Milton's Ludlow
       Mask," Milton: Modern Essays in Criticism. (A
       Galaxy Book). Edited by Arthur E. Barker. (New
       York: Oxford University Press, 1965), 88-111.
              A revised article that appeared in PMLA,
       LXXIV (1959), 533-543. Proposes that Milton's
       Platonism in the work is the Renaissance Pla-
       tonism of Ficino.

689   Kirkconnell, Watson. That Invincible Samson: The
       Theme of Samson Agonistes in World Literature
       With Translations of the Major Analogues. Toronto:
       University of Toronto Press, 1964. 218 pp.
              Notes 107 versions of Samson Agonistes from
       the 12th century B. C. to 1944.

690   Klein, Joan Larsen. "Some Spenserian Influences
       on Milton's Comus." Annuale Mediaevale, V
       (1964), 27-47.

691   Kranidas, Thomas. "Dalila's Role in Samson Agonis-
       tes." Studies in English Literature, 1500-1900,
       VI (1966), 125-137.
              A study of Dalila's speeches that attempts
       to test the validity of her arguments and to
       justify Samson's outraged responses.

692   --"Milton's Concept of Decorum." Ph.D. University
       of Washington, 1962. (Order No. 63-3123).
              Decorum as a concept which contributes to
       "unity" as well as to consistency in the parts
       of discourse. Discusses Samson's moving toward

"wholeness" in Samson Agonistes.

693   Krouse, F. M. Milton's Samson and the Christian
        Tradition. Hamden, Connecticut: The Shoe String
        Press, 1963.

694   Landy, Marcia. "Character Portrayal in Samson
        Agonistes." Texas Studies in Literature and
        Language, VII (1965), 239-253.
            Milton's characters are less allegorizations
        than individuals realized with human depth and
        complexity.

695   Landy, Marcia K. "Of Highest Wisdom: a Study of
        John Milton's Samson Agonistes as a Dramatization
        of Christian Conversion." Ph.D. The University
        of Rochester, 1962. (Order No. 62-6668).
            Samson experiences conversion before regene-
        ration. He undergoes the steps of conversion
        as outlined by Christian writers of the Renais-
        sance and Seventeenth Century.

696   Lemay, J.A.Leo. "Jonson and Milton: Two Influences
        in Oakes's Elegie." The New England Quarterly,
        XXXVIII (1965), 90-92.
            The influence of Samson Agonistes on Ameri-
        can poet, Urian Oakes's An Elegie upon the Death
        of the Reverend Mr. Thomas Shepard (1677).

697   Long, Anne Bowers. "The Relation Between Classical
        and Biblical Allusions in Milton's Later Poems."
        Ph.D. University of Illinois, 1967.(Order No.
        68-8151).
            Examines Samson Agonistes as well as
        Paradise Lost and Paradise Regained.

698   Low, Anthony. "Milton Bibliography." Seventeenth
        Century News, XXV (1967), 2.
            Contributes four items, including essays by
        Johnson and Richard Cumberland, as addenda to
        Carl J. Stratman, C.S.V., "Milton's Samson
        Agonistes: A Checklist of Criticism," Restoration
        and Eighteenth Century Theatre Research, (1965),
        2-10.

699   Madsen, William G. "From Shadowy Types to Truth,"
        The Lyric and Dramatic Milton. Selected Papers
        from the English Institute. Edited with a
        Foreword by Joseph H. Summers. (New York and
        London: Columbia University Press, 1965), 95-114.
            A typological interpretation of Samson
        Agonistes suggests that it is both non-Christian
        and Christian in much the same way as the Old
        Testament may be considered non-Christian and
        Christian, and that the play may be regarded as
        a companion piece to Paradise Regained.

700   Major, John M. "Milton's View of Rhetoric."
        Studies in Philology, LXIV(1967), 685-711.
            Studies the relationship between Milton's
        attitudes toward rhetoric and his training and
        beliefs. Discusses the debate between the Lady
        and Comus in Comus and the character of Dalila
        as sophist-orator in Samson Agonistes.

701   Merchant, W. Moelwyn. Creed and Drama: An Essay in
        Religious Drama. London: S. P. C. K., 1965,
        119 pp.
            Includes a discussion of Samson Agonistes.

702   Miriam Clare, Sister. Samson Agonistes: A Study
        in Contrast. New York: Pageant Press, 1964,
        153 pp.
            Investigates the use of the classical
        figures of contrast, particularly Antithesis,
        in the characterization, action, key concepts,
        and grammar of the play.

703   Mish, Charles C. "Comus and Bryce Blair's Vision
        of Theodorus Verax." Milton Newsletter, I (1967),
        39-40.
            Blair also used Milton's source, the Comus
        of Erycius Puteanus, for his version of the story.

704   Mitchell, Charles. "Dalila's Return: The Importance
        of Pardon." College English, XXVI(1965), 614-
        620.
            Samson does not become conscious of God's
        pardon until after the appearance of Dalila who,
        in contrast to the hero, seeks pardon without
        having earned it through penance.

705   Moss, Leonard. "The Rhetorical Style of Samson
        Agonistes. Modern Philology, LXII (1965), 296-
        301.
                Milton's use of classical rhetoric, parti-
        cularly the device of synonymia, for the crucial
        arguments of Samson Agonistes.

706   Mueller, Martin. "Sixteenth-Century Italian Criti-
        cism and Milton's Theory of Catharsis," Studies
        in English Literature, 1500-1900 VI (1966),
        139-150.
                Milton was indebted to Italian theories of
        cartharsis current in the sixteenth century. His
        chief debt was to Florence and to the scholarly
        tradition represented by men like Pietro Vettori
        and Lorenzo Giacomini.

707   Mueller, Martin E. "Pathos and Katharsis in Sam-
        son Agonistes." Journal of English Literary
        History, XXXI (1964), 156-174.
                Samson differs from Greek tragedy in that
        "the catastrophe has no immediate bearing on
        any human relationship but is only meaningful as
        the final event in the relationship of Samson
        and God."

708   Neuse, Richard. "Metamorphosis and Symbolic Action
        in Comus." Journal of English Literary History,
        XXXIV (1967), 49-64.
                The Lady's enchantment and release are not
        a mere concluding flourish to her refusal of the
        cup. The Lady's paralysis and liberation by
        Sabrina present a genuine complication and reso-
        lution initiated by the original clash between
        the Lady and Comus.

709   Nicolson, Marjorie Hope. John Milton: A Reader's
        Guide to His Poetry. New York: Farrar, Straus
        and Company, 1963. 385 pp.
                Surveys Milton's writings for undergraduates.
        Includes a discussion of Milton's dramatic pie-
        ces.

710   Parker, W.R. Milton's Debt to Greek Tragedy in Sam-
        son Agonistes. Hamden: The Shoe String Press, 1963.

711   Parker, William Riley. "Notes on the Text of <u>Samson</u>
       <u>Agonistes</u>." <u>Journal of English and Germanic</u>
       <u>Philology</u>, LX (1961), 688-698.
             A discussion and illustration of problems
       of spelling and punctuation in modern editions
       of Milton's text.

712   Radzinowicz, M.A.N. "<u>Samson Agonistes</u> and Milton
       the Politician in Defeat." <u>Philological Quar-</u>
       <u>terly</u>, XLIV (1965), 454-471.
             An "epic of defeat," <u>Samson Agonistes</u>
       represents Milton's attempt to justify God's
       ways in the fall of the Commonwealth.

713   Rajan, B. "Milton Seen Anew." <u>Canadian Literature</u>,
       No. 21, (1964), 55-58.
             Review article of Roy Daniells' <u>Milton,</u>
       <u>Mannerism, and Baroque</u> (Toronto: University of
       Toronto Press, 1963). Comments on Daniells'
       interpretation of <u>Comus</u> and <u>Samson Agonistes</u>.

714   Raleigh, Sir Walter. <u>Milton</u>. New York: Benjamin
       Blom, 1967. 286 pp.
             A reissue of the 1900 edition in which
       Raleigh presents a brief biography and discusses
       the major works, their themes, characters, style
       and influence.

715   Ricks, Christopher. <u>Milton's Grand Style</u>. Oxford:
       Clarendon Press, 1963, 154 pp.
             Milton's style is not only powerful and
       grand, it is also delicate and subtle. Chapter
       II includes a study of metaphors in <u>Samson</u>
       <u>Agonistes</u>.

716   Riese, Teut Andreas. "Die Theatralik der Tugend in
       Milton <u>Comus</u>," <u>Festschrift fur Walter Hubner</u>, eds.
       Dieter Riesner and Helmut Gneuss. (Berlin:
       Schmidt, 1964), 192-202.
             On the artistic unity of <u>Comus</u>.

717   Riley, Sister Mary Geraldine, R.S.M. "Infinite
       Variety in Milton: A Study of John Milton's Con-
       cept of Woman as Shown in His Works." Ph. D.
       Rutgers University, 1962. (Order No. 62-5316).
             Milton's attitude toward women is typical

133

of a seventeenth-century gentleman. Considers
Comus and Samson Agonistes.

718   Rosenberg, Donald M. "Milton and the Laughter of
        God." Ph.D. Wayne State University, 1965.
            Specific comic elements can be recognized
        in the point of view, tone, structure, charac-
        terization and style of Comus,Paradise Lost,
        Paradise Regained, and Samson Agonistes to show
        that Milton is sensitive to contradictions
        fundamental to man's condition.

719   Rudrum, Alan. A Critical Commentary on Milton's
        Comus and Shorter Poems. (Macmillan Critical
        Commentaries). London: Macmillan Co., 1967,
        113 pp.
            A line by line analysis of the play's plot,
        characters and theme.

720   Sadler, Mary Lynn Veach. "Samson Agonistes and the
        Theme of Consolation." Ph.D. University of
        Illinois, 1967. (Order No. 68-8210).
            For Milton, consolation is regeneration.
        The theme also brings together two foci of Mil-
        ton's criticism: his reading of the ways of God
        in historical dispensations and of the psychology
        of religious experience.

721   Saillens, Emile. John Milton: Man, Poet, Polemicist.
        New York: Barnes and Noble, 1964, 371 pp.
            First published in 1959 as John Milton,
        poete combattant and intended as a popular
        biography. Chapter XIX concerns Samson Agonistes.

722   Samuels, Charles T. "Milton's Samson Agonistes
        and Rational Christianity." Dalhousie Review,
        XLIII (1963), 495-506.
            In Samson Agonistes Milton departs from his
        lifelong commitment to make God seem "humanly,
        rationally correct."

723   San Juan, E.,Jr. "The Natural Context of Spiritual
        Renewal in Samson Agonistes." Ball State University
        Forum, VI, iii (1965),55-60.
            Studies Samson's human nature as it "under-
        goes its regeneration when it begins to partici-
        pate in the organic processes of nature subsumed

within a Divine Order of things."

724   Sellin, Paul R. "Milton's Epithet Agonistes."
       Studies in English Literature, 1500-1900,
       IV (1964), 137-162.
              Agonistes may mean "dissembling,""assuming
       a mask," "playing a part," and "acting". These
       meanings are relevant to the structure of the
       play and especially important for the theme ex-
       pressed by the chorus in its final ode.

725   Sensabaugh, George F. Milton in Early America.
       Princeton: Princeton University Press, 1964,
       320 pp.
              Studies American interest in Milton during
       the colonial period. Includes occasional refer-
       ences to Samson Agonistes.

726   Shawcross, John T. "Henry Lawes's Settings of Songs
       for Milton's Comus." Journal of the Rutgers
       University Library. XXVIII (1964), 22-28.
              Revisions in the songs of Comus are pointed
       up by a collation of the British Museum MS with
       the Lawes MS.

727   --"A Metaphoric Approach to Reading Milton."   Ball
       State University Forum, VIII (1967), 17-22.
              A metaphoric reading of specific words
       suggests somewhat different or deeper interpre-
       tations of lines and passages in which they
       appear, and it echoes motives found elsewhere in
       the work. Includes a discussion of lines from
       Samson Agonistes.

728   Smith, Logan Pearsall. Milton and His Modern Critics.
       Hamden, Conn.: Archon Books, 1967, 87 pp.
              A reprint of the 1941 edition.

729   Steadman, John M. "'Faithful Champion': The Theolo-
       gical Basis of Milton's Hero of Faith," Milton:
       Modern Essays in Criticism. (A Galaxy Book).
       Edited by Arthur E. Barker. (New York: Oxford
       University Press, 1965), 467-483.
              Reprinted from Anglia, LXXVII (1959), 12-28.
       Contends that the dominant motif of the tragedy
       is the hero's spiritual rebirth or sanctification

so that Milton's primary emphasis falls on what
happens in the hero's soul.

730   --Milton and the Renaissance Hero. New York: Oxford University Press, 1967.
The first six chapters analyze Milton's
treatment of the most important formulae for an
epic hero; another chapter relates his heroic
image to the Biblical archetypes and classical
prototypes.

731   --"Notes: Dalila, The Ulysses Myth, and Renaissance
Allegorical Tradition." Modern Language Review,
LVII (1962), 560-565.
In rejecting Dalila, Samson uses terms and
figures from classical mythology.

732   --"The Tragic Glass: Milton, Minturno, and the
Condition Humaine," Th' Upright Heart and Pure:
Essays on John Milton Commemorating the Tercen-
tenary of the Publication of Paradise Lost.
Edited by Amadeus P. Fiore, O.F.M. (Pittsburgh:
Duquesne University Press, 1967), pp. 101-115.
Takes issue with critics who see Milton's
later work only as an expression of subjective
feeling. In Minturno's L'Arte Poetica Milton
could have found ideas and images that led to
the conception of Samson as an emblem of humanity.

733   Stratman, Carl J., C.S.V. "Milton's Samson Agonistes: A Checklist of Criticism." Restoration and
Eighteenth Century Theatre Research, IV (November,
1965), 2-10.
141 items arranged chronologically from
1751 to 1964.

734   Stroup, Thomas B. "The Cestus: Manuscript of an
Anonymous Eighteenth Century Imitation of Comus."
Studies in English Literature, 1500-1900, II
(1962), 47-55.
Contends that the play has considerable
literary merit and suggests likely candidates
for authorship. Shows influence of Milton.

735   Summers, Joseph H. "The Movements of the Drama,"
The Lyric and Dramatic Milton. Selected Papers
from the English Institute. Edited with a

Foreword by Joseph H. Summers. (New York and
London: Columbia University Press, 1965), 153-175.
The dramatic movements of <u>Samson Agonistes</u>
are often ironical or paradoxical and cannot be
simply reduced to a formula of "degradation and
suffering to triumph."

736   Sundell, Roger Henry. "Internal Commentary in the
        Major Poems of John Milton." Ph.D. Washington
        University, 1965. (Order No. 66-1626).
            Within his major poems Milton consciously
        included "interpretative commentary" to insure
        that the works would be properly understood. The
        Attendant Spirit in <u>Comus</u> and the Chorus in
        <u>Samson Agonistes</u> prepare and guide the audience's
        sympathies while highlighting the dramatic action.

737   Teunissen, John James. "Of Patience and Heroic Mar-
        tyrdom: The Book of Job and Milton's Conception
        of Patient Suffering in 'Paradise Regained' and
        'Samson Agonistes.'" Ph.D. University of Rochester,
        1967. (Order No. 67-13, 652).
            A large part of Samson's suffering stems
        from his very ignorance of the fact that he is
        being afflicted not because of past sins but be-
        cause, as in the case of Job, God wishes to ex-
        pose him to a period of probation.

738   Thorpe, James. "On the Pronunciation of Names in
        <u>Samson Agonistes</u>." <u>Huntington Library Quarterly</u>,
        XXXI (1967), 65-74.
            Scansion of Milton's lines shows that he
        intended the names of Dalila, Manoa, and Harapha
        to be accented on the first syllable.

739   Tillyard, E. M. <u>Milton</u>. Rev. ed. With a Preface by
        Phyllis B. Tillyard. London: Chatto and Windus,
        1966. 390 pp.
            The biographical and critical study origin-
        ally published in 1930. Part I, Chapter VI treats
        <u>Comus</u>; Part III, Chapters XI-XIV treat <u>Samson
        Agonistes</u>, its origin, quality, the dramatic
        motive, and its relation to Milton's experience
        and thought.

740   Tung, Mason. "The Search for Perfection in John
        Milton." Ph.D. Stanford University, 1962. (Order
        No. 62-5521).
            The search for perfection in Milton's life
        and works as a "secure principle" with which
        much Milton scholarship can be coordinated.

741   Tyson, John Patrick. "The Elements of Aristotelian
        Tragedy in Paradise Lost." Ph.D. Tulane Univer-
        sity, 1967. (Order No. 68-4071).
            Aristotle's plot, character, thought, diction,
        spectacle, and song from the Poetics serves as
        the basis for analysis.

742   Van Kluyve, Robert A. "Out, Out Hyaena!" American
        Notes and Queries, I (1963), 99-101.
            Deals with the encounter of Samson and
        Dalila.

743   Weismiller, Edward. "The 'Dry' and Rugged Verse,
        The Lyric and Dramatic Milton. Selected Papers
        from the English Institute. Edited with a fore-
        word by Joseph H. Summers. (New York and London:
        Columbia University Press, 1965), 115-152.
            A prosodic study of Samson Agonistes, parti-
        cularly of the choral odes which may be written
        "in that ultimate form of seventeenth-century
        English irregular verse, the blank or near-blank
        Italianate Pindaric."

744   Wilkenfield, Roger B. "Act and Emblem: The Conclu-
        sion of Samson Agonistes." Journal of English
        Literary History, XXXII (1965), 160-168.
            Discusses the relationship between the
        phoenix symbol and the motifs of freedom and
        transformation.

745   --"Act and Emblem: A Study of Narrative and
        Dramatic Patterns in Three Poems of John Milton."
        Ph.D. The University of Rochester, 1964. (Order
        No. 64-12, 453).
            The "dramatic" in Comus and Samson Agonistes
        derives from a complex system of ironic and ver-
        bal motifs. Their power rests in the expansive
        emblems of the Paralyzed Lady and the Rising
        Phoenix.

138

746 --"The Seat at the Center" An Interpretation of
Comus." Journal of English Literary History,
XXXIII (1966), 170-197.
The center or "hinge" in the structure of
Comus is an emblem, "the concrete, visual, drama-
tically viable emblem of the Lady paralyzed in
the seat of Comus."

747 --"Theoretics or Polemics? Milton Criticism and
the 'Dramatic Axiom.'" Publications of the Modern
Language Association, LXXXII (1967), 505-515.
Because Milton critics do not make an effort
to separate the "vocal" and "modal" definitions
of the dramatic, it is impossible to say whether
they are defining a technique, the results of a
technique, or an aspect of personality. Includes
references to Comus and Samson Agonistes. See
Also No. 571

748 Wilkes, G.A. "The Interpretation of Samson Agonistes." Huntington Library Quarterly, XXVI
(August, 1963), 363-379.
Samson Agonistes is the story not only of
Samson but also of the Chorus, Manoah, and other
characters who arrive gradually at an understanding of the power of providence.

749 Williamson, George. "The Context of Comus." Milton
and Others (London, 1965), 26-41.
Interprets Comus in the light of Milton's
elegiac utterances and his unrealized play on the
fall of Sodom, Cupids Funeral Pile.

750 --"Tension in Samson Agonistes." Milton and Others
(London, 1965), 85-102.
In Samson Agonistes Milton gives vent to his
own personal anxiety and frustrations. He
utilizes a theory of tragedy based on the Paracel-
sian principle of similia similibus.

751 Woodhouse, A.S.P. "Tragic Effect in Samson Agonistes,"
Milton: Modern Essays in Criticism. (A Galaxy
Book). Edited by Arthur E. Barker. (New York:
Oxford University Press, 1965), 447-466.
Reprinted from the University of Toronto
Quarterly, XXVIII (1958-59), 205-222. Interprets

Samson Agonistes as a classical tragedy with a
Christian theme and outlook. See Also Nos. 46,
386

752   Woodman, Ross. "Literature and Life." Queen's
       Quarterly, LXVIII (Winter, 1962), 621-631.
             Uses Samson Agonistes, along with the work
       of Shakespeare and Keats to show that literature
       is more comprehensible, and therefore, in some
       respects, greater than life.

     MISCELLANEOUS
753   Avery, Emmett L. "The London Stage". 17th and 18th
       Century Theatre Research, I (May, 1962), 12.
             Suggestions for further study of the music,
       dancing, and periodicals related to Restoration
       and Eighteenth Century theatre.

754   Boswell, Eleanore. The Restoration Court Stage.
       London: George Allen and Unwin, 1966, 370 pp.
             A reprint of the work originally published
       in 1932. Part I concerns the court theatres,
       Part II problems of maintenance and production,
       and Part III the masque Calisto (1675).

755   Broich, Ulrich. "Libertin und heroischer Held:
       Das Drama der englischen Restaurationzeit und
       seine Leitbilder." Anglia, LXXXV (1967), 34-57.

756   Camden, Carroll, editor. Restoration and Eight-
       eenth-Century Literature: Essays in Honor of
       Alan Dugald McKillop. Chicago: University of
       Chicago Press for William Marsh Rice University,
       1963. 435 pp.
             Includes papers on such writers as Dryden,
       Blake, Johnson, Steevens, and Steele.

757   Cautero, Gerard Salvatore. "Studies in the In-
       fluence of the Commedia dell' arte on English
       Drama: 1650-1800." Ph.D. University of Southern
       California, 1962. (Order No. 62-6045).
             The influence of the Commedia on the bour-
       geois comedy of Jephson, Garrick and Colman.

758   Clunes, Alec. The British Theatre. London:
       Cassell, 1964.

Slight text accompanies this popular pictorial treatment of Restoration and 18th Century
dramatists, characters, types, and players.

759   Day, Cyrus L. "The W. N. H. Harding Music Collection."
       Restoration and 18th Century Theatre Research,
       III (May, 1964), 23-24.
               On editions and copies of Restoration and
       Augustan dramas, operas, and pantomimes in the
       private library of the Chicago book collector
       Harding.

760   Dobrée, Bonamy. Essays in Biography, 1680-1726.
       Freeport, New York: Books for Libraries Press,
       1967. 362 pp.
               A reprint of the 1925 edition contains
       biographies of Etherege, Vanbrugh and Addison.

761   --Variety of Ways: Discussions on Six Authors.
       Freeport, New York: Books for Libraries Press,
       1967. 118 pp.
               A reprint of the 1932 edition includes dis-
       cussions of Congreve, Dryden and Steele.

762   Dobson, Austin. First Series: Eighteenth Century
       Vignettes. New York: Benjamin Blom, 1967. 264
       pp.
               A reprint of the 1892 edition includes essays
       on Goldsmith's library and on Steele.

763   --Second Series: Eighteenth Century Vignettes. New
       York: Benjamin Blom, 1967, 312 pp.
               A reprint of the 1894 edition includes
       essays on Richardson, Johnson, and Swift.

764   --Third Series: Eighteenth Century Vignettes. New
       York: Benjamin Blom, 1967, 376 pp.
               A reprint of the 1896 edition includes essays
       on the last performances of Garrick and on Colman.

765   Downer, Alan S. and Arthur C. Kirsch, eds. Restora-
       tion. (The Laurel Masterpieces of World Literature).
       New York: Dell Publishing Company, 1965. 512 pp.
               A paperback anthology. Includes Rymer's
       Othello, Dryden's An Essay of Dramatic Poesy, and
       verse from several Restoration dramas.

766   Emery, John P. "Restoration Dualism of the Court
        Writers." Révue des Langues Vivantes, XXXII,
        iii (1966), 238-265.
                Includes study of the plays of Buckingham,
        Rochester, Etherege, and Wycherley, among others.

767   Erskine-Hill, Howard. "Augustans on Augustanism:
        England, 1665-1759." Renaissance and Modern
        Studies, XI (1967), 55-83.
                Examines some of the more important passages
        in which Augustans use the word "Augustan,"
        express their understanding of it, and explicitly
        or implicitly apply it to their own age. Includes
        references to Dryden, Rowe and Goldsmith.

768   An Exhibition to Honor William B. Van Lennep, Cura-
        tor of the Harvard Theatre Collection from 1940
        to 1960. Cambridge: The Houghton Library, Spring,
        1963. 32 pp.
                Pamphlet in honor of one of the authors of
        The London Stage, 1660-1800, describes some of
        the holdings of the Houghton Theatre Collection.

769   Fletcher, Richard M. English Romantic Drama, 1795-
        1843: A Critical History. New York: Exposition
        Press, 1966, 226 pp.
                Purposes to bring poetic tragedy as a genre
        into sharper focus, both as it reflected and as
        it delineated the spirit of its age. Chapter 1,
        "Romantic Drama and Its Theatre," refers to 18th
        century theatre.

770   Foxon, David. Libertine Literature in England,
        1660-1745. New Hyde Park, New York: University
        Books, 1965, 70 pp.
                Concerned primarily with a bibliographical
        description of pornographic novels, the work
        makes only occasional references to Restoration
        comedy.

771   Gray, Charles Harold. Theatrical Criticism in
        London to 1795. New York: Benjamin Blom, 1964,
        333 pp.
                Reprint of Gray's 1931 compendium of con-
        temporary reaction to plays and players between
        1730 and 1795. Arranged Chronologically.

772   Gunther, R. "Vienna's Popular Theatre." The Ameri-
       can German Review, XXVIII (August-September, 1962)
       12-13.
              Review of contemporary theatre in Vienna.
       Short references to the "Teutsche Komödie"and
       Parvlatschentheter of the Eighteenth Century in
       recent seasons and revivals.

773   Hartnoll, Phyllis, ed. The Oxford Companion to the
       Theatre. Third Edition, New York: Oxford Univer-
       sity Press, 1967.
              Articles by twenty-nine new contributors
       bring this reference work, originally published
       in 1951, up to date.

774   Hogan, Charles Beecher. "The London Theatres,
       1776-1800: A Brief Consideration." Theatre Note-
       book, XXI (Autumn, 1966), 13-14.
              A brief comment on the importance of the
       last quarter of the 18th century for theatrical
       developments.

~ 775 Hogan, Floriana T. "Notes on Thirty-One English
       Plays and Their Spanish Sources." Restoration
       and Eighteenth Century Theatre Research, VI
       (May, 1967), 56-59.
              Lists thirty-one Restoration and 18th cen-
       tury plays and their actual, erroneous, or
       questionable Spanish sources. Includes references
       to Dryden, Wycherley, Behn, Killigrew, Cibber
       and Centlivre.

776   Hook, Lucyle, ed. The Female Wits (Anonymous),
       (1704). (ARS Publication, 124). Los Angeles:
       Clark Memorial Library, U.C.L.A., 1967.
              First played around October 1696 at the
       Theatre Royal in Drury Lane. "A devastating satire
       in the manner of Buckingham's The Rehearsal, it
       attacks all plays by women playwrights but Mary
       de la Riviere Manley's blood and thunder female
       tragedy, The Royal Mischief (1696), in particular."

777   Howard, Gordon S. "An Analysis of the Contribution
       of the English Stage Manager to the Evolution of
       the Director." M.S. University of Oregon, 1963.

778   Hoy, Cyrus. "The Effect of the Restoration on
       Drama." Tennessee Studies in Literature, VI

(1961), 85-91.
A brief study of Restoration drama as affec-
ted by tendencies present in English drama from
the early seventeenth century, as well as the
influences of Tudor and Stuart comedy and tragedy.

779   --"Renaissance and Restoration Dramatic Plotting."
       Renaissance Drama, IX (1966), 247-264.
           Examines the dramatic plotting in the tragi-
       comedies and comedies of the late Jacobean and
       Caroline periods and in the Restoration heroic
       plays. Since plays of both periods are concerned
       with erotic passion, they exhibit similarities
       in theme and in the arrangement and movement of
       the action.

780   Hynes, Samuel, editor. English Literary Criticism:
       Restoration and 18th Century (Goldentree Books).
       New York: Appleton-Century-Crofts, 1963, 322 pp.
           An anthology. Includes essays on drama by
       Dryden, Collier, Congreve, Vanbrugh, Steele,
       Hume and Goldsmith. Brief notes and bibliography
       precede each selection.

781   Igo, John, "A Calendar of Fausts." Bulletin of the
       New York Public Library, LXXI (1967), 5-24.
           A list of most of the Fausts created in the
       last four hundred and fifty years includes nine-
       teen titles of plays, pantomimes, operas, prose
       works, and engravings published in England be-
       tween 1664 and 1798.

782   Kaul, R.K. "Rhyme and Blank Verse in Drama: A Note
       on Eliot." English (London), XV (1964), 96-99.
           Considers T. S. Eliot's pronouncements on
       verse drama in light of the writings of Johnson,
       Addison, and Dryden.

783   Keesey, Donald Earl. "Dramatic Criticism in the
       Gentleman's Magazine, 1747-1784." Ph.D. Michigan
       State University, 1964. (Order No. 65-1760).
           Attempts to show how the theatrical criti-
       cism of the Gentleman's Magazine differed from
       that of other 18th century journals, especially
       the London Magazine, the Monthly, and Critical
       Review.

784   Knight, G. Wilson. The Golden Labyrinth: A Study of
British Drama. London: Phoenix House: New York:
Norton Press, 1962, xiv. 402 pp.
     Historical and critical survey. Chapter VII,
"Restoration," pp. 130-170. Chapter VIII, "Augustan,"
pp. 171-200.

785   Langhans, Edward A. "Restoration Manuscript Notes
in Seventeenth Century Plays." Restoration and
18th Century Theatre Research V (May, 1966),
30-39, V (November, 1966), 3-17.
     A list of 252 manuscript notes in printed
and manuscript plays, prologues, and epilogues
that provide information on performances and
publication dates, casts and cast changes, and
staging practices. Includes a bibliography of
recent books and articles that cite or discuss
many of the items.

786   --"Restoration Theatre Scholarship 1960-66: A
Resume and Suggestions for Future Work." Restoration and Eighteenth Century Theatre Research,
VI (May, 1967), 8-11.
     Most of the theatre scholarship of the last
six years has been devoted to performance information, scenery and staging methods, actors and
acting, theatre architecture, costumes, music,
promptbooks, and theatre management. One pressing need is for critical editions or facsimile
reprints of existing primary source material.

787   Loftis, John. The Politics of Drama in Augustan
England. Oxford: Oxford University Press, 1963,
173 pp.
     A thorough examination of the political back-
ground of early eighteenth century drama. Discusses litigation affecting the theatres, political
affiliations of playwrights and actors, as well
as specific plays on topical subjects.

788   --Restoration Drama: Modern Essays in Criticism.
New York: Oxford University Press, 1966. Pp. xi,
376.

789   McManaway, James G. "Unrecorded Performances in London about 1700." Theatre Notebook, XIX (Winter,
1964-5), 68-70.

Notes several productions not mentioned in
The London Stage, Part II.

790   Mandel, Oscar. The Theatre of Don Juan: A Collection of Plays and Views, 1630-1963. Edited with
a Commentary. Lincoln: University of Nebraska
Press, 1963, 731 pp.
        Includes the text of Shadwell's The Liber-
tine (1676) based on Montague Summers's edition
in The Complete Works of Thomas Shadwell. Introduction to the play discusses its Restoration
spirit and Shadwell's indebtedness to Rosimond's
Lennouveau Festin de Pierre, ou l'Atheé foudroyé
(1669).

791   Mellers, Wilfrid. Harmonious Meeting: A Study of
the Relationship Between English Music, Poetry
and Theatre, c. 1600-1900. London: Denis Dobson,
1965, 318 pp.
        Deals with the union of poetry and music
from the time of Elizabethan composers to the end
of the Romantic Movement. Although the work concentrates heavily on the seventeenth century,
some chapters consider Purcell, Handel, Gay and
Pepusch.

792   Miner, Earl. "Introduction." Restoration Dramatists:
A Collection of Critical Essays. (Twentieth Century Views). Edited by Earl Miner. (Englewood
Cliffs, N.J.: Prentice-Hall, Inc., 1966), 1-18.
        A survey of the subjects, forms, and styles
that characterize Restoration drama.

793   Mitchell, Louis Thomas D. "The Aesthetic and Finan-
cial Impact of 'Command Performances' on the
London Stage in the First Quarter of the Eighteenth
Century." Ph.D. New York University, 1967.
(Order No. 68-6087)
        The study considers those factors pertinent
to a command production: text, actors and acting,
entr'act performers, the play's position in the
regular repertory, dramatic theory, and the
economic advantages gained.

794   Moody, William Vaughn and Robert M. Lovett. A
History of English Literature. 8th edition. Revised by Fred B.Millett, New York:Scribners, 1964.

602 pp.
Neoclassical drama is briefly treated in
this paperback edition of a standard literary
history. Includes updated bibliographies.

795   Otten, Terry Ralph. "The Empty Stage: A Comment on
the Search for Dramatic Form in the Early Nineteenth Century." Ph.D. Ohio University, 1966.
(Order No. 66-11, 898).
Although the study concentrates on the
efforts of Shelley, Byron, Tennyson, and Browning,
some references are made to the eighteenth century
concepts and dramatic forms rejected by these
poets.

796   Rankin, Hugh F. The Theatre in Colonial America.
Chapel Hill: University of North Carolina Press,
1965, 239 pp.
Includes information on the popularity of
Restoration and 18th century plays and play-
wrights in colonial America.

797   Renwick, W. L. English Literature: 1789-1815. (Oxford History of English Literature, edited by
F. P. Wilson, and Bonamy Dobree, Vol. IX). Oxford: Clarendon Press, 1963, 293 pp.
Chapter on drama outlines briefly the
dramatic careers of Mrs. Inchbald, and Thomas
Holcroft.

798   Righter, Anne. Restoration Theatre. (Stratford-Upon-
Avon Studies, 6), New York: St. Martin's Press,
1965.

799   Roberts, Edgar V. "An Unrecorded Meaning of 'Joke'
(or Joak) in England." American Speech, XXXVII
(1962), 137-140.
A bawdy meaning of "joke" which would have
been familiar to Eighteenth Century Englishmen.
References to this meaning found in Charles Coffey's The Beggar's Wedding, and Fielding's
Tumble Down Dick, and The Letter Writers.

800   Rosenfeld, Sybil. "Private Theatricals at Bowman's
Lodge, Dartford." Theatre Notebook, XVI (Summer,
1962), 125-126.
Theatrical activities of the Society of
Kentish Bowmen, 1785-1802.

147

801   Ross, Judy Joy. "Marriage, Morals, and the Muse:
       The Vindication of Matrimony on the Eighteenth
       Century Stage." Ph.D. New York University, 1962.
       (Order No. 63-7199).
              Examines both Restoration and eighteenth
       century views of marriage and women; analyzes
       the various types of sentimental drama, and dis-
       tinguishes the emotional drama of sensibility from
       "uplift" drama.

802   Saxon, A.H. "A Brief History of the Claque".Theatre
       Survey, V (1964), 10-26.
              Outlines the history of the claque from an-
       cient to modern times and offers an explanation
       of its organization and function. Includes refer-
       ences to Cibber, Garrick, Goldsmith, and Fielding
       in a brief discussion of the claque in Restoration
       and 18th century theatres.

803   Schless, Howard H. "The Yale Edition of Poems on
       Affairs of State." Restoration and Eighteenth
       Century Theatre Research, IV (May, 1965), 17-19.
              An explanation of items in the edition that
       are of special interest to scholars in Restoration
       and Eighteenth Century Theatre: political verse
       by Restoration dramatists, prologues, and ballad
       materials.

804   Schoenbaum,. Samuel. "Research Opportunities in
       Late 17th Century Drama." Restoration and 18th
       Century Theatre Research, II (May, 1963),5-8.
              Textual and bibliographical problems in
       seventeenth century theatre which merit investi-
       gation.

805   Singh, Amrih. "The Argument on Poetic Justice.
       (Addison versus Dennis). " Indian Journal of
       English Studies, III (1962), 61-77.

806   Singh. Sarup. The Theory of Drama in the Restora-
       tion Period. Calcutta: Orient Longmans, 1963, 299
       pp.
              Analyzes Restoration drama from the view-
       point of dedications, prefaces, prologues, and
       epilogues.

807   Sorelius, Gunnar. "The Giant Race Before the Flood."
       Pre-Restoration Drama on the Stage and in the
       Criticism of the Restoration. (Acta Universitatis
       Upsaliensis, Studia Anglistica Upsaliensia 4).
       Uppsala: Almquist and Wiksells, 1966. 227 pp.
           Concerned with the repertory of old plays
       that was the background of the Restoration stage.
       Discusses the changing conditions of the theatre,
       repertories and companies from 1660 to 1700 and
       transitions that occurred in comedy and tragedy.

808   Thaler, Alwin.   Shakespeare to Sheridan: A Book
       about the Theatre of Yesterday and To-Day. New
       York: Benjamin Bloom, 1963, 339 pp.
           Reprint of Thaler's 1922 study of the indebt-
       edness of the seventeenth and eighteenth century
       theatre to that of Shakespeare and his contem-
       poraries. Points of comparison includes players,
       managers, dramatists, financing, staging, publicity.
       Illustrations and three appendices.

809   Troubridge, St. Vincent. "OED Antedatings from Play
       Titles, 1660-1900--I." Notes and Queries, New
       Ser., X (1963), 104-106.
           Notes four play titles from the period 1660-
       1800 containing phrases which antedate the cita-
       tions in OED.

810   --"OED Antedatings from Play Titles 1660-1900-II."
       Notes and Queries, New Ser., X (1963), 136-138.
           Part two of Troubridge's study lists two
       play titles between 1660-1800.

811   Wells, James M. "The Newberry Library Holdings."
       Restoration and 18th Century Theatre Research,
       III, (May, 1964), 11-14.
           A brief description of the 17th and 18th cen-
       tury dramatic and theatrical material available
       at Newberry Library, Chicago, Illinois.

812   Willard, Helen C. "The Harvard Library Collections."
       Restoration and 18th Century Theatre Research, III
       (1964), 14-22.
           Surveys the 17th and 18th century playbills,
       prints, books and manuscripts found in the theatri-
       cal holdings of Houghton Library.

8 13   Wilson, John Harold. A Preface to Restoration Drama.
        (Riverside Studies in Literature). Boston:
        Houghton Mifflin Company, 1965, 208 pp.
                Intended as an introduction to Restoration
        drama for students, includes chapters on the
        nature of Restoration theatre, tragedy, comedy,
        and a selected bibliography.

8 14   --"A Theatre in York House." Theatre Notebook, XVI
        (Spring, 1962), 75-78.
                Evidence for the existence of a theatre at
        York House from 1672-1674.

8 15   --Six Eighteenth-Century Plays. With an Introduction.
        (Riverside Eds., B 85). Boston: Houghton Mifflin,
        1963, 374 pp.
                Includes The Fair Penitent, The Conscious
        Lovers, The Beggar's Opera, The London Merchant,
        She Stoops to Conquer, The School for Scandal.

8 16   Zielske, Harald. "Handlungsort und Buhnenbild in
        17. Jahrhunder Untersuchungen zur Raumdarstel-
        lung in europaischen Barock-theater." Ph. D.
        Freie Universitat Berlin, 1965.

        MOLIERE, See Nos. 164, 1166, 1176

        MONMOUTH, See No. 307

        MONTAGU
8 17   Boulton, James T. "Mrs. Elizabeth Montagu (1720-
        1800)." Burke Newsletter, III (Winter-Spring,
        1961-62), 96-98.
                The personality and talent of Mrs. Elizabeth
        Montagu. Friendships with Burke, Johnson, Sterne,
        and Reynolds.

8 18   "Simplicity." Johnsonian Newsletter, XXVII (1967), 2.
                A brief discussion of Lady Mary Wortley
        Montagu's Simplicity (c. 1735) adapted from
        Marivaux's Le Jeu de l'amour et du hasard (1730).

        MONTAGUE, See No. 955

        MONTHLY MAGAZINE, See No. 783

        MOORE, See Nos. 101, 568, 946, 1120

                                150

MUNFORD
819   Baine, Rodney M. Robert Munford: America's First
       Comic Dramatist, Athens, Georgia: University
       of Goergia Press, 1967,   132 pp.
          A critical biography of the 18th century
       American playwright includes references to
       Restoration and 18th century English drama.

MURPHY
820   New Essays by Arthur Murphy. Edited with an intro-
       duction by Arthur Sherbo.   East Lansing: Michigan
       State University Press, 1963, 217 pp.
          Theatrical criticism attributed to Murphy,
       chiefly from dramatic periodicals of the period.
       Approximately thirty-five essays.   See Also No.
       249

821   Lehnert, Martin. "Arthur Murphy's Hamlet-Parodie
       (1772) auf David Garrick." Shakespear Jahrbuch,
       CII (1966), 97-167.
          Studies the history of Murphy's parody and
       includes the full text of his play.

822   Miller, Henry Knight. "Internal Evidence: Professor
       Sherbo and the Case of Arthur Murphy." Bulletin
       of the New York Public Library, LXIX (1965), 459-
       470.
          Contends that Sherbo's evidence is not
       scientific or weighty enough to attribute The
       Entertainer and several other theatrical writings
       to Arthur Murphy.

823   Sherbo, Arthur. "Imitation or Concealment: Who Wrote
       the Entertainer Essays?" Bulletin of the New York
       Public Library, LXIX (1965), 471-486.
          Strengthens his original arguments for Mur-
       phy's authorship of The Entertainer with statistics
       on diction and vocabulary.

824   Trefman, Simon. "Arthur Murphy's Long Lost English-
       man From Paris: A Manuscript Discovered."Theatre
       Notebook, XX(Summer, 1966), 137-141.
          Comments on the manuscript at the Newberry
       Library, Chicago, and on the play's production
       on April 3, 1756 at Drury Lane, particularly its
       competition with Samuel Foote's Englishman Re-
       turned From Paris. See Also No. 146

MURPHY, See Also Nos. 71, 133, 1088

MUSEUM, See No. 856

MUSIC
825   Henigan, Robert Hamilton, "English Dramma Per
        Musica: A Study of Musical Drama in England from
        The Siege of Rhodes to the Opening of the Hay-
        market Theatre." Ph.D. University of Missouri,
        1961. 417 pp. (Order No. 61-4068).
            Stresses the importance of "Dramma per Musi-
        ca" in the Restoration, and demonstrates how
        typical it is of the period.

MUSIC, See Also Nos. 832, 967, 968

                        N

NATURE, See Nos. 370, 477, 580, 581

NEWBERRY LIBRARY, See No. 811

NEWDIGATE
826   Wilson, John Harold. "More Theatre Notes from The
        Newdigate Newsletters." Theatre Notebook, XVI
        (Winter, 1961-2), 59.
            A continuation of material in Theatre Note-
        book XV (Spring, 1961). From Feb. 4, 1681-2, to
        Jan. 11, 1693-4.

827   --"More Theatre Notes from the Newdigate Newsletters."
        Theatre Notebook, XVI (Winter, 1962), 59.
            Supplement to those already published in
        Theatre Notebook, XVI (1961), 79.

828   --"Theatre Notes from the Newdigate Newsletters."
        Theatre Notebook, XV (Spring, 1961), 79-84.
            Newsletters from 1674 through 1715. The
        collection, totalling 3,950 letters are at the
        Folger Shakespeare Library. Professor Wilson has
        culled the theatre news from them, and prints
        the entries in chronological order, from March
        21, 1673-4, to May 10, 1715.

NEW YORK PUBLIC LIBRARY, See No. 962

NIPCLOSE, See No. 475

NORWICH, See No. 1

NOUVERRE, See No. 1039

NURSERY, See No. 1

O

O'HARA
829   Maxwell, Margaret F. "Olympus at Billingsgate:
The Burlettas of Kane O'Hara." Educational Theatre
Journal, XV (1963), 130-135
        O'Hara's Midas and The Golden Pippin are
two of the best examples of burlesque oc classical myths popular in the eighteenth century. See
Also No. 93

OHIO STATE UNIVERSITY, See No. 542

OLDMIXON
830   Oldmixon, John. An Essay on Criticism (1728).
With an introduction by R. J. Madden, C.S.B.
Los Angeles: Clark Memorial Library, University
of California, Los Angeles, 1964, 94 pp.
        Scattered references to Restoration drama
in this facsimile reproduction of the 1728 edition of Oldmixon's critical essay. (Augustan
Reprint Society Publication No. 107-108).

831   Shepperson, Wilbur S., and John G. Folkes. "Biographical Notes on Sir John Oldmixon." Notes and
Queries, New Ser., IX (1962), 4-5.
        Discussion and a correction of erroneous
statements concerning the biography of Sir John
Oldmixon published in Notes and Queries in 1867,
and in other periodicals.

OPERA
832   Fiske, Roger. "The 'Macbeth' Music." Music and
Letters, XLV (1964), 114-125.

The history of <u>Macbeth</u> as a tragic opera
during the Restoration and 18th century. Takes
into account scores by Davenant, Matthew Locke,
Eccles, and Leveridge.

833 Krummel, Donald W. "Viva tutti': the Musical
Journeys of an Eighteenth-Century Part-Song."
<u>Bulletin of the New York Public Library</u>, LXVII
(1963), 57-64.
The use of "Viva tutti" in eighteenth century London comic opera.

834 Lord, Phillip. "The English-Italian Opera Companies,
1732-3." <u>Music and Letters</u>, XLV(1964), 239-251.
Highlights the main events in the 1732
attempts of Lampe and Arne to create an English
national opera.

835 McManaway, James G. "Entertainment for the Grand
Duke of Tuscany." <u>Theatre Notebook</u>, XVI (Autumn
1961), 20-21.
Reproduces the passage recording a performance of an opera and ballet based on the story
of Psyche, performed before Cosimo the Third
Grand Duke of Tuscany, at Drury Lane, June 3,
1669. See Also Nos. 446, 491, 563

836 Rosenfeld, Sybil. "An Opera House Account Book."
<u>Theatre Notebook</u>, XVI (Spring, 1962), 83-88.
Account Book for the 1716-17 season of the
King's Theatre, Haymarket, from a manuscript in
the Hampshire Record Office in Winchester.

837 Sands, Mollie. "The Rehearsal of an Opera." <u>Theatre
Notebook</u>, XIX (Autumn, 1964), 30-31.
Marco Ricci's paintings of a rehearsal of
<u>Pirro e Demetrio</u> are based on an actual incident
which took place on December 9, 1708, at the
Queen's Theatre. See Also No. 982

838 Temperley, Nicholas. "The English Romantic Opera."
<u>Victorian Studies</u>, IX (1966), 293-301.
A study of nineteenth century English opera
includes brief references to the English opera
of the eighteenth century.

839   White, Eric Walter. "English Opera Research, the
        immediate Past and the Future: A Personal View-
        point." Theatre Notebook, XXI (Autumn, 1966),
        32-37.
               Comments on English Opera research during
        the last fifteen years. Includes references to
        English versions of 17th century Italian Operas,
        to works by Purcell and Handel, and to 18th cen-
        tury Ballad Operas, Pasticcio Operas, Burlettas,
        and Comic Operas. See Also No. 1119

OPERA, See Also Nos. 954, 967, 968

ORRERY, See Nos. 88, 550, 551

OTWAY
840   Gillespie, Gerald. "The Rebel in Seventeenth Century
        Tragedy." Comparative Literature, XVIII (1966),
        324-336.
               A comparative study of Savinien Cyrano de
        Bergerac's La Mort d'Agrippine (1633), Daniel
        Casper von Lohenstein's Epicharis (1665), and
        Otway's Venice Preserv'd (1682) outlines the
        development of the 17th century rebel from
        satanic antagonist to sentimental villain.

841   Hauser, David R. "Otway Preserved: Theme and Form
        in Venice Preserv'd." Restoration Dramatists: A
        Collection of Critical Essays. (Twentieth Cen-
        tury Views). Edited by Earl Miner. (Englewood
        Cliffs, N.J.: Prentice-Hall, Inc., 1966), 139-149.
               Reprinted from Studies in Philology, LV
        (1958), 481-493. Purposes to demonstrate "how
        Otway partially overcomes the obstructions of
        the heroic conventions to reanimate the dramatic
        mechanism of his age." and "to explore means by
        which the play may be viewed as more organic and
        more highly wrought artistically than has pre-
        viously been allowed."

842   Kleineberger, H.R. "Otway's 'Venice Preserv'd'
        and Hofmannsthal's 'Das Gerettete Venedig.'"
        Modern Language Review, LXII (1967), 292-297.
               Discusses Hofmannsthal's 1903-04 adaptation
        of Otway's play and notes particularly the
        changes the author made in the relationship of

Pierre and Jaffier to reflect his own relationship with his fellow poet, Stefan George.

843   Marshall, Geoffrey. "Themes and Structures in the
        Plays of Thomas Otway." Ph.D. Rice University,
        1964. (Order No. 64-10, 181).
            A study of Otway's literary techniques
        illustrates that there is greater artistic unity
        in his plays than has been previously indicated.
        His The Orphan and Venice Preserv'd are ventures
        into new areas of subject matter rather than en-
        deavors to create a new genre.

844   Stroup, Thomas B. "Otway's Bitter Pessimism."
        Essays in English Literature of the Classical
        Period Presented to Dougald MacMillan. Edited by
        Daniel W. Patterson and Albrecht B. Strauss.
        Studies in Philology, (Extra Series, January,
        1967), pp. 54-75.
            Studies the outgrowth of Otway's pessimism
        as it finds expression in dramatic devices and
        contrivances, in the elements of structure, and
        in the quality and meaning of the plays, especial-
        ly the tragedies.

845   Taylor, Aline Mackenzie. "Venice Preserv'd." Restora-
        tion Drama: Modern Essays in Criticism. (A Galaxy
        Book), Edited by John Loftis. (New York: Oxford
        University Press, 1966), 195-228.
            Reprinted from Next to Shakespeare: Otway's
        Venice Preserv'd and The Orphan (Durham: Duke
        University Press, 1950), pp. 39-72. An analysis
        of the plot, characterization and theme of the
        play attempts to explain the play's early popu-
        larity and the conflicting impressions modern
        readers derive from the text. See Also Nos. 551,
        877

846   Van Voris, W. "Tragedy through Restoration Eyes:
        Venice Preserv'd in its own Theatre." Hermathena,
        XCIX (1964), 55-65.
            If viewed through the eyes of Dryden, the
        Duchess of Portsmouth, and Charles II, the aspects
        of Venice Preserv'd which seem gross and senti-
        mental to the modern playgoer are the foundation
        for the play's strength. See Also Nos. 7, 30,
        36.

847   Williams, Gordon. "The Sex-Death Motive in Otway's
       Venice Preserv'd." Trivium, II (1967), 59-70.

OTWAY, See Also Nos. 225, 305

                              P

PAINTINGS, See No. 908

PALMER
848   Spencer, David G. "Gentleman John and Jack Plausible."
       Notes and Queries, New Ser., VIII (February,
       1961), 60-61.
              Clarifies the confusion between the two John
       Palmers who appeared as leading actors at Drury
       Lane in the eighteenth century.

PANTHEON THEATRE, See No. 1096

PANTOMIME, See No. 1060

PARSONS, See No. 293

PASTORAL OPERA, See No. 495

PATENT COMPANIES, See No. 3

PEPYS
849   McAfee, Helen. Pepys on the Restoration Stage. New
       York: Benjamin Bloom, 1963, 353 pp.
              Reprint of the 1916 edition of passages
       selected from Pepys's Diary relating to the theatre
       and drama. An elaborate introduction deals with
       Pepys as a dramatic historian, his reputation as
       a drama critic, and his relationship with the
       Restoration theatre. References in Pepys's Diary
       to the theatre are arranged by subject. Includes
       bibliography, notes, and illustrations.

PERIODICALS, See DRAMATIC PERIODICALS

PERIODICALS
850   Lams, Victor J.,Jr. "A Study of the Connoisseur
       (1754-56)." Ph.D. Northwestern University, 1965.

(Order No. 65-12, 119).
A description and analysis of the essay
journal written chiefly by George Colman the elder
and Bonnell Thornton. The journal treated manners and morals as well as language, literature,
and the arts.

851   Todd, William B. "A Bibliographical Account of The
       Gentleman's Magazine, 1731-1754." Studies in
       Bibliography, XVIII (1965), 81-109.

852   White, Robert Benjamin, Jr. "A Study of the Female
       Tatler (1709-1710). Ph.D. University of North
       Carolina, 1966. (Order No. 67-1065).
       Studies the backgrounds and development of
       the periodical, the later issues of which have
       been attributed to Susanna Centlivre. The con-
       tents of the periodical include dramatic criticism.
       See Also No. 552

PHILIPS, See No. 507

PIZARRO, See No. 909

PLATONISM, See No. 688

PLAY LISTS
853   Stratman, Carl J., C.S.V. "Dramatic Play Lists:
       1591-1963." Bulletin of the New York Public
       Library, LXX (1966), 71-85.
       A chronological arrangement of play lists
       that gives full title to each list, indicates
       the scope and relative merits of each as a refer-
       ence work. Includes information on subsequent
       editions, additions, changes and scholarly studies
       of particular lists. Part I of the collection
       contains 34 entries; 31 entries published during
       the Restoration and 18th century.

854   --"Dramatic Play Lists: 1591-1963." Bulletin of
       the New York Public Library, LXX(1966), 169-178.
       Part II of the collection contains 65 en-
       tries; 3 entries published during the 18th cen-
       tury.

PLAYBILLS
855   Fletcher, Ifan Kyrle. "British Playbills Before
       1718." Theatre Notebook, XVII (Winter, 1962-63),
       48-50.
           List of eight illustrations of the earliest
       British playbills.

856   Kilfoil, Thomas F. "The Brander Matthews Dramatic
       Museum." Restoration and Eighteenth Century
       Theatre Research, IV (May, 1965), 10-12.
           This theatre collection at Columbia Univer-
       sity contains models of stages (Lisle's Tennis-
       Court Theatre and Drury Lane), playbills (dating
       from 1753 for Drury Lane, from 1774 for the Hay-
       market, from 1790 for Covent Garden, eighteenth-
       century engravings and theatre tokens.

857   Rachow, Louis A. "The Players--The Walter Hampden
       Memorial Library." Restoration and Eighteenth
       Century Theatre Research, IV (May, 1965), 15-16.
           The library contains the William Henderson
       Collection of English Playbills--forty albums
       containing 4,000 bills and dating from 1750 to
       1888. See Also No. 570

PLAYWRIGHTS, See No. 434

PLOT, See No. 43

POETIC JUSTICE, See No. 598

POETIC STYLE, See No. 1126

POLISH ENLIGHTENMENT, See No. 568

POLITICIAN, See No. 712

POLITICS
858   Loftis, John. "The Political Strain in Augustan
       Drama." Restoration Drama: Modern Essays in
       Criticism. (A Galaxy Book). Edited by John Loftis.
       (New York: Oxford University Press, 1966), 229-
       235.
           Reprinted from The Politics of Drama in
       Augustan England (Oxford: Oxford University Press,
       1963), pp. 154-161. Studies the shortcomings of
       the period's political drama, "a political drama

159

that is clever rather than profound." See Also
Nos. 277, 499

POPE
859   Creeth, Ned H., editor. "The Preface of the Editor--
       Alexander Pope." Shakespeare Newsletter, XVI
       (1966), 25.
            A reprint of Pope's preface to his 1725 edi-
       tion of Shakespeare's works. Discusses Pope's
       virtues and shortcomings as an editor. "When
       Pope 'improved' Shakespeare he believed honestly
       he was gaining for him a wider readership."

860   Dixon, P. "Edward Bysshe and Pope's 'Shakespear.'"
       Notes and Queries, New Ser., XI (1964), 292-293.
            Correspondences between Bysshe's Art of
       English Poetry (1702) and Pope's Shakespear
       indicate that "Pope's taste in Shakespeare was
       not quite the unique thing that it has some-
       times been thought."

861   --"Pope's Shakespeare." Journal of English and
       Germanic Philology, LXIII (1964), 191-203.
            A study of Pope's selection of the best
       passages and outstanding scenes reveals his
       "strong preference for the crisply satiric, for
       passages of scorn and lofty denunciation."

862   Fuller, John. "A New Epilogue by Pope?" Review of
       English Studies, XVII (1966), 409-413.
            The epilogue to Gay's The Wife of Bath(1713).

863   Huseboe, Arthur R. "Pope's Critical Views of the
       London Stage." Restoration and 18th Century
       Theatre Research, III (May, 1964), 25-37.
            Pope's attack on the Augustan theatre in To
       Augustus, Peri Bathos, and the Dunciad "is based
       on his tendency to judge the minor dramatic gen-
       res not by their own traditions but by those of
       Aristotle and Horace." See Also Nos. 116, 194,
       956

864   Huseboe, Arthur Robert. "Alexander Pope's Dramatic
       Imagination." Ph.D. Indiana University, 1963.
       (Order No. 64-476).
            Pope's relation to drama and the theatre;
       its effect on his life and work.

160

865   McAleer, John J. "Alexander Pope--Shakespeare's
       Second Editor." Shakespeare Newsletter, XVI
       (1966), 32.

866   Maxwell, J.C. "Classic." Notes and Queries, New
       Ser., X (1963), 220.
            George Sewell's use of the term "classic"
       in his Preface to Pope's Shakespeare, Vol. VII
       (1725), to refer to literature other than Greek
       or Latin, antedates the earliest question in
       O.E.D. See Also No. 114

867   Rogal, Samuel J. "Pope's Treatment of Colley Cib-
       ber." Lock Haven Review, No. 8 (1966), pp. 25-30.
       See Also No. 109

868   Williams, George W. "Shakespeare's Antony and Cleo-
       patra III, xiii, 26." Explicator, XX (1962),
       Item 79.
            Discussion of Pope's emendation of "gay com-
       parisons" to "gay caparisons."

       PORRETT, See No. 890

       PORTRAIT, See No. 969

       PORTRAITS
869   Kerslake, J.F., ed. Catalogue of Theatrical Por-
       traits in London Public Collections. London:
       Society for Theatre Research, 1961, xi. 63 pp.
            A handlist of portraits, other than en-
       gravings, of performers in the theatre, which
       can be located in public collections in London.
       Includes protraits of professional performers,
       individually and in groups, in drama, opera,
       music hall, variety, the circus, and ballet,
       both British and foreign. (Modelled on the Har-
       vard Catalogue of Theatrical Portraits.)

       PRATT
870   Jason, Philip K. "Samuel Johnson Pratt's Unpub-
       lished Comedy of Joseph Andrews." Notes and
       Queries, XIV (1967), 416-418.
            Pratt successfully dramatizes some of the
       major incidents in the first and fourth books
       of Fielding's novel in this play which was
       presented as an after-piece at Drury Lane on

April 20, 1778.

PREFACES, See No. 434

PROLOGUE
871   Ausprich, Harry. "A Rhetorical Analysis of the
       Restoration Prologue and Epilogue." Ph.D. Michi-
       gan State University, 1963. (Order No. 64-4932).
           Considers the prologues and epilogues of the
       Restoration theatre with reference to the rhetori-
       cal principles of the period.

872   Sutherland, James. "Prologues Epilogues and Audience
       in the Restoration Theatre." Of Books and Human-
       kind: Essays and Poems Presented to Bonamy Dobrée,
       ed. John Butt et al. (London: Routledge and K.
       Paul, 1964), 37-54.
           Critics were among the favorite objects of
       witty and satirical attack as Prologues and Epi-
       logues came to be addressed to the various sec-
       tions of the audience to praise, ridicule or
       condemn them. Special attention is given to
       Dryden. See Also No. 1181

PROLOGUES
873   Avery, Emmett L. "Some New Prologues and Epilogues,
       1704-1708." Studies in English Literature, 1500-
       1900, V (1965), 455-467.
           Six Prologues and Epilogues, which appeared
       between 1704-1708 and were preserved by Narcissus
       Luttrell, are reprinted with introductory notes.

874   Knapp, Mary E. Prologues and Epilogues of the Eigh-
       teenth Century. New Haven: Yale University Press,
       1961, xi, 350 pp. (Yale Studies in English, No.
       149).
           First real work on the subject. Analysis of
       the prologues and epilogues. Gives a good picture
       of the taste of the audiences.

PROMPT BOOKS
875   Kerr, Barlyn B. "A Study of Selected Prompt Books
       for the Productions of Measure for Measure Between
       1772 and 1846." M.A. Ohio State University, 1962.

PROMPT COPIES, See No. 126

PROMPTBOOKS

876   Langhans, Edward A. "Research Opportunities in
       Early Promptbooks." Educational Theatre Journal,
       XVII (March, 1966), 73-76.

877   --"Three Early Eighteenth Century Promptbooks."
       Theatre Notebook, XX (Summer, 1966), 142-150.
             Presents information on promptbooks pre-
       pared for Settle's Pastor Fido, c. 1706; Behn's
       The Rover, c. 1720's; and Otway's The Cheats
       of Sapin, c. 1730's. See Also Nos. 958, 997

878   --"Three Early Eighteenth Century Manuscript
       Promptbooks." Modern Philology, LXV (1967),
       114-129.
             Provides a transcription of three prompt-
       books and comments on them. The three manu-
       scripts (Theobald's The Perfidious Brother,
       Settle's The Lady's Triumph, and Southerne's
       Money, the Mistress) were probably prepared
       by John Steed for production during the 1710's
       and 1720's at Rich's Lincoln's Inn Fields.

PROMPTER, See Nos. 243, 552

PROSODY, See No. 743

PROVINCES, See No. 1

PUNS, See No. 130

PURCELL

879   Bicknell, Joan Colleen Patton. "Interdependence
       of Word and Tone in the Dramatic Music of Henry
       Purcell." Ph.D. Stanford University, 1961,
       273 pp. (Order No. Mic 61-1216).

880   Moore, Robert Etheridge. Henry Purcell and the
       Restoration Theatre. Foreword by Sir Jack West-
       rup. London: Heinemann; Cambridge, Massachusetts:
       Harvard University Press, 1961, xvi, 223 pp.

881   Zimmerman, Franklin B. Henry Purcell, 1659-1695.
       London: Macmillan Co., 1967, 429 pp.

PURITAN

882   Morgan, Edmund S. "Puritan Hostility to the
       Theatre." Proceedings of the American Philosophi-

163

<u>cal Society</u>, CX (1966), 340-347.
An analysis of Puritan arguments attempts
to account for the intensity of hostility
against the theatre. Although most of the
article is devoted to events of the late 16th
century, there are many references to the Restoration and 18th century.

Q

QUEEN"S THEATRE, See No. 1108

R

RAILLERY, See No. 131

RAKE, See Nos. 168, 170

RALPH
883   Bastian, J. M. "James Ralph's Second Adaptation
        from John Banks." <u>Huntington Library Quarterly</u>,
        XXV (1962), 181-188.
            Ralph's adaptation of Banks' <u>Anna Bullen,</u>
        (1682) into <u>Vertue Betray'd; or, Anna Bullen</u>
        (ca. 1735). Grace and strength of Ralph's
        poetry makes the adaptation superior to the
        original.

884   Shipley, John Burke. "James Ralph: Pretender
        to Genius." Ph.D. Columbia University, 1963.
        (Order No. 63-7433).
            Surveys his theatrical career, his rela-
        tionship with Garrick and Fielding.

RANELAGH GARDENS, See No. 1096

REED
885   McAleer, John J. "Isaac Reed: Editor of the
        'First Variorum.'" <u>Shakespeare Newsletter</u>,
        XIII(1963), 26.
            Brief biography of the eighteenth cen-

tury Shakespeare scholar. Includes excerpts
from his Biographia Dramatica (1782) on specific Shakespearean plays. See Also No. 485

RESTORATION, See No. 813

RHETORIC
886   Fussell, Paul. The Rhetorical World of Augustan
       Humanism: Ethics and Imagery from Swift to
       Burke. Oxford: Clarendon Press, 1965, 314 pp.
           Concentrating on the rhetorical techni-
       ques, especially the polemic imagery of Swift,
       Pope, Johnson, Reynolds, Gibbon, and Burke,
       the work mes occasional references to Augus-
       tan drama. See Also Nos. 288, 1122

RICH, See Nos. 705, 1060, 1093

RICHARDSON
887   Dussinger, John A. "Richardson's Tragic Muse."
       Philological Quarterly, XLVI (1967), 18-33.
           Examines Richardson's interest in the
       drama and its effect on Clarissa, appreciated
       by his contemporaries as "a work of tragic
       species." Includes references to Hill, Field-
       ing and Cibber.

888   Konigsberg, Ira. "The Tragedy of Clarissa."
       Modern Language Quarterly, XXVII (1966), 285-
       298.
           Discusses the novel's relationship to a
       theory of tragedy and to 18th century tragedies.
       See Also No. 763

889   Sherburn, George. "Samuel Richardson's Novels
       and the Theatre: A Theory Sketched." Philo-
       logical Quarterly, XLI (1962), 325-329.
           The possible indebtedness of Richardson
       to the theatre for plot-focus, character types
       and conversation.

890   Wilson, Stuart. "The First Dramatic Version of
       Clarissa." English Language Notes, II (1964),
       21-25.
           Though never produced, Robert Porrett's
       Clarissa; or, The Fatal Seduction (1788) is
       the first dramatic version of Richardson's

work and demonstrates the influence of the
Gothic on late 18th century drama.

ROCHESTER
891   Bror, Danielsson and David M. Vieth, Eds.
The Gyldenstolpe Manuscript Miscellany of
Poems by John Wilmot, Earl of Rochester, and
Other Restoration Authors. Stockholm Studies
in English, XVII. (Acta Universitatis Stock-
holmiensis) Stockholm: Almqvist and Wiksells,
1967.

892   De Sola Pinto, Vivian. Enthusiast in Wit: A Portrait of John Wilmot, Earl of Rochester, 1647-
1680. Lincoln: University of Nebraska Press,
1962.
         Revised edition of the 1935 biography of
Wilmot. "Extensive revision, rewriting, and
supplementation" of the original version in
light of recent scholarship.

ROWE
893   Rowe, Nicholas. Tamerlane, a Tragedy. Edited
by Landon C. Burns, Jr., Philadelphia: University of Pennsylvania Press, 1966.
         With introduction and notes.

894   Boddy, Margaret. "Tonson's 'Loss of Rowe.'"
Notes and Queries, New Ser., XIII (1966), 213-
214.
         The rivalry of Lintot and Tonson in pub-
lishing Rowe's plays and translation.

895   Ingram, William. "Theobald, Rowe, Jackson: Whose
Ajax?" The Library Chronicle, XXXI (1965), 91-
96.
         Bibliographical and biographical evidence
points to Rowe as the probable translator of
Sophocles' Ajax, published by Lintot in 1714.

896   Kearful, Frank J. "The Nature of Tragedy in
Rowe's The Fair Penitent." Papers on Language
and Literature, II (1966), 351-360.
         "The function of tragedy in The Fair
Penitent is not merely to arouse vicarious
suffering: it is also to instruct Rowe's
audience in the kind of moral knowledge

requisite to their own lives."

897   Kleitz, Philip Rex. "Nicholas Rowe: Developer
       of the Drama of Sympathy." Ph.D. University
       of Minnesota, 1967. (Order No. 68-7342).
       Discusses the transition in Rowe's Works
       from the heroic to sentimental tragedy and
       his development of language and the pitiful
       heroine for the latter form.

898   McAleer, John J. "Nicholas Rowe--Matrix of
       Shakespearean Scholarship." Shakespeare
       Newsletter, XVII (1967), 6.
       A brief biography of Rowe that con-
       siders the qualities of his edition of Shake-
       speare. See Also Nos. 507, 571, 767, 974,
       1122.

899   Rowan, D. F. "Shore's Wife." Studies in English
       Literature, 1500-1900, VI (1966), 447-464.
       Traces the popular and literary treatments
       of Jane Shore from her own day to Rowe's
       Tragedy of Jane Shore (1714).

900   Schwarz, Alfred. "An Example of Eighteenth-
       Century Pathetic Tragedy: Rowe's Jane Shore."
       Modern Language Quarterly, XXII (1961), 236-
       247.
       A study of Rowe's purpose and success
       with a pathetic family tragedy, a type well
       received by the London audience in spite of
       its disregard for the outmoded rules dictated
       by the neoclassical critics.

901   Wyman, Lindley A. "The Tradition of the Formal
       Meditation in Rowe's The Fair Penitent."
       Philological Quarterly, XLII (1963), 412-416.
       Rowe's use of the Elizabethan formal
       meditation accounts for the melodramatic as-
       pects of the final act. See Also No. 815

ROWLANDSON, See No, 1042

RYMER, See Nos. 381, 765, 1005, 1009

S

SALISBURY COURT, See No. 1101

SATIRE, See Nos. 32, 145, 146, 162, 251, 286, 462, 499, 505, 626, 1184

SAUNDERS, See No. 1096

SAVAGE
902   Shugrue, Michael. "Richard Savage in the Columns of 'Applebee's Original Weekly Journal.'" Notes and Queries, New Ser., VIII (February, 1961), 51-52.
        From 1723-1727. One is the reprint of the epilogue written by Aaron Hill, Esq., and spoken by Mrs. Breet, of Savage's play, Sir Thomas Overbury, June 22, 1723.

903   Tracy, Clarence. "Some Uncollected Authors XXXVI: Richard Savage, d. 1743." Book Collector, XII (1963), 340-349.
        Theatrical writings included in checklist of Savage's separate printed works.

SCENE PAINTERS, See Nos. 914, 915, 916, 917, 918, 919

SCENERY
904   Barker, Kathleen. "Michael Edkins, Painter." Theatre Notebook, XVI (Winter, 1961-62), 39-55.
        Edkins' work for the Theatre Royal, Bristol. Entries from Edkins' ledger for 1768 to 1783.

905   Jackson, Allan S. "Restoration Scenery, 1656-1680." Restoration and 18th Century Theatre Research, III (November, 1964), 25-38.
        Studies the use of set pieces, semipractical flats, the painting of sets by professional artists, and lighting effects in Restoration staging practices before 1680. Includes illustrations.

906   McManaway, James G. "L'héritage de la Renaissance dans la mise en scène en Angleterre

(1642-1700)." Le lieu théâtral à la Renaissance.
Edited by Jean Jacquot, Elie Konigson, and
Marcel Oddon. (Paris: Eds. du Centre National
de la Recherche Scientifique, 1964), pp. 459-
472.

907   Mander, Raymond, and Joe Mitchenson. "De Loutherbourg and Pizarro, 1779." Theatre Notebook,
XX (Summer, 1966), 160.
    Additional information on De Louther-
bourg's relationship to the scenery for Pizarro
discussed in Theatre Notebook, XX (Autumn,
1965), 30-32.

908   --"The Village Lawyer by Samuel De Wilde. Some
Information on the Paintings." Theatre Notebook, XX (Autumn, 1965), 33-34.
    De Wilde's paintings of the characters
from William Macready's play, performed at the
Theatre Royal, Haymarket, August 28, 1787,
6 plates.

909   Oliver, Anthony, and John Saunders. "De Loutherbourg and Pizarro, 1799". Theatre Notebook,
XX (Autumn, 1965), 30-32.
    De Loutherbourg's relationship to the
scenery for Pizarro, the translated and adapted
version of Kotzebue's Die Spanier in Peru,
first performed at Drury Lane on May 24, 1799.

910   Peet, Alice Lida. "The History and Development
of Simultaneous Scenery in the West from the
Middle Ages to Modern United States." Ph.D.
University of Wisconsin, 1961. 393 pp.
(L.C. Card No. Mic 61-1547).
    A study of simultaneous scenery "which
is characterized by its recognizable, repre-
sentational quality and the use of multiple
locales which remain essentially in view of
the audience during the entire performance,"
from its beginnings in the Middle Ages to
modern United States. Includes a discussion
of the stage sets of the neo-classical drama.

911   Peterson, William M. and Richard Morton. "Mirrors
        on the Restoration Stage." Notes and Queries,
        New Ser., IX (1962), 10-13, 63-67.
            Traditional and new uses of mirrors in
        drama." . . . in general, the Restoration stage
        used mirrors to insure observance of its
        elaborate and formal code of decorum."

912   Rosenfeld, Sybil. "Scene Painters at the London
        Theatres in the 18th Century." Theatre Notebook
        XX (Spring, 1966), 113-118.
            An appendix to "A Checklist of Scene
        Painters" which appeared in Volumes XIX and
        XX (1964-1966) of Theatre Notebook. The tables
        enable readers to trace the painters who were
        operating at the London theatres in any parti-
        cular season. See Also Nos. 7, 604, 625

913   --"A Transparency by Thomas Greenwood the Elder."
        Theatre Notebook, XIX (Autumn, 1964), 21-22.
            A description of a Greenwood transparency
        used in the 1779 Sadler's Wells production of
        The Prophecy or Queen Elizabeth at Tilbury
        demonstrates the high calibre of entertainment
        at certain minor theatres in 18th century
        England.

914   Rosenfeld, Sybil and Edward Croft-Murray. "A
        Checklist of Scene Painters Working in Great
        Britain and Ireland in the 18th Century."
        Theatre Notebook, XIX (Autumn, 1964), 6-20.
            A much needed index to 18th century scene
        painters and their works. Entries are arranged
        alphabetically by artist, and whenever pos-
        sible include biographical and bibliographical
        material. 39 painters in this first of four
        installments.

915   --"A Checklist of Scene Painters Working in
        Great Britain and Ireland in the 18th Century
        (2)." Theatre Notebook, XIX (Winter, 1964-5),
        49-64.
            Continues list of scene painters begun
        in Theatre Notebook, XIX, 1. 36 entries; 5 plates.

916   --"A Checklist of Scene Painters Working in Great
        Britain and Ireland in the 18th Century (3)."
        Theatre Notebook, XIX (Spring, 1965), 102-113.
            The third installment of an index to 18th
        Century scene painters begun in Theatre Note-
        book, XIX (Autumn, 1964). Entries are arranged
        alphabetically by artist and include biographi-
        cal and bibliographical material. 18 entries,
        including De Loutherbourg.

917   --"A Checklist of Scene Painters Working in Great
        Britain and Ireland in the 18th Century (4)."
        Theatre Notebook, XIX (Summer, 1965), 133-
        145.
            Continues list of scene painters begun
        in Theatre Notebook, XIX (Autumn, 1964). 38
        entries.

918   --"A Checklist of Scene Painters Working in Great
        Britain and Ireland in the 18th Century (5)."
        Theatre Notebook, XX(Autumn, 1965), 36-44.
            The fifth installment of the list of scene
        painters begun in Theatre Notebook,XIX (Autumn
        1964). 37 entries.

919   --"A Checklist of Scene Painters Working in Great
        Britain and Ireland in the 18th Century, Addi-
        tions and Corrections." Theatre Notebook, XX
        (Winter, 1965-6), 69-72.
            11 additions, 14 corrections. See Also
        Nos. 466, 542.

       SCOTT, See No. 287

       SCUDERY, See Nos. 320, 335

       SEDLEY, See No. 282

       SEEDO
920   Roberts, Edgar V. "Mr. Seedo's London Career and
        His Work with Henry Fielding." Philological
        Quarterly, XLV (1966), 179-190.
            Uses The London Stage to describe the
        career of Seedo, theatre music director, com-
        poser and organist in London from the mid
        1720's until 1736, who collaborated with wri-
        ters of ballad operas, including Fielding and
        Charles Coffey.

SENTIMENTAL DRAMA
921 Parnell, Paul E. "The Sentimental Mask." Publications of the Modern Language Association,
LXXVIII (1963), 529-535.
A study of the moral ambiguity of sentimentalism. Reviews previous scholarship on
the definition of sentimentalism and includes
references to Cumberlan's West Indian(1771),
Lillo's The London Merchant(1731), Steele's
The Lying Lover(1703), and The Conscious Lovers
(1722), Cibber's Love's Last Shift(1722), and
The Careless Husband (1704).

922 --"The Sentimental Mask." Restoration Drama:
Modern Essays in Criticism. (A Galaxy Book).
Edited by John Loftis. New York: Oxford University Press, 1966). 285-297.
Reprinted from PMLA, LXXVIII(1963) 529-
535. Attempts to define the basic relationship
between sentimentalism and virtue or morality,
and to explain why the term carries a general-
ly unfavorable connotation. See Also No.103

SENTIMENTAL, See Also Nos. 108, 124, 126, 423, 462,
532, 897

SETTING, See No. 183

SETTLE
923 Barsam, Richard Meran. "A Critical Edition of
Elkanah Settle's Cambyses, King of Persia."
Ph.D. University of California, 1967. (Order
No. 67-13, 736).
Provides text with relevant critical and
textual apparatus.

924 Doyle, Ann Therese. "The Empress of Morocco; a
Critical Edition of the Play and the Contro-
versy Surrounding it." Ph.D. University of
Illinois, 1963. (Order No. 63-5089).
Investigates the attack of Dryden, Crowne,
and Shadwell on the play and Settle's response.

925 Zielske, Harald. "Handlungsort und Buhnenbild im
17. Jahrhundert. Untersuchungen zur Raumdar-
stellung im europäischen Barock-theater." Ph.D.
FU Berlin, 1965.

Includes a study of scenery in Settle's
The Empress of Morocco. See Also Nos. 550, 878

SETTLE, See Also Nos. 285, 877, 950

SHADWELL
926   Shadwell, Thomas. The Virtuoso. Edited by Marjorie Hope Nicolson and David Stuart Rodes.
(Regents Restoration Drama Series). Lincoln:
University of Nebraska Press, 1966.
    Includes critical introduction and notes.

927   Alssid, Michael W. Thomas Shadwell. New York:
Twayne Publishers, Inc., 1967, 191 pp.
    A biographical and critical study of Shad-
well's life and works whose general purpose
is to show "how highly conscious an artist
Shadwell was and how intelligently and percep-
tively he translated into his plays many of
the profound and ironic views of man, society,
and art which he and his age held."

928   Dearmin, Michael G. "Thomas Shadwell: Playwright."
Ph.D. University of Wisconsin, 1967. (Order
No. 66-9899).
    Studies Shadwell as the best of the Restor-
ation dramatists of character and situation
and examines his plays in light of his own
theories of drama.

929   Edmunds, John. "Shadwell and the Anonymous Timon"
Notes and Queries, XIV (1967), 218-221.
    Discusses the extent of Shadwell's bor-
rowing from the anonymous play for his 1678
adaptation of Shakespeare's Timon of Athens.
See Also Nos. 264, 265, 342, 368

930   Love, H.H.R. "The Authorship of the Postscript of
Notes and Observations on The Empress of Morocco." Notes and Queries, New Ser., XIII (1966),
27-28.
    Attributes the postscript to Thomas Shad-
well.

931   Pearsall, Ronald. "The Case for Shadwell." Month,
New Ser., XXIX (1963), 364-367.

Suggests that Shadwell's reputation might
have equaled that of his contemporaries had he
not have been involved in a series of unhappy
events.

932   Smith, John Harrington. "Shadwell, the Ladies,
        and the Change in Comedy." Restoration Drama:
        Modern Essays in Criticism. (A Galaxy Book).
        Edited by John Loftis. (New York: Oxford Uni-
        versity Press, 1966), 236-252.
                Reprinted from Modern Philology, XLVI
        (1948), 22-33.Differences between Restoration
        comedy and the comedy of the early 18th cen-
        tury may be attributed to Shadwell's attempt
        to correct the dubious morality of the plays of
        his contemporaries and to ladies of the audi-
        ence who deplored the stage's cynicism and
        immorality. See Also Nos. 217, 285, 986

933   Sorelius, Gunnar. "Shadwell Deviating into
        Sense: Timon of Athens and the Duke of Bucking-
        ham." Studia Neophilologica,XXXVI(1964),232-244.
                The influence of Buckingham and the country
        party on the aesthetic, political, and moral
        concepts in Shadwell's adaptation. Shadwell's
        Timon reflects Buckingham. See Also No. 171,
        223

934   Towers, Tom H. "The Lineage of Shadwell: An
        Approach to MacFlecknoe."Studies in English
        Literature, 1500-1900, III(1963), 323-334.
                Examines the poem as a theatrical docu-
        ment in terms of dramatic allusions and struc-
        ture.

935   Vernon, P.F. "Social Satire in Shadwell's Timon."
        Studia Neophilologica, XXXV(1963),221-226.
                Shadwell's adaptation is a satirical re-
        flection on the evil effects of money on
        society. See Also No. 924

        SHAFTESBURY
936   Alderman, William E. "English Editions of
        Shaftesbury's Characteristics." Papers of the
        Bibliographical Society of America, LXI (1967),
        315,334.

Lists 17 "authenticated English editions"
between 1711 and 1964. 13 editions were published in the 18th century.

937   Tuveson, Ernest. "The Importance of Shaftes-
       bury." Restoration Drama: Modern Essays in
       Criticism. (A Galaxy Book). Edited by John
       Loftis. (New York: Oxford University Press,
       1966), 253-284.
            Reprinted from A Journal of English Liter-
       ary History, XX(1953),267-299. Discusses the
       extent of Shaftesbury's influence on the 18th
       century through his theory of the "moral sense"
       and his glorification of external nature.

938   --"Shaftesbury and the Age of Sensibility."
       Studies in Criticism and Aesthetics, 1660-1800:
       Essays in Honour of Samuel Holt Monk. Edited
       by Howard Anderson and John S. Shea.(Minneapolis:
       University of Minnesota Press,1967),73-93.
            Corrects misinterpretations of Shaftes-
       bury's philosophy and discusses his influence
       on his own time and thereafter.

SHAKESPEARE
939   "Acting Characteristics via EDP."Shakespeare
       Newsletter, XVI (1966), 49.
            A review of the Data Processing project
       of Ben R. Schneider, Jr. of Lawrence University,
       whose work on The London Stage may lead to
       evidence for interpretation of Shakespearean
       roles on the 18th century English stage.

940   Alexander, Peter, editor. Studies in Shakespeare.
       Oxford: Oxford University Press, 1964.
            Paperback reprint of 10 British Academy
       Shakespeare Lectures. Includes Alice Walker's
       "Edward Capell and his Edition of Shakespeare."

941   Angus, William. "Acting Shakespeare." Queen's
       Quarterly, LXXII(1965), 313-333.
            Brief section on the acting styles of
       Betterton, Garrick, and Macklin.

942   Bell, Mary. "Walter Whiter's Notes on Shakespeare."
       Shakespeare Survey, XX(1967),83-94.

A selection and discussion of notes not
included in Walter Whiter's Specimen of a Commentary on Shakespeare (1794).

943   Brennecke, Ernest. Shakespeare in Germany, 1590-
       1700. Chicago: The University of Chicago Press,
       1964, 301 pp.
            A translation of five German versions of
       Shakespeare's plays. A brief introduction to
       each work demonstrates the role played by
       quasi-Shakespearean material in the development
       of Shakespeare's reputation on the Continent.

944   Brockbank, J.P. "Shakespeare and the Fashion of
       These Times." Shakespeare Survey, XVI (1963),
       30-41.
            Considers eighteenth century interpreta-
       tions of Cleopatra's suicide speech opening
       Act V, Scene ii of Antony and Cleopatra.

945   Brown, Arthur. "The Great Variety of Readers."
       Shakespeare Survey, XVIII (1965), 11-21.
            A critical study of Shakespearean editions,
       notes that the 18th century editors of Shake-
       speare established a tradition of publishing
       'modern' texts designed for the general reading
       public and therefore containing a minimum of
       scholarly explication.

946   Brown, F. Andrew. "Shakespeare and English Drama
       in the German Popular Journals, 1717-1759."
       Kentucky Foreign Language Quarterly, XII (1965).
       13-27.
            Presents samples and discussion of German
       journals that demonstrate an interest in Shake-
       speare and English drama even before Lessing's
       Literaturbrief. Includes references to a dis-
       cussion of Moore's Gamester and Lillo's London
       Merchant in the Hamburgische Beytrage (1753).

947   --"Shakespeare in Germany: Dryden, Langbaine,
       and the Acta Eruditorum." The Germanic Review,
       XL (1965), 86-95.
            Acta Eruditorum, a scholarly journal
       founded by Otto Mencke in 1682, set the tone
       of subsequent German studies in Shakespeare and
       Dryden with its introduction of the controversy

176

regarding "ingenio" and "arte."

948   Camden, Carroll. "Songs and Choruses in The Tem-
       pest." Philological Quarterly, XLI(1962), 114-122.
       Suggests that two songs in a unique copy
       of Songs and Choruses in the Tempest were written
       by Sheridan for production in 1777.

949   Campbell, Oscar James, editor: Edward G. Quinn,
       associate editor. The Reader's Encyclopedia
       of Shakespeare. New York: Crowell, 1966, 1014 pp.
       Provides information on productions,
       actors, and critics of the 18th century.

950   Carlisle, Carol J. "Hamlet's 'Cruelty' in the
       Nunnery Scene: The Actors' Views." Shakespeare
       Quarterly, XVIII(1967), 129-140.
       A review of Actors' interpretations of
       the Nunnery scene includes references to Gar-
       rick, Charles Dibdin and William Oxberry.

951   Coleman, William S.E. "Shylock from Dogget to
       Macready." Ph.D. University of Pittsburgh, 1965.
       This chronological account of the London
       productions of The Merchant of Venice reveals
       a change in attitude among Englishmen towards
       those of the Jewish race. Interpretations of
       Shylock rendered by Charles Macklin, Thomas
       King, John Henderson and John Kemble are ana-
       lyzed in detail.

952   Creeth, Edmund. "Landmarks of Criticism." The
       Shakespeare Newsletter, XIV(1964), 83.
       Reviews Some Remarks on the Tragedy of
       Hamlet, Prince of Denmark (London, 1736),
       attributed to Sir Thomas Hammer and sometimes
       cited as the first extended work of Shakespear-
       ean criticism.

953   Cudworth, Charles. "Two Georgian Classics: Arne
       and Stevens." Music and Letters, XLV(1964),
       146-153.
       Outlines the careers of two eighteenth
       century Shakespearean lyricists and chronicles
       the composition and publication of their most
       famous songs.

954   Dean, Winton. "Shakespeare in the Opera House."
       Shakespeare Survey, XVIII (1965), 75-93.
       Brief mention of Restoration and 18th
       century operatic adaptations of Shakespeare. A
       valuable list of composers, titles, and libret-
       tists of known operas based on Shakespeare's
       dramas concludes the article.

955   Donohue, Joseph Walter." Toward the Romantic Con-
       cept of Dramatic Character: Richard III and
       Macbeth in Criticism and Performance, 1740-1820."
       Ph.D. Princeton University, 1965. (Order No.
       66-4991).
       The 18th century "closet" criticism of
       Johnson, Montague, and Whately, and the thea-
       trical productions of Garrick and Mrs. Siddons
       reveal the increasing tendency to interpret
       Shakespeare's heroes in terms of their "mental
       processes."

956   Eastman, A.M. and G.B. Harrison, editors. Shake-
       speare's Critics: From Jonson to Auden: A
       Medley of Judgments. Ann Arbor: University of
       Michigan Press, 1964, 346 pp.
       Popular anthology of Shakespearean cri-
       ticism arranged in a series of "debates."
       Includes critical comments by Johnson and Pope.

957   Evans, G. Blakemore. "The Douai Manuscript--Six
       Shakespearean Transcripts (1694-95)." Philo-
       logical Quarterly, XLI (1962), 158-172.
       Discusses transcripts of Twelfth Night,
       As You Like It, The Comedy of Errors, Romeo
       and Juliet, Julius Caesar, and Macbeth. See
       Also Nos. 469, 483, 574, 868

958   --Shakespearean Prompt-books of the Seventeenth
       Century. Vol. LV:Part i. (Published for the
       Bibliographical Society of the University of
       Virginia). Charlottesville: University of Vir-
       ginia Press, 1966.
       Reproduces the text of the Smock Alley
       Hamlet (c.1676-1679), the earliest prompt-book
       of the play now extant. Includes introduction
       and collations.

959   Francis, F.C. "The Shakespeare Collection in the
      British Museum." Theatre Research, VI(1964),
      51-56.
          On the theatre collection which David Gar-
      rick bequeathed to the Museum in 1779.

960   Fried, Gisela. "Das Charakterbild Shakespeares
      im 17. und 18. Jahrhundert." Deutsche Shake-
      speare-Gesellschaft West (Jahrbuch, 1965), 161-
      183.
          Concerns 17th and 18th century critical
      assessments of Shakespeare's personal qualities.

961   Geckle, George Leo. "A History of the Literary
      Criticism of Shakespeare's Measure for Measure."
      Ph.D. University of Virginia, 1965, (Order No.
      66-3183).
          See the eighteenth century criticism of
      Measure for Measure as primarily an outgrowth
      of the era's philosophical penchant for order
      and balance.

962   Gordan, John D. "The Bard and the Book: Editions
      of Shakespeare in the Seventeenth Century."
      Bulletin of the New York Public Library, LXVIII
      (1964), 462-476.
          Describes the New York Public Library's
      Shakespeare holdings printed between 1600 and
      1685.

963   Grover, P.R. "The Ghost of Dr. Johnson: L. C.
      Knights and D.A. Traversi on Hamlet." Essays
      in Criticism, XVII(1967), 143-157.
          The criticism of L.C. Knights in An Approach
      to Hamlet and D.A. Traversi in An Approach to
      Shakespeare reflects the pre-Romantic and now
      outdated moral criticism of Johnson.

964   Gruber, Christian P. "Falstaff on an 18th Cen-
      tury Battlefield." Theatre Notebook, XXI
      (Spring, 1967), 120-121.
          Affirms that the I Henry IV plate from
      Robert Walker's edition of Shakespeare (Lon-
      don, 1734) provides authentic evidence of
      current stage practice.

965   Halliday, F.E. "Four Centuries of Shakespearean
Production." History Today, XIV(1964),98-106.
Mentions interpretations by Davenant,
Betterton, Garrick, and Macklin.

966   Harbage, Alfred. Conceptions of Shakespeare.
Cambridge: Harvard University Press, 1966, 164 pp.
A series of five lectures with three reprinted and revised for this edition. While
references to the Restoration and 18th century
are made throughout the book, Chapter 3, "These
Our Actors," contains matter of special interest, concerning Betterton and Garrick.

967   Hartnoll, Phyllis, editor. Shakespeare in Music.
London: Macmillan and Company, 1964, 333 pp.
Essays on musical achievements which drew
their inspiration directly from Shakespeare's
plays and poems. In "Song and Part-Song Settings of Shakespeare's Lyrics, 1660-1900",
pp. 50-87, Charles Cudworth outlines the history of compositions written especially for
theatrical productions of Shakespeare. Winton
Dean, "Shakespeare and Opera," pp. 89-175,
surveys briefly the operatic expressions of
Purcell, Leveridge, and Smith. A "Catalogue of
Musical Works Based on the Plays and Poetry of
Shakespeare" is appended to the work.

968   Hoffman, D.S. "Some Shakespearian Music, 1660-1900."
Shakespeare Survey, XVIII(1965), 94-101.
Traces the musical elements in Shakespeare's
plays from Davenant's Macbeth to the late 18th
century operatic interpretations of Mrs. Jordan,
Michael Kelly, and Mrs. Crouch.

969   Hyde, Mary. "Shakespeare's Head." Shakespeare
Quarterly, XVI (1965), 139-143.
The Shakespeare protrait, discovered by
Mr. Jacques Vellerkoop in 1962 and exhibited at
the Morgan Library in 1964, probably belonged
to Jacob Tonson (1656-1736), publisher, book-
seller and collector. It was probably viewed
by Dryden, Wycherley, Johnson, and many other
writers of Tonson's acquaintance.

970   Jackson, MacD. P. "Langbaine and the Memorial

Versions of 'Henry VI, Parts II and III.'"
Notes and Queries, New Ser., XI (1964), 134.
Langbaine's New Catalogue of English Plays
(1688) confirms modern scholarly opinion that
The Contention and The True Tragedy (corrupt
versions of Henry VI, Parts II and III) were
derived from Shakespeare's play and not vice
versa.

971   Jenkins, Harold. "'Hamlet' Then Till Now." Shakespeare Survey, XIII (1965), 34-45.
An historical view of Hamlet's reputation.
Early 18th century treatments of Hamlet stressed
the virtue, boldness and manliness of the hero
(e.g. Betterton's portrayal). Those after 1763
were hymed for their sensitivity in capturing
the personality of an irresolute, inconsistent
and pathetic young man.

972   Jensen, Niels, Lyhnne. "Shakespeare in Denmark."
Durham University Journal, LVI (1964), 91-98.
On Shakespearean criticism and transla-
tion in Denmark during the 18th century.

973   Knight, G. Wilson. "Timon of Athens and Its
Dramatic Descendants." A Review of English
Literature, II (October, 1961), 9-18.
A brief study of the themes of Timon of
Athens and its influence on English drama and
dramatists of the eighteenth and nineteenth
centuries.

974   Kujoory, Parvin. "The Development of Shakespeare
Biography From 1592 Through 1790." Ph.D. Catholic University of America, 1967. (Order No.
67-15, 450).
Discusses biographers' scholarship, their
sources for facts, and their opinions and attitudes. Includes a study of Rowe's biography
and its use by Pope, Johnson, Warburton, and
Stevens.

975   Laver, James. Costume in the Theatre. London:
George G. Harrap, 1964. 223 pp.
Contains a popular account of the staging
of Shakespeare's plays from Davenant to Keane.
Includes 25 illustrations of 18th century ac-
tors and actresses in key roles.

181

976   Leech, Clifford. "Shakespeare, Cibber, and the
       Tudor Myth." Shakespearean Essays. (Knoxville,
       Tennessee: The University of Tennessee Press,
       1964), 79-95.

977   Lelyveld, Toby Bookholtz. Shylock on the Stage.
       Western Reserve University Press, 1960; Lon-
       don: Routledge, 1961, 149 pp.
            A careful tracing of the Shylock role
       from the beginning to the present. Contains
       references to portrayals by Edmund Kean, Wil-
       liam Charles Macready, Edwin Booth, and
       Charles Macklin.

978   Levin, Richard. "Anatomical Geography in 'The
       Tempest,' IV, i. 235-238." Notes and Queries
       New Ser., XI, (1964), 142-146.
            Steevens' 1778 edition of Shakespeare
       provides the most satisfactory interpretation
       of Stephano's joke in The Tempest, IV, i.

979   McAleer, John J. "Malone and Ritson." Shake-
       speare Newsletter, XIII(1963), 12.
            Clears Malone of the charge that he
       bought three volumes of Ritson's manuscripts
       for the latter's proposed edition of Shake-
       speare in order to destroy them.

980   McCredie, Andrew D. "John Christopher Smith as
       a Dramatic Composer." Music and Letters,
       XLV (1964), 22-38.
            Reevaluates the work of Handel's assist-
       ant, especially his composition of two Shake-
       spearean operas.

981   McManaway, James G. "A 'Hamlet' Reminiscence in
       1660." Notes and Queries, CCVI(1961), 388.
            In Thomas Jordan's Speech Made to ...the
       Lord General Monk.

982   --"Richard II at Covent Garden." Shakespeare
       Quarterly, XV (Spring, 1964), 161-175.
            Discusses the manuscript transcribed by
       John Roberts for the revival of Richard II
       at Covent Garden in 1738.

983   Marder, Louis. His Exits and his Entrances: The
       Story of Shakespeare's Reputation. Philadelphia
       and New York: J.B. Lippincott, 1963, 386 pp.
           Frequent allusions to Neoclassical Shake-
       spearean critics, actors, adaptations, festi-
       vals, and productions.

984   --"Shakespeare Concordances: 1787-1967."
       Shakespeare Newsletter, XVII (1967), 33-34.
           Includes descriptions of concordances by
       Pope, Andrew Beckett, and Samuel Ayscough.

985   Meldrum, Ronald Murray. "Changing Attitudes
       Toward Selected Characters of Shakespeare."
       Ph.D. Arizona State University, 1965.(Order
       No. 65-10377).
           Interest in Shakespeare's characters dur-
       ing the Restoration and eighteenth century
       was both literary and theatrical. The acting
       style of David Garrick had a significant in-
       fluence on contemporary interpretations of
       Shakespearian heroes.

986   Merchant, W. Moelwyn. "Shakespeare 'Made Fit.'"
       Restoration Theatre. Edited by John Russell
       Brown and Bernard Harris. (Stratford-Upon-
       Avon Studies, 6). (London: Edward Arnold;
       New York: St. Martin's Press, 1965,195-219.
           Discusses the principles used especially
       by Tate, Dryden, and Shadwell in adapting
       Shakespeare to the Restoration stage.

987   Moore, Robert E. "The Music to Macbeth."Musical
       Quarterly, XLVII (1961), 22-40.
           On the eighteenth century "original mu-
       sick."

988   Muir, Kenneth. "Shakespeare's Imagery--Then and
       Now." Shakespeare Survey,XVIII(1965), 46-57.
           Includes an analysis of Rev. Walter Whiter's
       A Specimen of a Commentary on Shakespeare pub-
       lished in 1794.

989   Nichols, James W. "Shakespeare as a Character in
       Drama:1679-1899." Educational Theatre Journal,
       XV (1963), 24-32.

Shakespeare was often used to criticize
contemporary drama in prologues and epilogues
as in Dryden's adaptation of Troilus and
Cressida, George Granville's The Jew of Venice,
and George Sewall's epilogue to The Tragedy
of Sir Walter Raleigh. Processions of Shakespearean characters were also popular as in
Garrick's Harlequin's Invasion.

990   Nilan, Mary Margaret. "The Stage History of The
       Tempest: A Question of Theatricality." Ph. D.
       Northwestern University, 1967. (Order No. 67-
       15, 305).
               Discusses how the theatricality of the
       play has been handled in productions over the
       years and how the various approaches have been
       received by audiences and reviewers. Includes
       a study of adaptations from 1667 to 1837.

991   Odell, G.C.D. Shakespeare from Betterton to
       Irving. 2 vols.,with a new introduction by
       Robert Hamilton Ball. New York: Dover Publica-
       tions, 1966.
               A paperback edition of the work originally
       published in 1920. Book I concerns Shakespeare
       on the London stage in the Age of Betterton
       (1660-1710); Book II, The Age of Cibber (1710-
       1742); and Book III, The Age of Garrick,(1742-
       1776). Each book treats the theatres, plays,
       scenery, staging and costumes.

992   Odell, George C. D. Shakespeare: From Betterton
       to Irving. New York: Benjamin Bloom, 1963. 2
       vols. 954 pp.
               Reprint of Professor Odell's chronological
       history of Shakespeare on the London Stage from
       1660 to 1902, first published in 1920. Vol.
       I concentrates on stage production during the
       theatrical careers of Betterton, Cibber, and
       Garrick. Illustrations.

993   Price, Joseph G. "From Farce to Romance: All's
       Well That Ends Well, 1756-1811." Shakespeare
       Jahrbuch, XCIX (1963), 57-71.
               A study of the eighteenth century adapta-
       tions of Garrick, Pilon, and Kemble. "The
       freedom and exuberance of the theatre in the

first half of the century were curbed by the
drift toward Romantic sentimentality and Vic-
torian prudery at the end of the century; that
drift is recorded in the increasing modifica-
tions of the original Shakespearean text which
led finally to the expurgated version of John
Kemble."

994 Schneider, Duane B. "Dr. Garth and Shakespeare:
a Borrowing." English Language Notes, I(1964),
200-202.
  Garth's description of an apothecary's
shop in The Dispensary (1699) was probably an
adaptation of a similar description in Romeo
and Juliet."Because of his acquaintance with
Dryden and Rowe, it would seem reasonable to
suggest that Garth had some knowledge of Shakespeare's plays."

995 Sen, Sailendra Kumar. "Shakespeare as a Borrower:
Kellet and Eighteenth-Century Critics." Notes
and Queries, New Ser.,X(1963), 332-334.
  Kellet's thesis about the gaps in Shakespeare's plays "was one which seems to have
been well understood and well illustrated in
Johnson's time."

996 Shattuck, Charles. "Shakespeare Promptbook Collections." Restoration and 18th Century
Theatre Research, III (May, 1964),9-11.
  Takes into account recent scholarship on
17th and 18th century promptbooks. See Also
Nos. 338, 364, 468, 471, 482, 484, 585, 586,
639, 832, 860, 861, 1079

997 Shattuck, Charles H. The Shakespeare Promptbooks:
A Descriptive Catalogue. Urbana: University
of Illinois Press, 1965, 553 pp.
  A catalogue describing all the marked
copies of Shakespeare used in English-language
professional theatre productions from the 1620's
to 1961 that are available in public collections,
in the production departments of the late Old
Vic and the Festival theatres at the three
Stratford. Entries are arranged alphabetically
with the title of the play and then chronologically.

998   Shoemaker, Neille. "The Aesthetic Criticism of
Hamlet from 1692 to 1699." Shakespeare Quar-
terly, XVI (1965), 99-103.
         The publication of replies to the studies
of Thomas Rymer and Jeremy Collier made a be-
ginning in the field of aesthetic criticism.
James Drake, author of The Ancient and Modern
Stages Survey'd, Or, Mr. Collier's View of the
Immorality and Profaneness of the English Stage
Set in a True Light (1699), is entitled to
rank as the first Hamlet critic.

999   Smith, David Nicol, editor. Eighteenth Century
Essays on Shakespeare. Second Edition. Oxford:
Clarendon Press, 1963, 340 pp.
         A new edition of an important work ori-
ginally published by Professor Smith in 1903.
Especially noteworthy is his revised commen-
tary on Johnson.

1000   --Shakespeare in the Eighteenth Century. New
York: Oxford University Press, 1967.
         A reprint of the 1928 edition which exa-
mines the ways in which 18th century critics,
scholars, and actors contributed to Shakespeare's fame.

1001   Spencer, Christopher. "'Count Paris's Wife':
Romeo and Juliet on the Early Restoration Stage."
Texas Studies in Literature and Language,VII
(1966), 309-316.
         Uses John Downes' description of the play's
performance at Lincoln's Inn Fields in the
early 1660's to discuss the possibilities of
an adaptation before that of James Howard.
See Also Nos. 86, 377, 489, 604, 821, 859,
865, 1055, 1080, 1084

1002   --ed. Five Restoration Adaptations of Shakespeare.
Urbana: University of Illinois Press, 1965.,
475 pp.
         Includes Tate's King Lear(1681), Cibber's
Richard III(1700), the operatic Tempest(1674),
Davenant's Macbeth(1674), and Granville's Jew
of Venice (1701).

1003   Spencer, Hazelton. Shakespeare Improved; the
        Restoration Versions in Quarto and on the Stage.
        New York: Ungar, 1963, 406 pp.
            A new edition of the 1927 study of Shake-
        speare's plays produced during the Restoration
        from 1660 to 1710, the year of Betterton's
        death. See Also Nos. 111, 121, 231, 295, 323,
        470, 866, 885, 935, 1050, 1083

1004   Spencer, T.J.B. "The Course of Shakespeare
        Criticism." Shakespeare's World, ed. James
        Sutherland and Joel Hurtsfield(London, 1964),
        156-173.
            Contains a brief survey of Restoration
        and 18th century Shakespearean scholarship.

1005   --"The Great Rival: Shakespeare and the Classical
        Dramatists," Shakespeare: 1564-1964.Edited by
        Edward A. Bloom. (Providence: Brown University
        Press, 1964), 177-193.
            An account of critical comparisons be-
        tween Shakespeare and the Ancients. Alludes to
        the comments of Johnson, Dryden, Rymer, and
        Collier.

1006   Steensma, Robert C. "Shakespeare Criticism in
        Eighteenth-Century England: A Bibliography of
        Modern Studies." Shakespeare Newsletter,XI
        (November, 1961), 39.
            A list of 57 books and articles from
        1863-1960. Not annotated.

1007   --"Shakespeare on the Eighteenth-Century English
        Stage: A Bibliography." Shakespeare Newsletter
        XI (September, 1961), 29.
            A list of forty-four of the more important
        books and articles. Not annotated.

1008   Summers, Montague, ed. Shakespeare Adaptations.
        New York: Haskell House, 1966, 282 pp.
            A reprint of the 1922 edition of Davenant
        and Dryden's The Tempest(1670), Duffett's
        The Mock-Tempest(1675), and Tate's King Lear
        (1681), includes introduction and notes.
        See Also Nos. 576, 580, 581, 587, 593, 596,
        603, 605, 612, 631, 898, 929, 1078, 1079, 1114,
        1115, 1148

1009   Weinmann, R. "Shakespeare's Publikum und Plat-
        formbuhne im Spiegel klassizistischer Kritik.
        (bei Rymer, Dryden, u.a.)." Bulletin de la
        Faculte des lettres de Strasbourg, XLIII
        (Mai-Juin, 1965), 891-1007.

1010   Wells, Stanley. "Shakespearian Burlesques."
        Shakespeare Quarterly, XVI(1965), 49-61.
                Although the article deals mainly with
        the burlesques of John Poole, introductory re-
        marks refer briefly to burlesques by Thomas
        Duffett and to the burlesque instinct surround-
        ing Buckingham's The Rehearsal. Fielding's
        Tom Thumb and Sheridan's The Critic. See Also
        Nos. 559, 569, 572, 573, 577, 591, 592

SHELDONIAN THEATRE,   See No. 1096

SHELTON,   See No. 1115

SHERBO,   See No. 822

SHERIDAN
1011   F. Russell, Norma H. "Some Uncollected Authors
        XXXVIII: Frances Sheridan, 1724-1766." Book
        Collector, XIII(1964), 196-205.
                Brief biography of the wife of R.B. Sheri-
        dan. Includes a checklist of her plays, novels,
        and prose pieces.

SHERIDAN, MRS..   See No. 133

SHERIDAN, RICHARD
1012   Sheridan, Richard Brinsley. The Critic, or A
        Tragedy Rehearsed. Edited with an Introduction,
        Translation, and Notes by Germaine Landré-
        Augier. Paris: Aubier, Editions Montaigne,
        Collection Bilingue, 1963,   231 pp.
                English text with French translations on
        opposite pages. The introduction in French re-
        views current scholarship on the play.

1013   --The Rivals. Edited by A. Norman Jeffares.
        (English Classics-New Series). London: Mac-
        millan; New York: St.Martin's Press, 1967.
                Includes general introduction, notes,
        critical extracts, and selected bibliography.

1014   --The School for Scandal. Edited by A. Norman
       Jeffares. (English Classics-New Series). Lon-
       don: Macmillan; New York: St.Martin's Press,
       1967.
               Besides general introduction, notes, cri-
       tical extracts, and selected bibliography this
       edition includes two appendices: one on Sheri-
       dan's rewriting of the play taken from Thomas
       Moore's Memoirs(1825) and the other on details
       of the play's history from R. Crompton Rhodes'
       Harlequin Sheridan (1933).

1015   --The School for Scandal. Edited by John Loftis.
       (Crofts Classics). New York: Appleton-Century-
       Crofts, 1966.
               With introduction, notes, and selected
       bibliography.

1016   Bradbrook, Frank W. "Lydia Languish, Lydia Ben-
       net, and Dr. Fordyce's Sermons." Notes and
       Queries, New Ser., XI(1964), 421-423.
               Further comment on the heroines of Sheri-
       dan and Austen supplementing E.E. Phare's
       article. See No. 147

1017   Cichoke, Anthony J. "The Rivals: A Production
       Book." M.A. Saint Louis University,1964.

1018   Coggin, Frederick Marsh. "The Design of the
       Setting for The Rivals." M.A. University of
       Georgia, 1964.

1019   Deelman, Christian. "The Original Cast of The
       School for Scandal." Review of English Studies,
       XIII(1962), 257-266.
               The success of The School for Scandal as
       a theatrical production can be traced to Sheri-
       dan's putting the play together "with a parti-
       cular cast in view."

1020   Delpech, Jeanine. "Sheridan, le Beaumarchais
       Anglais." Nouvelles Litteraires, (17 Mai,1962),
       p. 3.

1021   Donaldson, Ian. "New Papers of Henry Holland
       and R.B. Sheridan: (1) Holland's Drury Lane,
       1794." Theatre Notebook,XVI(Spring,1962)90-96.

Concerns the correspondence between
Holland and Sheridan on the rebuilding of
Drury Lane in 1794.

1022 --"New Papers of Henry Holland and R.B. Sheridan:
(11) The Hyde Park Corner Operas and the Dor-
mant Patent." Theatre Notebook,XVI (Summer,
1962,) 117-125.
Sheridan's attempts to defend the monopoly
rights of Drury Lane and the Covent Gardens by
proposing a new theatre and two opera houses
at Hyde Park Corner which woudl be under the
control of the two major theatres.

1023 Dulck, Jean. Les Comédies de R. B. Sheridan.
Paris: Didier, 1962, 611 pp.
Historical, formal, textual and compara-
tive study of the comedies.

1024 Fiske, Roger. "A Score for 'The Duenna.'"
Music and Letters, XLII (April, 1961), 132-141.
The author attempts to discover the original score, or parts of it, that were evidently
taken from existing airs. Comment on the
popularity of the opera, for which Sheridan
provided the libretto.

1025 g.n. [sic.] "Kritische Rückschau." Forum, VIII
(October, 1961), 454.
On the School for Scandal.

1026 Jackson, J.R. de J. "The Importance of Witty
Dialogue in The School for Scandal." Modern
Language Notes, LXXVI(November,1961),601-607.

1027 Landfield, Jerome. "Sheridan." Quarterly Journal
of Speech, XLVIII (1962), 5-7.
Sheridan's uncertain position in British
public address.

1028 Lutaud, Oliver. "Des acharniens d'Aristophane au
critique de Sheridan." Les Langues Modernes,
LX (1966), 433-438.

1029 Niederauer, Rev.George Hugh. "Wit and Sentiment
in Sheridan's Comedies of Manners." Ph.D. University of Southern California, 1966. (Order

190

No. 66-11, 579).
Analyzes the plots, characters, and dialogue of The Rivals and The School for Scandal to determine the extent to which Sheridan combined conventions of the Restoration and sentimental comic traditions in his two most successful comedies of manners.

1030   Nussbaum, R.D. "Poetry and Music in 'The Duenna.'" Westerly, No. 1 (1963), 58-63.
Sheridan's The Duenna, with music by Thomas Linley and son, is considered in "the history of light music drama from Gilbert and Sullivan."

1031   Phare, E.E. "Lydia Languish, Lydia Bennet, and Dr. Fordyce's Sermons." Notes and Queries, New Ser.,XI (1964), 182-183.
The disrespect of Sheridan's heroine in The Rivals and Jane Austen's Lydia in Pride and Prejudice for Dr. James Fordyce's Sermons for Young Women (1765).

1032   Price, C.J.L. "The Completion of The School for Scandal." Times Literary Supplement.(December 28, 1967), p.1265.
Discusses circumstances surrounding the composition of the play. Events and personalities contemporary with Sheridan may explain incidents and characterizations in the play.

1033   --"The Second Crewe MS of The School for Scandal." Papers of the Bibliographical Society of America, LXI(1967), 351-356.
A description of the recently discovered Hodgson Ms. reveals that it is not the second Crewe Ms. but that a third Crewe Ms. is or was in existence.

1034   --"Sheridan-Linley Documents." Theatre Notebook, XXI (Summer, 1967), 165-167.
Describes the papers of Sheridan and his wife now at the British Museum. The best of them is a copy of their marriage articles.

1035   Price, Cecil. "Another Crewe MS. of The School for Scandal?" Papers of the Bibliographical Society of America, LVII(1963),79-81.

191

Textual differences between G.H. Nettleton's text, the Yale MS and the Dublin edition
of 1799 suggest that there might have been two
Crewe MSS.

1036   --"The Columbia Manuscript of The School for
        Scandal." Columbia Library Columns, XI(1961),
        25-29.

1037   --"The Larpent Manuscript of St. Patrick's Day."
        Huntington Library Quarterly,XXIX(1966),183-
        189.
            More than any other copy of the play, the
        Larpent manuscript shows most clearly Sheridan's
        personal touch.

1038   --editor. The Letters of Richard Brinsley Sheridan. Oxford: The Clarendon Press, 1966, 3 vols.
            A chronological arrangement of 937 letters
        written by Sheridan between 1766 and 1816.
        Includes introduction and index.   See Also
        Nos. 30, 146, 616, 626

1039   --"Nouverre and Sheridan, 1776." Theatre Research, VII,(1965), 45-46.
            A hitherto unpublished letter of Charles
        Greville contains details on the attempts of
        Richard Sheridan to obtain the services of
        the balletmaster, Jean-Georges Nouverre for
        Drury Lane.

1040   --"Sheridan's Doxology." London Times Literary
        Supplement, 4 May, 1962, p. 309.
            Sheridan's signature on the manuscript
        of The School For Scandal.

1041   Pryce-Jones, Alan. "The School for Scandal."
        Theatre Arts, XLVII (March,1963), 57.
            The January 24, 1963 production of Sheridan's play at the Majestic Theatre in New
        York.

1042   Rothwell, Kenneth S. "The School for Scandal:
        The Comic Spirit in Sheridan and Rowlandson."
        The School for Scandal: Thomas Rowlandson's
        London.(Lawrence: Kansas University Museum
        of Art, 1967), 23-45.

Analyzes and compares the comic spirit
in Sheridan's play and in Rowlandson's water-
color of Vauxhall Gardens.

1043   Skinner, Quentin. "Sheridan and Whitbread at
        Drury Lane, 1809-1815." Theatre Notebook,
        XVII (Winter, 1962-63), 40-46.
            Presents problems which seem to have been
        ignored in the appreciation of Whitbread's
        works after the fire of 1809.

1044   --"Sheridan and Whitbread at Drury Lane, 1809-
        1815, II ." Theatre Notebook, XVII (Spring,
        1963), 74-79.
            Because of Sheridan's contention that
        Whitbread was "the scoundrel," the latter's
        positive achievements have been underrated.
        Part I of this article appeared in Theatre
        Notebook, XVII (Winter, 1962-63), 40-46.
        See Also Nos. 249, 815

1045   Tillett, Jeffrey, editor. Shakespeare, Sheridan,
        Shaw. London: Heinimann Educational Books, 1965.
            Sheridan's St. Patrick's Day. See Also
        Nos. 153, 623, 1010

1046   Willoughby, Donna Elaine. "A Comparison of
        Techniques Used by Richard Brinsley Sheridan,
        the Dramatist and Public Speaker, with an
        Evaluation of His Speech Techniques." M.A.
        University of Florida, 1964. See Also Nos.
        128, 568

        SHERIDAN, THOMAS
1047   Sheridan, Thomas. A Course of Lectures on Elo-
        cution: Together With Two Dissertations on
        Language. New York: Benjamin Blom, 1967, 392
        pp.
            A reprint of the 1798 edition includes
        Sheridan's remarks on the art of speaking in
        the theatre.

1048   Bacon, Wallace A. "The Elocutionary Career of
        Thomas Sheridan (1719-1788)." Speech Monographs,
        XXXI (1964), 1-53.
            Although primarily concerned with Sheri-
        dan's interest in the arts of reading and

speaking, this monograph also contains commentaries on Sheridan's career as actor, playwright, theatre manager, and his relationship
to Garrick.

Two appendices present "Sheridan and Garrick as Compared by Thomas Davies," and "Sheridan's and Garrick's Prescriptions for Reading
Prayer."

1049   Bryant, Donald C. "London Notes, 1769-1774."
Quarterly Journal of Speech, LII(1966), 179-
181.
Reprints an advertisement in the July
30, 1774 Middlesex Journal for a performance
by the popular mimic George Saville Carey and
a comment condemning Sheridan's "Attic Entertainment" in 1769.

1050   Sheldon, Esther K. "Sheridan's Coriolanus: An
18th Century Compromise." Shakespeare Quarterly
XIV (1963), 153-161.
Acts I and II of Sheridan's Coriolanus;
or, The Roman Matron (1752) are from Shakespeare's play: Acts III, IV, and V are chiefly
from Thomson's Coriolanus.

1051   --"Thomas Sheridan: Gentleman or Actor?" Theatre
Survey, II (1961), 3-14.
On the Kelly riots, Smock Alley Theatre,
Dublin, 1747, together with associated pamphlet
literature, and Sheridan's refusal to appease
a faction of the audience.

1052   --Thomas Sheridan of Smock-Alley. Princeton:
Princeton University Press, 1967, 530 pp.
An account of Sheridan's career as theatre
manager based on biographies of his contemporaries on 18th century newspapers, pamphlets,
playbills and on letters written to and by
Sheridan. Includes information about Sheridan's
relations with Garrick and a Smock-Alley Calendar that gives a daily record of performances
and casts.

1053   Spence, Rhoda. "Mr. Sheridan Comes to Edinburgh."
Irish Digest, LXXXI (1964), 65-67.
On the Irish actor's lectures in Scotland.

194

SHERIDAN, T. See Also No. 1081

SHUTER, See No. 13

SIDDONS, See No. 603

SIDNEY
1054   Andrews, Michael Cameron. "Sidney's Arcadia on
        the English Stage: A Study of the Dramatic
        Adaptions [sic] of The Countess of Pembroke's
        Arcadia." Ph.D. Duke University, 1966,(Order
        No. 67-6094).
            Studies nine plays that constitute all
        the English drama known to draw upon Sidney's
        Arcadia as their primary source. One 18th
        century play, Philoclea (1754), reflects the
        influence of decadent heroic drama.

SMITH
1055   Lothian, John M. "Adam Smith as a Critic of
        Shakespeare." Papers, Mainly Shakespearean.
        Edited by G.I. Duthie. (Aberdeen University
        Studies, 147). Edinburgh: Oliver and Boyd,
        1964, pp. 109. See Also No. 15

SOCIAL CRITICISM, See No. 166

SOCIAL THEME, See No. 42

SONGS, See Nos. 236, 284, 405, 428

SOPHOCLES, See No. 895

SOUTHERNE
1056   Thornton, Ralph Rees. "The Wives Excuse by
        Thomas Southerne: A Critical Edition." Ph.D.
        University of Pennsylvania, 1966.(Order No.
        66-10, 678).
            Includes a study of the play's composi-
        tion, earlier editions, staging, popular
        success, and its importance in the revival of
        the comedy of manners. See Also No. 878

SPAIN, See No. 775

SPECTACLE, See No. 1063

195

STAGE, See Nos. 78, 434, 570

STAGE MANAGER, See No. 777

STAGING

1057   Allen, Ralph G. "De Loutherbourg and Captain
        Cook. Theatre Research, IV (1962),195-211.
        The staging of Omai with settings by De
        Loutherbourg in 1785.". . . undoubtedly the
        most spectacular and costly entertainment ever
        produced in London up to that time."

1058   Banks, Howard Milton. "A Historical Survey of
        the Mise-en-Scene Employed in Shakespearean
        Productions from the Elizabethan Period to
        the Present." Ph.D. University of Southern
        California, 1963.
        Considers what changes occurred in the
        structure of the stage between 1660 and 1800,
        especially the scenic innovations of Davenant.

1059   Gage, John. "Loutherbourg: Mystagogue of the
        Sublime." History Today, XIII(1963), 332-339.
        A brief history of the theatrical
        Eidophusikon. Loutherbourg's association with
        Garrick.

1060   Green, Elvena M. "John Rich's Art of Pantomime
        as Seen in his The Necromancer, or Harlequin
        Doctor Faustus: A Comparison of the Two Faustus
        Pantomimes at Lincoln's-Inn-Fields and Drury
        Lane." Restoration and Eighteenth Century
        Theatre Research, IV (May,1965), 47-60.
        More successful and artistic than the
        rival Drury Lane production of John Thurmond's
        Harlequin Doctor Faustus, John Rich's The
        Necromancer (1723) surpasses its rival not in
        spectacular effects but in the greater care
        taken with the selection and arrangement of
        major sequences and with the development of
        the protagonist's character.

1061   Jackson, Allan Stuart. "The Perspective Land-
        scape Scene in the English Theatre, 1660-1682."
        Ph.D. The Ohio State University, 1962. (Order
        No. 63-4670).
        Studies in the pictorial appearance of

the perspective landscapes painted upon
theatrical scenery during the Restoration.
Appendices include a list of printed stage
directions, and two catalogues of paintings
representative of taste during the period.

1062 Kennedy, James Keith. "The Restoration Theatre:
A study in Period Vision." Ph.D. University
of Florida, 1963.
   Designed to meet the visual requirements
of the day, the Restoration stage combined the
best elements of the classical and the baroque
theatres.

1063 Langhans, Edward Allen. "Staging Practices in
the Restoration Theatres 1660-1682." Ph.D.
Yale University, 1965. (Order No. 65-9469).
   The development of machines, lighting,
and other theatrical effects to meet the de-
mand of Restoration audiences for spectacle
was in part responsible for the type of play
Dryden and his compatriots wrote. See Also
No. 480

1064 Martin, Lee J. "From Forestage to Proscenium:
a Study of Restoration Staging Techniques."
Theatre Survey, IV (1963), 3-28.
   From a study of text and stage directions
in several plays, it is evident that the Restoration stage increased acting space by
gradually removing it from the forestage to
the area behind the proscenium arch.

1065 Payne, Rhoda. "Stage Direction during the Restoration." Theatre Annual, XX(1963), 41-63.
   Concludes that "although the director's
role has grown in importance, its germ may
certainly be seen in the practices of directing
during the Restoration." Examines the direc-
torship of Davenant, Betterton, Cibber, Dryden,
and others. Includes illustrations.

1066 Rosenfeld, Sybil. "The Eidophusikon Illustrated."
Theatre Notebook, XVIII(Winter, 1963-64), 52-54.
   An explanation and reprinted illustration
of Philip James de Loutherbourg's "Eidophusikon; or, Various Imitations of Natural Pheno-

mena, Represented by Moving Pictures," recently
acquired by the British Museum. See Also Nos.
905, 913, 914, 915, 964, 965, 975

STEELE
1067   Steele, Richard. The Tender Husband. Edited by
        Calhoun Winton. (Regents Restoration Drama
        Series). Lincoln: University of Nebraska Press,
        1967.
            Includes introduction, notes and chrono-
        logy. See Also Nos. 761, 762, 1072, 1088

1068   Fisher, Walt. "Steele's Great Indian Merchant."
        Loch Haven Review, No. 6 (1964), 30-35.
            In The Conscious Lovers Steele voices
        his approbation of the Whig merchant class.

1069   Loftis, John, ed. Richard Steele's The Theatre,
        1720. Oxford, Clarendon Press, 1962.
            First edition of the work since the
        Eighteenth century. Contains Steele's views
        on theatre, politics, economics, morals, manners
        and personalities. With introduction and ex-
        planatory notes.

1070   Nickerson, Charles C. "Gibbon's Copy of Steele's
        Dramatick Works." Book Collector,XIII (1964),207.
            Describes a volume of The Dramatick
        Works found in Gibbon's Library at Lausanne.

1071   Parnell, Paul E. "A Source for the Duel Scene
        in The Conscious Lovers." Notes and Queries,
        New Ser., IX (1962), 13-15.
            Discussion of the relationship between
        Act IV, Sc. i of The Conscious Lovers, and
        Colley Cibber's Woman's Wit (1697).

STEELE, See Also Nos. 26, 756, 780, 815, 921

STEEVENS, See No. 978

STERNE
1072   Anderson, Howard. "A Version of Pastoral: Class
        and Society in Tristram Shandy." Studies in
        English Literature, 1500-1900, VII (1967),
        509-529.

A study of Sterne's use of pastoral to
reflect on the contemporary world includes references to Steele's The Conscious Lovers and
Gay's The Beggar's Opera. See Also No. 473

STEVENS
1073   Thomas, Robert Blaine. "The Life and Works of
        George Alexander Stevens." Ph.D. Louisiana
        State University, 1961. 241 pp. (Order No.
        61-5156.
            Minor literary figure of the eighteenth
        century: writer who was an actor, puppeteer,
        poet, novelist, dramatist, essayist, and
        lecturer. Some plays were never intended for
        the stage, although his farces were. See
        Also No. 953

STRATFORD, See Nos. 469, 483

STROLLING COMPANY, See No. 1

STRUCTURE, See Nos. 184, 262, 456

STYLE, See Nos. 705, 715

SWIFT
1074   Mayhew, George. "Some Dramatizations of Swift's
        Polite Conversations (1738)." Philological
        Quarterly, XLIV, (1965), 51-72.
            Productions of Swift's prose work in
        Dublin theatres shortly after its publica-
        tion in 1738.

1075   Williams, Kathleen. "Restoration Themes in the
        Major Satires of Swift." Review of English
        Studies, XVI(1965), 258-271.
            Includes a brief references to Dryden,
        Wycherley, and Etherege. "Like them, he is
        affected by the view of man as animal or auto-
        mation, and by the moral narrowness and de-
        featism and the intellectual pride of the new
        age, and in the three major satires he can be
        seen as coming to terms with the disturbing
        views of the later seventeenth century."
        See Also Nos. 287, 346, 763

SYMBOL, See No. 744

TASSO, See No. 359

TATE

1076   Tate, Nahum, and Henry Purcell. Dido and
        Aeneas. Libretto Facsimile of The First Edi-
        tion. London: Boosey and Hankins, 1961. [3]
        8 pp.

1077   Ayres, James Bernard. "Shakespeare in the Res-
        toration: Nahum Tate's The History of King
        Richard the Second, The History of King Lear,
        and The Ingratitude of a Commonwealth." Ph.D.
        The Ohio State University, 1964. (Order No.
        65-3820).
              Tate's revisions of Shakespeare are
        justified in terms of the political, linguis-
        tic, and dramatic milieu of the period 1678-
        1682.

1078   Black, James. "An Augustan Stage-History: Nahum
        Tate's King Lear." Restoration and Eighteenth
        Century Theatre Research, VI (May, 1967), 36-54.
              Reviews comprehensively the productions
        of Tate's play from 1680 to the present and
        gives information on casts, scenery, and con-
        temporary criticism. Includes a discussion of
        Garrick's relationship to Tate and the play.

1079   --"The Influence of Hobbes on Nahum Tate's King
        Lear." Studies in English Literature, 1500-1900,
        VII (1967), 377-385.
              Tate possessed more than the popular no-
        tion of Hobbes' doctrines and saw in Shake-
        speare's Edmund an adumbration, if not an
        actual type, of the Hobbesian "natural" man.
        See Also No. 1008

1080   Hodson, Geoffrey. "The Nahum Tate 'Lear' at Rich-
        mond." Drama, No. 81 (Summer, 1966), 36-39.
              An account of a modern production of Tate's
        play under the auspices of the Inner London
        Education Authority.

1081   McGugan, Ruth Ella. "Nahum Tate and the Corio-
        lanus Tradition of English Drama with a
        Critical Edition of Tate's The Ingratitude
        of a Commonwealth."Ph.D. University of Illi-
        nois, 1965. (Order No. 66-4234).
               A scholarly introduction traces the pro-
        bable sources and subsequent influence of Tate's
        Ingratitude.Tables appended to the work com-
        pare Tate's version with those of Dennis,
        Thomson, and Thomas Sheridan.

1082   Morris, Helen. Shakespeare's King Lear. New York:
        Barnes and Noble, 1965, 73 pp.
               See Chapter IV on Tate's version of King
        Lear. See Also No. 1002

1083   Spencer, Christopher. "A Word for Tate's King
        Lear." Studies in English Literature, 1500-
        1900, III (1963), 241-251.
               Suggests that Tate's adaptation of Shakes-
        peare's play is in keeping with his own drama-
        tic purposes.

1084   Williams, T.D. Duncan. "Mr. Nahum Tate's King
        Lear." Studia Neophilologica,XXXVIII(1966),
        290-300.
               Examines the validity of charges made
        against Tate's adaptation and discusses the
        reasons for the play's long popularity, not
        the least of which is the age's taste for di-
        dactic novels and sentimental drama. See
        Also Nos. 293, 920

        TATHAM
1085   Tatham, John. The Dramatic Works of John Tatham.
        Edited by James Maidment and W.H. Logan, New
        York: Benjamin Blom, 1967, 320 pp.
               A reprint of the 1874 edition includes
        five plays by Tatham.

TECHNIQUE, See Nos. 153, 477

TENNIS-COURT THEATRE, See No. 856

THEATRE ACT OF 1737, See No. 457

THEATRE DESIGN, See No. 1096

THEATRE ROYAL, See Nos. 908, 1103, 1109, 1110

THEATRES

1086   Avery, Emmett L. "Dorset Garden Theatre (T.N.
        XVIII,4)." Theatre Notebook, XIX(Autumn,1964),
        40.
            Notes a variant version of the 1706 poem
        on Dorset Garden.

1087   --"A Poem on Dorset Garden Theatre." Theatre
        Notebook, XVIII (Summer, 1964), 121-124.
            A review and reprint of a satirical
        description of the playhouse written in 1706
        and now part of the Louis Silver Collection
        of Newberry Library, Chicago, Illinois.

1088   Barker, Kathleen, M.D. "The First Night of the
        Theatre Royal, Bristol." Notes and Queries
        XIV (1967), 419-421.
            A playbill for the opening of the
        Theatre Royal in Bristol on May 30, 1766 shows
        the farce accompanying Steele's The Conscious
        Lovers that night to have been Murphy's The
        Citizen.

1089   --"The Theatre Proprietors' Story." Theatre
        Notebook, XVIII (Spring,1964), 79-91.
            Peruses the Minute Books of Theatre
        Royal, Bristol, from 1764 to 1815, and from
        1908 to 1925, to determine what problems
        faced the provincial theatre owner.

1090   Cameron, Kenneth M. "The Edinburgh Theatre,
        1668-1682." Theatre Notebook, XVIII (Autumn
        1963), 18-25.
            An historical account reveals the acti-
        vities of the Edinburgh Theatre which was
        especially vigorous from 1668 to 1673.

1091   Carter, Rand. "The Architecture of English
        Theatres: 1760-1860." Ph.D. Princeton Univer-
        sity, 1966. (Order No. 66-13, 298).
            Studies the evolution of theatre archi-
        tecture in the major and minor London Theatres
        of the period.

1092   Highfill, Philip H.,Jr. "Rich's 1744 Inventory
        of Covent Garden Properties." Restoration and
        18th Century Theatre Research, V (May, 1966),
        7-17; V(November,1966), 17-26.
        Lists of costumes, scenery and other
        properties at Covent Garden in 1744 are re-
        produced from the British Museum manuscript
        (BM Add. MSS. 12, 201).

1093   --"Rich's 1744 Inventory of Covent Garden
        Properties, Part 3." Restoration and Eighteenth
        Century Theatre Research, VI(May, 1967),27-35.
        Lists of costumes, scenery and other
        properties at Covent Garden in 1744 are re-
        produced from the British Museum manuscript
        (BM Add. Mss. 12,201). Concludes the articles
        from Restoration and Eighteenth Century Re-
        search, V(May, 1966),7-17 and V (November, 1966)
        17-26.

1094   Joseph, Bertram L. "Famous Theatres; 1 The Theatre
        Royal, Bristol." Drama Survey, II(1962),139-145.

1095   Joseph, Stephen. The Story of the Playhouse in
        England. London: Barne and Rockliff, 1963,
        156 pp.
        Contains a popular account of Restoration
        and 18th century theatres.

1096   Kallop, Edward L. "Theatre Designs in the Cooper
        Union Museum." Restoration and Eighteenth Cen-
        tury Theatre Research, IV(May, 1965), 12-15.
        Of special interest in this collection
        are "A Treatise on Theatres" by George Saunders
        (London, 1790), and views of the rotunda in
        Ranelagh Gardens (1794), of the Sheldonian
        Theatre, and of the Pantheon Theatre(1784).

1097   Kennedy-Skipton, Laetitia. "Notes on a Copy of
        William Capon's Plan of Goodman's Fields
        Theatre, 1786 and 1802, and on a Copy of One
        of the Ceiling Paintings in the Folger Shake-
        speare Library." Theatre Notebook, XVII
        (Spring, 1963), 86-89.
        Descriptions of James Winston's copy of
        Capon's plan for Goodman's and the Folger's
        watercolor copies of the ceiling painting of

203

Apollo and the Muses at this theatre.

1098   Langhans, Edward A. "The Dorset Garden Theatre
        in Pictures." Theatre Survey, VI(1965), 134-146.
            Twelve new prints of the theatre's ex-
        terior discovered in the Harvard Theatre Col-
        lection, the Brander Matthews Dramatic Museum
        and the British Museum.

1099   --"New Restoration Theatre Accounts, 1682-1692."
        Theatre Notebook, XVII(Summer, 1963), 118-134.
            Two documents in the Chancery Masters
        Exhibits at the Public Record Office give
        valuable information on performance dates and
        schedules of the United Company.

1100   --"Pictorial Material on the Bridges Street and
        Drury Lane Theatres." Theatre Survey, VII
        (1966), 80-100.
            New information about the architectural
        designs of the two theatres. 18 illustrations.

1101   --"A Picture of the Salisbury Court Theatre."
        Theatre Notebook, XIX (Spring, 1965), 100-101.
            The Dorset Garden Theatre pictured on
        the Lea and Glynne map of London (1706) may
        actually represent the old Salisbury Court
        playhouse. 2 plates.

1102   Lea, John Kepler. "A Study of the Management of
        Theatre Royal, Drury Lane, Between 1663 and
        1791." M.A. Miami University(Ohio), 1964.

1103   Little, Bryan. The Theatre Royal: The Beginning
        of a Bicentenary. Bristol: Bristol Building
        Design Centre, 1964, 12 pp.
            Commemorative pamphlet on the foundation
        of the "Theatre in King Street," 1764. 9
        illustrations.

1104   McNamara, Brooks. "The English Playhouse in Amer-
        ica." The Connoisseur, CLXVI(December, 1967),
        262-267.
            The English tradition of stagecraft and
        theatre architecture dominated the 18th cen-
        tury American playhouse. Includes ten illus-
        trations.

1105   McNamara, Brooks Barry. "The Development of the
        American Playhouse in the Eighteenth Century."
        Ph.D. Tulane University, 1965. (Order No.66-
        1562).
            American theatres in the 1800's owe their
        design and construction to the English play-
        houses of the 17th and 18th centuries. See
        Also No. 813

1106   Mander, Raymond, and Joe Mitchenson. The Theatres
        of London. Illustrated by Timothy Birdsall.
        New York, 1961.
            History of existing theatres in London:
        their location, architecture, audience capa-
        city, and chronological listing of major plays
        produced. An illustration of the theatre
        building accompanies each of the sixty-four
        entries. Chronological list of theatres and
        alphabetical list of architects included.
        See Also Nos. 70, 80, 90

1107   Morley, Malcolm. Margate and its Theatres,
        1730-1965. London Museum Press, 1966, 176 pp.
            A history of the Theatre Royal includes
        illustrations and an index of plays.

1108   Mullin, Donald C. "The Queen's Theatre, Hay-
        market; Vanbrugh's Opera House." Theatre Sur-
        vey, VIII(1967), 84-105.
            Studies the development of the theatre
        designed by Vanbrugh and begun in 1704.

1109   --"The Theatre Royal, Bridges Street: A Con-
        jectural Restoration." Educational Theatre
        Journal, XIX(1967), 17-29.
            Reviews available evidence concerning the
        form of the theatre before Wren's reconstruc-
        tion in 1674.

1110   --and Bruce Koenig. "Christopher Wren's Theatre
        Royal." Theatre Notebook, XXI(Summer,1967),
        180-187.
            Uses memorabilia from the period to trace
        the development of Wren's original design.

1111   Pedicord, Harry William. "'The Second Chronicler':
        A Tentative Identification of the Unhuman Hand

in The MS. Diaries of the Drury Lane Theatre."
Theatre Survey, V(1964), 79-86.
        Identifies the second chronicler as John
Brownsmith, under-prompter at Drury Lane
Theatre in Cross's life-time, and prompter at
the Theatre-Royal in the Haymarket during
Foote's management.

1112   Rosenfeld, Sybil. "Early Lyceum Theatres."
        Theatre Notebook,XVIII(Summer, 1964),129-132.
                Traces the history of the Lyceum play-
        houses from 1765 through 1817.

1113   --"Some British Private Theatres in the 18th
        Century." Maske und Kothurn (Graz-Wien), X
        (1964), 422-431.

        THEME, See Nos. 42, 43, 1075

        THEOBALD
1114   Frazier, Harriet Cornelia. "Shakespeare, Cer-
        vantes, and Theobald: An Investigation into
        the Cardenio-Double Falsehood Problem."
        Ph.D. Wayne State University, 1967. (Order
        No. 68-2090).
                Presents evidence to assert that the
        numerous echoes of Hamlet, which Theobald
        edited in 1726, and of other Shakespearean
        plays in the apocryphal work point to its
        being a deliberate forgery on Theobald's
        part rather than Shakespeare's work or that
        of another Jacobean dramatist.

1115   --"Theobald's The Double Falsehood: A Revision
        of Shakespeare's Cardenio?" Comparative Drama,
        I(1967), 219-233.
                Theobald's play does not have its source
        in a manuscript by Shakespeare and Fletcher
        as Theobald claimed but in Shelton's Don
        Quixote,(1725). See Also No.878

1116   Kaul, R.K. "What Theobald Did to Webster."
        Indian Journal of English Studies, II (1961),
        138-144.
                Versification of The Fatal Secret com-
        pared with that of its source, The Duchess of
        Malfi.

206

THEOBALD, See Also Nos. 101, 415, 895, 1121

THEOLOGY, See No. 729

THOMSON, See No. 1081

THOMSON, A., See No. 626

THOMSON, J.
1117   Kern, Jean B. "James Thomson's Revision of Aga-
        memnon." Philological Quarterly, XLV (1966).
        289-303.
            Studies the differences in the Huntington
        Library Larpent Collection's manuscript ver-
        sion of Thomson's play and the two printed
        versions of 1738 and 1752. See Also No. 1121

1118   McKillop, Alan D. "Two More Thomson Letters."
        Modern Philology, LX (1962), 128-130.
            Second letter to an anonymous lady makes
        reference to her collection for Tancred and
        Sigismunda and to Thomson's new play on
        "Titus Marcius Coriolanus."

THORNTON, See No. 850

TILLOTSON, See No. 310

TOFTS
1119   Sands, Mollie. "Mrs. Tofts, 1685-1756." Theatre
        Notebook, XX (Spring, 1966), 100-113.
            A biographical study of Catherine Tofts,
        her life and career as an opera singer.

TONSON, See No. 969

TORY, See No. 499

TRAGEDY
1120   Booth, Michael R., editor. Eighteenth Century
        Tragedy, World's Classics. London: Oxford Uni-
        versity Press, 1965, 394 pp.
            Anthology with introduction. Includes
        Lillo's The London Merchant, Johnson's Irene
        Moore's The Gamester, Home's Douglas, and
        George Colman the Younger's The Iron Chest.
        See Also Nos. 251, 390, 729, 750, 751, 813

1121 Ingram, William Henry. "Greek Drama and the Augustan Stage: Dennis, Theobald, Thomson." Ph.D. University of Pennsylvania, 1966. (Order No. 66-10, 625).

   Studies Augustan theories of translation, particularly Dryden's; the state of classical scholarship at the time, centering on Richard Bentley; the split between scholarly and polite learning, particularly in the Phalaris controversy. Separate chapters are then devoted to the <u>Iphigenia</u> (1700) of John Dennis, the <u>Orestes</u> (1731) of Lewis Theobald, and the <u>Agamemnon</u> (1737) of James Thomson.

1122 Kearful, Frank Jerome. "The Rhetoric of Augustan Tragedy." Ph.D. University of Wisconsin, 1966. (Order No.66-9154).

   Studies the linguistic devices and patterns used to affect the appeals of Augustan tragedy. Special attention is given to Rowe, Addison, Dennis, and Lillo.

1123 Kenion, Alonzo Williams. "The Influence of Criticism upon English Tragedy, 1700-1750." Ph.D. Duke University, 1963 (Order No.63-4245).

   An examination of one hundred and forty tragedies written between 1700 and 1750 reveals that criticism, "though by no means a dead force, did not dominate tragedy." Writers "tended to bow to the demands of popular taste rather than to the injunctions of criticism." See Also Nos. 214, 355, 391

1124 Leech, Clifford. "Restoration Tragedy: A Reconsideration." <u>Restoration Drama: Modern Essays</u> in Criticism. (A Galaxy Book). Edited by John Loftis. (New York: Oxford University Press, 1966), 144-160.

   Reprinted from <u>Durham University Journal</u> XI (1950), 106-115. Considers the relationship of Restoration tragedy to earlier tragedy and the special problem faced by Restoration tragedians.

1125 Mavrocordato, A. "La Critique Anglaise et la Fonction de la Tragedie (1660-1720)." <u>Etudes Anglaises</u>, XIV (January-March, 1961), 10-24.

1126   Ridland, John Murray. "Poetic Style in Augustan Tragedy(1700-1750)." Ph.D. Claremont Graduate School and University Center, 1964. (Order No. 66-3348.)

           The central reason for the failure of English tragedy in the first half of the 18th century is the poets' incapacity to write a poetically valid style which was also dramatically effective.

1127   Righter, Anne. "Heroic Tragedy." Restoration Theatre. Edited by John Russell Brown and Bernard Harris. (Stratford-Upon-Avon Studies,6). (London: Edward Arnold, 1965; New York: St. Martin's Press,1965), 135-137.

           Studies the opposition of Restoration comedy and tragedy in their subject matter, language, setting, manner of presentation, acting style, and effects on the audience. See Also Nos. 575, 583, 769, 840, 896

1128   Rothstein, Eric. "English Tragic Theory in the Late Seventeenth Century." Journal of English Literary History, XXIX(1962),306-323.

           Discusses the parallel between dramatic theory and the practice of English tragedians during the late 17th century. Indicates the critical channels (particularly in Dryden and Rapin) through which sentimental tragedy came to succeed heroic tragedy.

1129   --Restoration Tragedy: Form and the Process of Change. Madison: University of Wisconsin Press, 1967, 194 pp.

           A study of Restoration tragedy, incidentally in terms of individual plays, specifically in terms of the developing genre. One chapter discusses tragic theory in the Restoration, others are devoted to the repertory tradition, the late heroic play, language, and the conventions of structure.

1130   --"Unrhymed Tragedy, 1660-1702." Ph.D. Princeton University, 1962. (Order No. 62-3638).

           The development of sentiment and "natural" speech in tragedy during Restoration and Orange Periods.

1131   Stratman, Carl J., C.S.V. "A Survey of the
        Bodleian Library's Holdings in the Field of
        English Printed Tragedy." The Bodleian Library
        Record, VII (1964), 133-143.
            Table I compares the Bodleian holdings in
        tragedy with those of the British Museum and
        with the total number of editions, issues and
        authors located; Table II graphs, century
        by century, both the total number of editions,
        issues and authors of tragedy and the Bodleian
        holdings. A survey of 45 tragedians for whom
        the Bodleian has the first edition of every
        tragedy is included.

1132   --"A Survey of the Huntington Library's Holdings
        in the Field of English Printed Drama."
        Huntington Library Quarterly, XXIV (February,
        1961), 171-174.
            Survey of the Huntington Library holdings
        in English tragedy, in comparison with the
        holdings of the British Museum, Folger Shake-
        speare Library, Harvard University, Yale Uni-
        versity, the New York Public Library, Columbia
        University, and Newberry Library. From 1565
        to 1900.

1133   --"Unpublished Dissertations in the History and
        Theory of Tragedy, 1889-1957: Addenda." Bulletin
        of Bibliography, XXIII(January-April, 1962),
        162-165.
            This and the following entry give some 397
        additional items, and carry the work through
        1959. Includes sections on European nations, in
        addition to England and the United States.

1134   --"Unpublished Dissertations in the History and
        Theory of Tragedy, 1899-1957: Addenda." Bulle-
        tin of Bibliography, XXIII(May-August, 1962),
        187-192.

1135   Warren, Bernice Sue. "A Critical Investigation
        of Eighteenth Century Domestic Tragedy." Ph.D.
        University of Missouri, 1967.(Order No.68-281).
            Studies the beginnings, climax, and de-
        cline of 18th century domestic tragedy, the
        relationship of the genre to current moral and
        religious concepts as well as to current literary

and theatrical history. See Also Nos. 887,
888, 1129, 1135

TRAGICOMEDY
1136   Guthke, Karl S. Modern Tragicomedy, An Investigation into the Nature of the Genre. New York:
Random House, 1966.
    Contains a chapter on English neoclassi-
cism.

TRANSLATIONS, See Nos. 139, 250, 943

TROTTER, See No. 1181

TYLER
1137   Péladeau, Marius B. "Royall Tyler's Other Plays."
New England Quarterly, XL (1967), 48-60.
    Studies four manuscript plays, three
manuscript fragments, and six other plays,
most of which were probably produced during
Tyler's lifetime but are now totally lost.
One of the lost plays, The Mock Doctor (1795)
was based on Moliere's Le Médicen Malgre Lui
or on Fielding's Mock Doctor.

1138   Tanselle, G. Thomas. "Author and Publisher in
1800: Letters of Royall Tyler and Joseph Nan-
crede." Harvard Library Bulletin, XV(1967),
129-139.
    Four letters reveal the awkward plight
of the gentleman of letters in the early re-
public and the cultivation, wit, and business
acumen of the early American publisher.

1139   --Royall Tyler. Cambridge, Mass.: Harvard University Press, 1967, 281 pp.
    A well-documented biography of Tyler
(1757-1828) that includes information on the
playwright's knowledge of the devices and
themes of 18th century British drama.

U

UNITIES, See No. 576

V

VANBRUGH
1140   Barnard, John. "Sir John Vanbrugh: Two Unpub-
        lished Letters." Huntington Library Quarterly,
        XXIX(1966), 347-352.
                Reprints and discusses two letters; the
        first in Vanbrugh's earliest extant letter
        (December 28, 1685), the second (May 14, 1708)
        concerns Vanbrugh's difficulties as an opera
        impresario for the season of 1707 and 1708.

1141   Harris, Barnard. Sir John Vanbrugh. London:
        Longmans, Green and Co., 1967. 43 pp.
                A brief survey of the playwright's life
        and works. Includes select bibliography.
        See Also Nos. 760, 1108

1142   Lloyd, Christopher. "Sir John Vanbrugh: 1664-
        1726." History Today,XIV (1964), 765-773.
                Tercentenary article on Vanbrugh's career
        as a dramatist and architect. See Also No. 171

1143   Patterson, Frank Morgan. "The Achievement of
        Sir John Vanbrugh." Ph.D. University of Iowa,
        1966. (Order No. 66-11, 689).
                Analyzes the structure and themes of Van-
        brugh's original plays, and studies im-
        provements on the five seventeenth-century
        French plays that he translated.

1144   --"The Revised Scenes of The Provok'd Wife."
        English Language Notes, IV (1966), 19-23.
                Suggests revisions were made between 1730
        and the play's first appearance in print in
        1743.

1145   Rosenberg, Albert. "New Light on Vanbrugh."
        Philological Quarterly, XLV(1966), 603-613.
                Eight letters by Vanbrugh. Four letters
        concern Vanbrugh's financial interest in the
        Haymarket Theatre. See Also Nos. 129, 137, 153,
        159, 161, 780

        VILLAIN, See No. 101

        VIRGIL, See No. 278

WALPOLE

1146   Bateson, F.W., editor. "Exhumations II: Horace Walpole's 'Thoughts on Comedy.'" Essays in Criticism, XV (1965), 162-170.
        Reprints Walpole's 1775-1776 essay on the comedy of manners, first published in 1798. See Also No. 499

1147   Parlakian, Nishan. "The Image of Sir Robert Walpole in English Drama, 1728-1742." Ph.D. Columbia University, 1967, (Order No. 67-14, 076).
        The image of Walpole can be found in the plot, character, dianoia, and diction of more than fifty plays written during the period. Special attention is given to Gay's The Beggar's Opera. See Also Nos. 94, 435

WARBURTON

1148   McAleer, John J. "William Warburton--Editor Ex Cathedra." Shakespeare Newsletter, XVII(1967), 40.
        A brief biography of Warburton that discusses his edition of Shakespeare.

WARD

1149   Kennedy-Skipton, A.L.D. "A Footnote to 'John Ward and Restoration Drama.'" Shakespeare Quarterly, XII(1961), 353.
        See also his earlier article, "John Ward and Restoration Drama." Shakespeare Quarterly, XI(1960), 493-94.

WEBSTER

1150   Moore, Don D. John Webster and His Critics, 1617-1964. Baton Rouge: Louisiana State University Press, 1966, 199 pp.
        Chapter 1, "Early Stagings and Scholarship," concerns Webster's reception in the 17th and 18th centuries. See Also No. 1170

WESTON, See No. 13

WHATELY, See No. 955

WHIG, See No. 308

WHITEHEAD, See No. 133

WHITER, See No. 942

WILLS, See No. 466a

WILSON
1151   Wilson, John. The Dramatic Works of John Wilson.
        Edited by James Maidment and W.H. Logan. New
        York: Benjamin Blom, 1967, 418 pp.
            A reprint of the 1874 edition contains
        four plays including The Cheats (1662).

WIT
1152   Milburn, D. Judson. The Age of Wit, 1650-1750.
        New York: Macmillan; London: Collier-Mac-
        millan, 1966, 348 pp.
            Attempts to identify and describe con-
        texts for meaning of wit by which the age
        understood itself. Includes references to
        the period's drama, and a part of Chapter 7
        is given to a study of the caricature of wit
        in Wycherley's The Country Wife.

WOFFINGTON
1153   Scott, W.S. "Peg Woffington and Her Circle."
        The New Rambler, Serial No.C. II(January,
        1967), 14-23.
            A brief biography of the Irish actress
        who played roles in Gay's The Beggar's Opera,
        Farquhar's Constant Couple, and Steele's
        Conscious Lovers. See Also No. 13

WOODWARD, See No. 13

WREN
1154   Langhans, Edward A. "Wren's Restoration Play-
        house." Theatre Notebook, XVIII(Spring,1964)
        91-100.
            Concerns Christopher Wren's architectural
        plan for a 17th century theatre. Includes
        several model reconstructions of the playhouse
        by the author and others. See Also No. 1110

WYCHERLEY
1155   Wycherley, William. The Complete Plays. Edited
        by Gerald Weales. (The Anchor Seventeenth-
        Century Series). Garden City, N.Y.: Doubleday

and Company, 1966).
Includes introduction, notes, and variants.

1156   Wycherley, William. The Country Wife. Edited
by Thomas H. Fujimura. (Regents Restoration
Drama Series). Lincoln: University of
Nebraska Press, 1965.
Includes critical introduction, notes
and bibliography.

1157   Wycherley, William. The Plain Dealer. Edited
by Leo Hughes. (Regents Restoration Drama
Series). Lincoln: University of Nebraska
Press, 1967.
Includes introduction, notes and chron-
ology.

1158   Auffret, J. "Wycherley et ses maitres les Mor-
alistes." Etudes Anglaises, XV (1962), 375-
387.
Wycherley is not a "repressed Puritan"
as John Palmer suggests, but a moralist in-
terested in human psychology and understanding
human nature.

1159   Auffret, J. M. "The Man of Mode and The Plain
Dealer. Common Origin and Parallels." Etudes
Anglaises, XIX (1966), 209-222.

1160   Berman, Ronald. "The Ethic of The Country Wife."
Texas Studies in Literature and Language, IX
(1967), 47-55.
Studies the ethical system in which the
action occurs, what institutions are recog-
nized and encountered, and what relationship
exists between ideals and reality in the play.

1161   Blakeslee, Richard C. "Wycherley's Use of the
Aside." Western Speech, XXVIII (1964), 212-
217.
Replies to Granville-Barker's contention
that his asides are often too long, too fre-
quent, and redundant. Though sometimes over-
done, asides in Wycherley's plays provide
information, witty or satirical comment, and
emphasis. Uses example of The Country Wife.

1162   Bowman, John S. "Dance, Chant and Mask in the Plays of Wycherley." Drama Survey, III (1963), 181-205.
          Concerns Wycherley's use of dance, chant and masks to project the ideas of his plays. The devices also demonstrate the significance of the plays for Restoration society.

1163   Brown, T.J. "English Literary Autograph XLI: William Wycherley, 1640?-1716, Sir John Vanbrugh, 1664-1726." Book Collector, XI (1962), 63.

1164   Donaldson, Ian. "'Tables Turned': The Plain Dealer." Essays in Criticism, XVII (1967), 304-321.
          The ambilvalence in Manly's character and the contradictoriness of the play are deliberate and controlled, the sources of the play's energy and Brilliance. The Plain Dealer, not The Country Wife, was considered his best play by Wycherley's friends and contemporaries.

1165   Foxon, David. "Libertine Literature in England, 1660-1745, I." Book Collector, XII (1963), 21-36.
          Allusions to Continental pornographic writings in the plays of Wycherley indicate that these writings were more widely known than is generally assumed.

1166   Friedson, A. M. "Wycherley and Molière: Satirical Point of View in The Plain Dealer." Modern Philology, LXIV (1967), 189-197.
          An analysis of The Plain Dealer and a comparison of this play with Molière's Le Misanthrope show that particular social follies, and not the subsidiary comedy of Manly's humor, are the main object of Wycherley's satire.

1167   Held, George M. C. "The Use of Comic Conventions in the Plays of William Wycherley." Ph.D. Rutgers, 1967. (Order No. 68-4539).
          Wycherley uses conventions characteristic not only of Restoration drama but of the comedy

of humours and romantic comedy as well.

1168   Holland, Norman N. "The Country Wife." Restoration Drama: Modern Essays in Criticism. (A Galaxy Book). Edited by John Loftis. (New York: Oxford University Press, 1966), 82-96.
Reprinted from The First Modern Comedies (Cambridge, Mass.: Harvard University Press, 1959), pp. 73-85. The significance of the play lies in the contrast and interaction of its three closely woven lines of intrigue.

1169   Jenkins, E. Valerie. "Plans for the Production of William Wycherley's The Plain Dealer." M.A. Kent State University, 1962.
See Also Nos. 125, 136

1170   Lagarde, Fernand. "Wycherley et Webster." Caliban, N.S.I., i (1965), 33-45.
Wycherley's indebtedness to Webster and other Jacobean playwrights.

1171   Matlack, Cynthia Sutherland. "Dramatic Techniques in the Plays of William Wycherley." Ph.D. University of Pennsylvania, 1967. (Order No. 68-9223).
Challenges the common and oversimplified criticisms of the plays' craft and content. Special attention is given to Wycherley's use of the technique of breaking the dramatic illusion.

1172   Messenger, Anne Carey Parshall. "The Comedy of William Wycherley: A Critical Reading of the Plays with Special Emphasis on The Plain Dealer." Ph.D. Cornell University, 1964.
Studies the theme of "the necessity of intelligence, particularly a kind of social shrewdness about others and a just estimation of oneself, for survival in the rough and tricky world of Restoration experience" in Love in a Wood, The Gentleman Dancing-Master, The Country Wife and The Plain Dealer. See Also Nos. 128, 145, 149, 171, 172, 409

1173   Mukherjee, Sujit. "Marriage as Punishment in the Plays of Wycherley." Review of English

Literature (Leeds), VII, iv (1966), 61-64.
Wycherley uses marriage as an instrument
of poetic justice; it is "the life sentence
given to erring human beings."

1174   Righter, Anne. "William Wycherley." Restoration Theatre. Edited by John Russell Brown
and Bernard Harris. (Stratford-Upon-Avon
Studies, 6). (London: Edward Arnold, 1965;
New York: St. Martin's Press, 1965), 71-91.
Also in Restoration Dramatists: A Collection
of Critical Essays. (Twentieth Century Views).
Edited by Earl Miner. (Englewood Cliffs, N.J.:
Prentice-Hall, Inc., 1966), 105-122.
        Traces Wycherley's development from his
indebtedness to Etherege to his movement
toward sentimentalism and a kind of "dark
comedy."

1175   Rogers, K.M. "Fatal Inconsistency: Wycherley
and The Plain Dealer." English Literary
History, XXVIII (1961), 148-162.
        Feels that "the play is written from two
incompatible levels of reality," because he
never made up his mind what he wished to do.

1176   Shepherd, James L. "Moliere and Wycherley's
Plain Dealer: Further Observations." South
Central Bulletin Studies, XXIII (1963), 37-40.
        Shows the influence of L'Ecole des
Femmes on Wycherley's hero and comic technique.

1177   Swander, Homer. "Morality in the Theatre: The
Country Wife." California English Journal, I,
iii (1965), 17-24.

1178   Vernon, P. F. William Wycherley. London: Longman's, Green and Company (for the British
Council and the National Book League), 1965,
44 pp.
        Brief introduction to Wycherley's life
and art with special emphasis on the nature of
his satiric temperament and social criticism.

1179   Vernon, P. F. "Wycherley's First Comedy and
        Its Spanish Source. Comparative Literature,
        XVIII (1966), 132-144.
            Wycherley's borrowings from Calderon's
        Mananas de abril y mayo for his Love in a Wood
        show that he borrowed with discrimination to
        create an English courtship comedy fused with
        realistic social satire.

1180   Vieth, David M. "Wycherley's The Country Wife:
        An Anatomy of Masculinity." Papers on Language
        and Literature, II (1966), 335-350.
            The play's central concern is with
        providing a definition of masculinity.

1181   Weales, Gerald. "A Wycherley Prologue." The
        Library Chronicle XXXII (1966), 101-104.
            Reprints and discusses the prologue
        written by Wycherley for Agnes de Castro (1696)
        by Catherine Trotter.

1182   Wolper, Roy S. "The Temper of The Country Wife."
        Humanities Association Bulletin, XVIII(1967),
        69-74.
            See Also Nos. 127, 775

1183   Wooton, Carl. "The Country Wife and Contem-
        porary Comedy: A World Apart." Drama Survey.
        II (1963), 333-343.
            Compares the moral attitude of The
        Country Wife with that of three modern plays
        written on the same theme: William Inge's
        The Seven Year Itch, Tennessee Williams's Baby
        Doll, and Terrence Rattigan's Tea and Sympathy.

1184   Zimbardo, Rose. Wycherley's Drama: A Link in
        the Development of English Satire. New York:
        Yale University Press, 1965, 174 pp.
            An investigation of Wycherley's position
        in the Roman-Anglo-Saxon-Elizabethan satiric
        tradition. Reviewed by Paul Parnell, RECTR,
        IV, 2 (November, 1965), 58-61. See Also
        Nos. 68, 129, 135, 969, 1075

1185   Zimbardo, Rose A. "The Satiric Design in The
        Plain Dealer." Studies in English Literature,
        I (Summer, 1961), 1-18.

Analysis in terms of "satirist" and "ad-
versarius" and the technique of formal satire.

1186   --"The Satiric Design in The Plain Dealer."
Restoration Dramatists: A Collection of Critical Essays. (Twentieth Century Views).
Edited by Earl Miner. (Englewood Cliffs, N.J.:
Prentice Hall, Inc., 1966), 123-138.
        Reprinted from Studies in English Litera-
ture, I (1961), 1-18. Wycherley's best work
bridges the two great periods in English satire,
the Elizabethan and the Augustan ages. The
structure of The Plain Dealer is based upon
the structure of Roman verse satire. See Also
Nos. 130, 147, 157, 161, 1152

X, Y, Z

YALE, See No. 803

YATES, See No. 13

AUTHOR INDEX

Adams, M. Ray 641

Aden, John M. 260

Ades, John I. 644

Aiken, W. Ralph, Jr. 404

Alderman, William E. 936

Alexander, Peter 940

Allain, Mathê 645

Allen, Ned Bliss 261

Allen, Ralph G. 623, 1057

Alssid, Michael W. 262, 263, 264, 927

Amory, Hugh 431

Anderson, Donald K., Jr. 222

Anderson, Howard 1072

Andrew, Richard H. 42

Andrews, Michael Cameron 1054

Angus, William 941

Anthony, Sister Rose 120

Appleton, William A. 430, 552

Appleton, William W. 103, 396

Arai, A. 646

Arbuthnot, John 516, 517

Archer, Stanley 265, 266

Archer, Stanley L. 267

Armens, Sven M. 493

Ashley, Leonard R. N. 105, 106

Auffret, J. M. 1158, 1159

Ausprich, Harry 871

Avery, Emmett L. 31, 78, 176, 753, 873, 1086, 1087

Ayres, James Bernard 1077

Bacon, Wallace A. 1048

Baer, Joel H. 524

Baine, Rodney M. 819

Baker, Sheridan 432

Ball, Robert Hamilton 991

Banhatti, G. S. 180

Banks, Howard M. 1058

Banks, Landrum 268

Barber, C. L. 100, 647

Barker, Arthur E. 648

Barker, Kathleen 90, 402, 904, 1088, 1089

Barnard, John 181, 269, 1140

Barnes, G. 572

222

223

224

227

228

229

233

234

Rodes, David Stuart 926

Rodway, Allan 541

Rogal, Samuel J. 867

Rogers, K. M. 1175

Roper, Alan 353

Rosenberg, Albert 1145

Rosenberg, Donald M.
718

Rosenfeld, Sybil 425,
800, 836, 912, 913,
914, 915, 916, 917,
918, 919, 1066, 1112,
1113

Ross, Judy J. 801

Rostvig, Maren-Sofie
354

Rothstein, Eric 426,
427, 1128, 1129,
1130

Rothwell, Kenneth S. 1042

Rowan, D. F. 899

Rouch, John S. 628

Rudrum, Alan 719

Russell, Norma H. 1011

Sachs, Arieh 591

Sadler, Mary Lynn Veach
720

Saillens, Emile 721

Samuels, Charles T. 722

Sands, Mollie 837, 1119

San Juan, E., Jr. 723

Saunders, John 909

Sawyer, Paul 485

Saxon, A. H. 802

Schenk, William M. 542

Schilling, Bernard N. 355

Schless, Howard H. 803

Schmunk, Thomas W. 48

Schneider, Duane B. 994

Schoenbaum, Samuel 60,
804

Schultz, William Eben
511

Schulz, Max F. 356

Schutz, Walter Stanley
158

Schwarz, Alfred 900

Schwarz, John Henry Jr.
609

Scott, Sir Walter 357

Scott, W. S. 1153

Scouten, Arthur H. 70,
78, 159

Sellin, Paul R. 724

Sen, Sailendra Kumar 995

Sensabaugh, George F. 725

237

Thomas, Robert Blaine 1073

Thompson, Keith Maybin 514

Thornton, Ralph Rees 1056

Thorpe, James 411, 738

Tiedje, Egon 167

Tillett, Jeffrey 1045

Tillinghast, A. J. 87

Tillyard, E. M. 739

Tillyard, Phyllis B. 739

Tisdall, E. E. P. 30

Tobin, J. E. 77

Todd, William B. 851

Torchiana, Donald T. 53, 54, 56

Towers, Tom H. 934

Tracy, Clarence 903

Traugott, John 168

Traylor, Eugene 119

Trefman, Simon 461, 824

Trowbridge, Hoyt 372

Trowbridge, St. V. 809, 810

Tumasz, Sister M. Florence 568

Tung, Mason 740

Tuveson, Ernest 937, 938

Tynan, Kenneth 419

Tyson, John Patrick 741

Underwood, Dale 412, 413

Ure, Peter 358

Van Kluyve, Robert A. 742

Van Lennep, William 78, 79, 80, 768

Van Voris, W. 846

Van Voris, W. H. 209

Vaughan, Jack A. 398, 399

Vaughn, Jack Alfred 400

Vernon, P. F. 81, 169, 935, 1178, 1179

Verrall, A. W. 373

Vieth, David M. 891, 1180

Wagenknecht, Edward 18

Wagner, Bernard M. 85

Waingrow, Marshall 598

Waith, Eugene M. 374, 375, 376

Wall, Donald Clark 170

Wallerstein, Ruth 377

Walton, J. K. 639

239

Ward, Charles E. 378, 379

Warner, Oliver 515

Warren, Bernice Sue 1135

Wasserman, George R. 380

Watson, George 82, 257,
381, 382

Weales, Gerald 179, 210,
1155, 1181

Weinbrot, Howard D. 383,
384

Weinmann, R. 1009

Weismiller, Edward 743

Welle, J. A. van der 385

Wells, James M. 811

Wells, Stanley 1010

Westbrook, Jean E. 63, 64,
65, 66

Wharton, Robert V. 462

White, Erie Walter 839

White, Robert Benjamin, Jr.
852

Wilcox, John 171

Wilkenfeld, Roger B. 744,
745, 746, 747

Wilkes, G. A. 748

Wilkinson, D. R. M. 172

Willard, Helen C. 812

Williams, George W. 868

Williams, Gordon 847

Williams, Kathleen 1075

Williams, T. D. D. 1084

Williamson, George 386,
387, 749, 750

Willoughby, Donna Elaine
1046

Wilson, James 224

Wilson, John 1151

Wilson, John Harold 19,
20, 21, 39, 218, 225,
226, 544, 813, 814,
815, 826, 827, 828

Wilson, Phoebe de K. 478

Wilson, Stuart 83, 890

Winterbottom, John A.
388, 389

Winton, Calhoun 1067

Wolf, Erwin 84

Wolfit, Donald 490, 638

Wolper, Roy S. 599, 1182

Woodbury, Lael J. 10

Woodhouse, A. S. P. 751

Woodman, Ross 752

Woods, Charles 452, 453

Woods, Charles B. 428,
454, 455

Wooton, Carl 1183

Wright, Andrew 456

Wright, Kenneth D. 457

Wycherley, William 1155, 1156, 1157

Wyman, Lindley A. 901

Zebouni, Selma A. 390, 391

Zesmer, David 392

Zielske, Harald 816, 925

Zimansky, Curt A. 53, 54 56

Zimbardo, Rose A. 1184, 1185, 1186

Zimmerman, Franklin B. 881

WITHDRAWAL